The F.A.
ENGLAND YEAR
1992–93

Brian Deane on the attack for England against Spain

The F.A. ENGLAND YEAR 1992–93

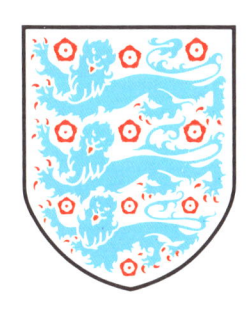

Stanley Paul
LONDON

The authors and publishers would like to thank the following for permission to reproduce copyright photographs: Action Images, Allsport, Colorsport, Eye to Eye Photographics, Mirror Group Newspapers, Press Association, Bob Thomas Sports Photography, Topham

Stanley Paul & Co Ltd

An imprint of Random House (UK) Ltd
20 Vauxhall Bridge Road, London SW1V 2SA

Random House Australia (Pty) Ltd
20 Alfred Street, Milsons Point, Sydney 2061

Random House New Zealand Ltd
18 Poland Road, Glenfield, Auckland 10

Random House South Africa (Pty) Ltd
PO Box 337, Bergvlei 2012, South Africa

First published 1992

Copyright © The Football Association 1992

The right of the Football Association to be identified as the author of this work has been asserted in accordance with the Copyright, Designs and Patents Act, 1988

Set in Helvetica and designed by Brian Folkard Design

Printed and bound in Great Britain by
Butler & Tanner Ltd, Frome and London

A catalogue record for this book is available upon request from the British Library

ISBN 0 09 177435 7

Wish me luck as you wave me goodbye, seems to be Neil Webb's message as he is escorted by David Seaman and Tony Dorigo

CONTENTS

Introduction
Gary Lineker – a Tribute **7**
   International Career Record **8**
Bryan Robson – England's Inspiration
   by Steve Curry **10**
   International Career Record **11**
Chris Waddle – International Career Record **14**

1/European Championship
Euro '92: Match Facts **16**
Denmark are Champions **30**

2/Road to Sweden
England's Qualification for Euro '92 **33**
England's Friendly Matches **36**

3/World Cup 1994
US as Hosts **39**
The Stadia and Schedule for the Finals **40**
England's World Cup Qualifiers **41**
The Other British Countries' Qualifiers **44**
Other Fixtures in Europe **45**

4/B International Year
Match Reports 1991–92 **46**

5/Under-21 Internationals
Match Reports 1991–92 **48**
Programme for 1992–93 **49**
Toulon Tournament **50**

6/England Youth Year
Introduction **51**
Under-18 **52**
   European Youth Championship **52**
   Tour to Sweden **53**
Under-16 **53**

7/Women's Football
Introduction **54**
Women's World Cup, China 1991 **54**
UEFA International Championship **55**
International Matches 1972–1992 **55**

Record Section
England
Full International Line-ups 1946–1992 **57**
Caps 1872–1992 **83**
International Goalscorers 1946–1992 **89**
International Season 1991–92 **89**
Country-by-Country Results 1872–1992 **91**
England's Managers Since Walter
   Winterbottom **98**

B Internationals
Caps 1949–1992 **98**
Country-by-Country Results 1949–1992 **99**

Under-21 Internationals
Caps 1976–1992 **100**
Goalscorers 1976–1992 **101**
Country-by-Country Results 1972–1992 **101**

Under-23 Internationals
Caps 1954–1976 **103**

Youth Internationals
Country-by-Country Results 1947–1992 **104**

World Cup
Results 1930–1990 **109**
Other Facts **118**

European Nations' Cup/European Championship
Results 1958–1992 **119**

British Home International Championships
Results 1883–1984 **126**

FA Fixtures for 1992–93
Diary Dates **127**

American Airlines

The Official Airline of the FA and the England Team

England's qualifying campaign for the 1994 World Cup finals in the United States will be supported by the Official Airline of the tournament, American Airlines. The appointment of American Airlines, the largest US transatlantic carrier from the UK, as the Official Airline of both The Football Association and the England team was made in October 1991.

All nine of the World Cup finals venues are served by American Airlines, from New York to Los Angeles and Dallas to Chicago. With up to 115 non-stop flights per week from London (Heathrow, Gatwick and Stansted), Manchester and Glasgow, American Airlines was the natural choice for the FA.

American Airlines' involvement with the game now extends worldwide. The airline is the official carrier not only to World Cup '94, the FA and England team, but also to the Scottish Football Association and Scottish team as well as to the Confederation of North, Central American and Caribbean Association Football (CONCACAF) and to several of the largest US and European international youth tournaments.

When the appointment was made, the FA's chief executive, Graham Kelly, said: 'We have been impressed by the commitment American Airlines have shown to the development of soccer in the United States and their desire to extend support to English football in particular. We are delighted to appoint American Airlines as our official airline and are confident that the high level of service provided can only help the team in their preparations for the World Cup.'

The England players benefit from a special Most Valued Player award, with American Airlines providing two return transatlantic Business Class tickets to the player making the greatest contribution to the England team as voted by the media at each home international. During the 1991–92 season, the presentation Crystal Eagle Trophy and air tickets were won by Stuart Pearce in the 1–0 victory over Turkey, Alan Shearer in the 2–0 victory over France (his international debut) and Chris Woods in the 1–1 draw with Brazil.

Where did that go? Stuart Pearce peers as Keith Curle (left), Alan Shearer and Tony Daley look on

INTRODUCTION

Gary Lineker – a Tribute

It takes genius to recognise the same in others. Bobby Charlton possessed that elusive, rare quality in his illustrious playing career with England and Manchester United. No one is therefore better qualified to pass judgement on Gary Lineker's phenomenal England career than Bobby Charlton, CBE.

Lineker bowed out of the European Championship just one goal short of immortality, his England career totalling only one less than Charlton's all-time record of 49.

As Charlton evaluates Lineker's international career, the Manchester United director and English soccer's worldwide ambassador has no doubts about the credentials of Lineker to take his place as one of England's greatest ever goal-scorers.

'He comes into the same group as Jimmy Greaves, Denis Law and Puskas – when they are given a goal-scoring chance, 99 times out of a 100 they will pop it in.

'I admire Gary Lineker's talents, a gift given to very few people, that is a goal-scoring knack, an awareness, a sixth sense, a feeling where he should be, the timing of his 'runs', the expectation of defenders making a mistake, a split second to find that space for a chance – and it only takes a split second . . . .'

Charlton was a scorer of spectacular goals, Lineker a prolific scorer of goals. Both have impeccable reputations. But it is Lineker's example to the youth of this country that sets him apart from any of his fellow professionals, contemporary or otherwise.

'He came off the field in his last game for his country completing a record without a single booking or sending off. I had a reasonably good record, but I must admit I could be very argumentative and I might have a shout at a ref. Gary has shown the kids the right way to conduct themselves on a football field, demonstrating the right sort of respect for officialdom. He can be held up as the perfect example.'

Bobby Charlton was willing Lineker to break his own record in Sweden during the eight-nations tournament. Lineker's illustrious international career came to an ignominious climax, substituted half an hour before the end of England's last match against Sweden.

'I hoped he would beat my record. I was more hoping that England would do well and naturally Gary get the goals. I was fully expecting Gary to break my record for the past three or four years; ever since he scored his first hat-trick for England the talk started about his potential to break my record. I was quite surprised when he didn't.

'I'll be perfectly honest, because the record became highlighted and increased in intensity the closer he got . . . . I'm pleased with myself that I am still the top goal-scorer for England.

'Certainly the record is not the be all and end all of Gary's England career, and I am sure that it will eventually be broken, although I've no idea how long it will now stand for. It depends on playing a high number of games, and being lucky enough to steer clear of injury. Both Gary and myself were fortunate to avoid major injuries.

'I feel someone will have to be selected at an early age for England and stay in the team long enough to accumulate the goals. I'm sure the record will stand for a long time. Gary had the best opportunity to break it.

'I've no doubt that Gary will be remembered more than anything for the way he finished his England career by being substituted, and I know that wasn't nice, really. We're all pundits, but the manager is responsible for results. The manager will be criticised for ever for the way he treated Gary Lineker, but he was the one with the responsibility. The manager was desperate to get a result, and many will disagree with his substitution of Gary. It was not a good way to go out. Never mind; that's water under the bridge.

'I hope he is remembered for his valuable contributions, his goals, and not for being substituted.'

Lineker heads for Japan and will never be out of the spotlight. Just like Charlton, his services will be required in a wide variety of fields – advertising, broadcasting, and even as an MCC batsman! Let's face it, there's no substitute for Gary Lineker.

GARY LINEKER'S INTERNATIONAL CAREER RECORD

*Denotes sub   WCQ World Cup Qualifier   FR Friendly   ECF European Championship Finals
WCF World Cup Finals   ECQ European Championship Qualifier   RC Rous Cup

1983–84 (as Leicester City player)

			Score	No of goals
1984 26 May	v Scotland*	Hampden Park	1–1	

1984–85

1985 26 March	v Republic of Ireland (FR)	Wembley	2–1	1
1985 1 May	v Romania* (WCQ)	Bucharest	0–0	
1985 25 May	v Scotland* (RC)	Hampden Park	0–1	
1985 6 June	v Italy* (FR)	Mexico City	1–2	
1865 12 June	v West Germany (FR)	Mexico City	3–0	
1985 16 June	v USA (FR)	Los Angeles	5–0	2

			Score	No of goals
1985–86 (as Everton player)				
1985 11 Sept	v Romania (WCQ)	Wembley	1–1	
1985 16 Oct	v Turkey (WCQ)	Wembley	5–0	3
1985 13 Nov	v Northern Ireland (WCQ)	Wembley	0–0	
1986 29 Jan	v Egypt (FR)	Cairo	4–0	
1986 26 March	v USSR (FR)	Tbilisi	1–0	
1986 24 May	v Canada (FR)	Vancouver	1–0	
1986 3 June	v Portugal (WCF)	Monterrey	0–1	
1986 6 June	v Morocco (WCF)	Monterrey	0–0	
1986 11 June	v Poland (WCF)	Monterrey	3–0	3
1986 18 June	v Paraguay (WCF)	Mexico City	3–0	2
1986 22 June	v Argentina (WCF)	Mexico City	1–2	1
1986–87 as (Barcelona player)				
1986 15 Oct	v Northern Ireland (ECQ)	Wembley	3–0	2
1986 12 Nov	v Yugoslavia (ECQ)	Wembley	2–0	
1987 18 Feb	v Spain (FR)	Madrid	4–2	4
1987 1 April	v Northern Ireland (ECQ)	Belfast	2–0	
1987 29 April	v Turkey (ECQ)	Izmir	0–0	
1987 19 May	v Brazil (RC)	Wembley	1–1	1
1987–88				
1987 9 Sept	v West Germany (FR)	Düsseldorf	1–3	1
1987 14 Oct	v Turkey (ECQ)	Wembley	8–0	3
1987 11 Nov	v Yugoslavia (ECQ)	Belgrade	4–1	
1988 23 March	v Holland (FR)	Wembley	2–2	1
1988 27 April	v Hungary (FR)	Budapest	0–0	
1988 21 May	v Scotland (RC)	Wembley	1–0	
1988 24 May	v Colombia (RC)	Wembley	1–1	1
1988 28 May	v Switzerland	Lausanne	1–0	1
1988 12 June	v Republic of Ireland (ECF)	Stuttgart	0–1	
1988 15 June	v Holland (ECF)	Düsseldorf	1–3	
1988 18 June	v USSR (ECF)	Frankfurt	1–3	
1988–89				
1988 19 Oct	v Sweden (WCQ)	Wembley	0–0	
1988 16 Nov	v Saudi Arabia (FR)	Riyadh	1–1	
1989 8 Feb	v Greece (FR)	Athens	2–1	
1989 8 March	v Albania (WCQ)	Tirana	2–0	
1989 26 April	v Albania (WCQ)	Wembley	5–0	1
1989 3 June	v Poland (WCQ)	Wembley	3–0	1
1989 7 June	v Denmark (FR)	Copenhagen	1–1	1
1989–90 (as Tottenham Hotspur player)				
1989 6 Sept	v Sweden (WCQ)	Stockholm	0–0	
1989 11 Oct	v Poland (WCQ)	Katowice	0–0	
1989 15 Nov	v Italy (FR)	Wembley	0–0	
1989 13 Dec	v Yugoslavia (FR)	Wembley	2–1	
1990 28 March	v Brazil (FR)	Wembley	1–0	1
1990 25 April	v Czechoslovakia (FR)	Wembley	4–2	
1990 15 May	v Denmark (FR)	Wembley	1–0	1
1990 22 May	v Uruguay (FR)	Wembley	1–2	
1990 2 June	v Tunisia (FR)	Tunis	1–1	
1990 11 June	v Republic of Ireland (WCF)	Cagliari	1–1	1
1990 16 June	v Holland (WCF)	Cagliari	0–0	
1990 21 June	v Egypt (WCF)	Cagliari	1–0	
1990 26 June	v Belgium (WCF)	Bologna	1–0	
1990 1 July	v Cameroon (WCF)	Naples	3–2	2
1990 4 July	v West Germany (WCF)	Turin	1–1	1
1990 7 July	v Italy (WCF)	Bari	1–2	
1990–91				
1990 12 Sept	v Hungary (FR)	Wembley	1–0	1
1990 17 Oct	v Poland (ECQ)	Wembley	2–0	1
1990 14 Nov	v Republic of Ireland (ECQ)	Dublin	1–1	
1991 6 Feb	v Cameroon (FR)	Wembley	2–0	2

Gary Lineker, the second-most prolific goalscorer in England international history, retired in June just one goal short of Bobby Charlton's record

			Score	No of goals
1991 27 March	v Republic of Ireland (ECQ)	Wembley	1–1	
1991 1 May	v Turkey (ECQ)	Izmir	1–0	
1991 25 May	v Argentina (FR)	Wembley	2–2	1
1991 1 June	v Australia (FR)	Sydney	1–0	
1991 3 June	v New Zealand (FR)	Auckland	1–0	1
1991 12 June	v Malaysia (FR)	Kuala Lumpur	4–2	4
1991–92				
1991 11 Sept	v Germany (FR)	Wembley	0–1	
1991 16 Oct	v Turkey (ECQ)	Wembley	1–0	
1991 13 Nov	v Poland (ECQ)	Poznan	1–1	1
1992 19 Feb	v France* (FR)	Wembley	2–0	1
1992 25 March	v Czechoslovakia* (FR)	Prague	2–2	
1992 29 April	v CIS (FR)	Moscow	2–2	1
1992 12 May	v Hungary (FR)	Budapest	1–0	
1992 17 May	v Brazil (FR)	Wembley	1–1	
1992 3 June	v Finland (FR)	Helsinki	2–1	
1992 11 June	v Denmark (ECF)	Malmö	0–0	
1992 14 June	v France (ECF)	Malmö	0–0	
1992 17 June	v Sweden (ECF)	Stockholm	1–2	

Bryan Robson – England's Inspiration

An appreciation by Steve Curry, Chief Football Writer of the **Daily Express** *who saw each of Robbo's 90 international appearances*

He always wore the England shirt as if it had been cut and sewn from the flag of St George, a prodigious patriot to the toe-end of his size eight boots. It is hard to comprehend that the familiar, easy smile will no longer beam out from the aisle seat on the front row of England's charter flights, the pole position that was his for over a decade. It is hard to believe that he will no longer lend to the national side his sublime talent, so inspirational, not just to those who played alongside him, but to all whose company he embraced.

I watched him first as a centre-half in the England Youth team, a teenager of abrasive commitment and towering confidence. You didn't need a soothsayer to predict an eminent international future. In the years that followed I watched his career blossom and flourish. I count myself privileged to have seen his every England performance, 90 of them in all. He always led from the front.

Only injury, the blight of his career, denied him a place among the international centurions. Given fitness, he would probably have accumulated 140 caps. He called it a day last October, and in a way I was glad. It might have ended after the 1990 World Cup when, typically, he had to come home for surgery halfway through the tournament. But his incomparable capacity to defy the years gave him such a stunning start to the season that Graham Taylor could not ignore his form.

Against Turkey in October 1991, however, the game passed him by. And it hurt him when it was implied next day that some players perhaps didn't pull their weight. He was no longer 'Captain Marvel'. Indeed he was no longer 'The Captain', the endearing term by which he was always addressed by Bobby Robson. But neither was he going to be made a scapegoat for a poor England performance. He had never been that. Manchester United's manager Alex Ferguson persuaded him not to call it a day then, to hang on and see if he would be picked for the last crusade, to steer England in Poland into the European Championship finals.

Taylor said: 'I didn't select him for the Poland game, so Bryan announced his retirement. But what neither Bryan nor myself wants is any suggestion that he has reached this decision because he wasn't picked.

'If I had selected him he would have announced his retirement after the Poland match. He performed no better or worse than anyone else in the Turkey game but those are not the standards by which he judges himself. He has always judged himself on being better than anyone else.'

And usually he was, whether it was for West Bromwich, where his career took root, for Manchester United where it grew stout as an oak, or for England where he won the status of a world-class midfield player.

What Robson embodied were qualities of leadership and courage, of vision and stealth, of explosive goalscoring. But, above all, he has an infectious personality which pervades any room he enters. Young players joining the England squad for the first time would regard him with not just respect but awe. He in turn always gave them his time, his encouragement and, when he got onto the pitch, his example. Robson never flinched from a challenge and got into areas few other players could reach. It was this refusal to give in that brought him many of his injuries. He never held back.

'Bryan has done more than his fair share for his country,' said Alex Ferguson. 'He has been a wonderful ambassador for his club and country. But I think he has made the right decision.'

Former England manager Bobby Robson added: 'Bryan was a natural leader and a fighter. He was an inspiration to everyone. I was lucky in my time as England manager to have him as the backbone of my side.'

The 34-year-old United skipper has made it clear he intends to play on at Old Trafford. 'I've had ten happy years with England but there are young lads coming through and I feel it is time to concentrate on my job with United.

'It was a big, even agonising, decision to take. At one stage I was looking forward to playing in the European Championship in Sweden last summer. But the game against Turkey finalised it for me. My aim was to win 100 caps. But at the end of the day those are only statistics. I have been to three World Cup finals and one European Championship and I've enjoyed every minute of it. But it was difficult coping with the physical demands of playing for England and leading Manchester United. I felt that for my club to get the best out of me for the next 12 months it was better for me to leave the international scene when I did.'

It was a typically unselfish attitude from a man who has always been a team member. England will miss him and he goes into the history books as one of the country's most loyal footballing ambassadors.

BRYAN ROBSON'S INTERNATIONAL CAREER RECORD

*Denotes captain   WCQ World Cup Qualifier   FR Friendly   ECF European Championship Finals
WCF World Cup Finals   ECQ European Championship Qualifier   RC Rous Cup

			Score	No of goals
1979–80 (as West Bromwich Albion player)				
1980 6 Feb	v Republic of Ireland (ECQ)	Wembley	2–0	
1980 31 May	v Australia (FR)	Sydney	2–1	
1980–81				
1980 10 Sept	v Norway (WCQ)	Wembley	4–0	
1980 15 Oct	v Romania (WCQ)	Bucharest	1–2	
1980 19 Nov	v Switzerland (WCQ)	Wembley	2–1	
1981 25 March	v Spain (FR)	Wembley	1–2	
1981 29 April	v Romania (WCQ)	Wembley	0–0	
1981 12 May	v Brazil (FR)	Wembley	0–1	
1981 20 May	v Wales (FR)	Wembley	0–0	
1981 23 May	v Scotland (FR)	Wembley	0–1	
1981 30 May	v Switzerland (WCQ)	Basle	1–2	
1981 6 June	v Hungary (WCQ)	Budapest	3–1	
1981–82 (as Manchester United player)				
1981 9 Sept	v Norway (WCQ)	Oslo	1–2	1

				Score	No of goals
1981 18 Nov	v Hungary (WCQ)	Wembley	1–0	
1982 23 Feb	v Northern Ireland (FR)	Wembley	4–0	1
1982 27 April	v Wales (FR)	Cardiff	1–0	
1982 25 May	v Holland (FR)	Wembley	2–0	
1982 29 May	v Scotland (FR)	Glasgow	1–0	
1982 3 June	v Finland (FR)	Helsinki	4–1	2
1982 16 June	v France (WCF)	Bilbao	3–1	2
1982 20 June	v Czechoslovakia (WCF)	Bilbao	2–0	
1982 29 June	v West Germany (WCF)	Madrid	0–0	
1982 5 July	v Spain (WCF)	Madrid	0–0	

1982–83

1982 22 Sept	v Denmark (ECQ)	Copenhagen	2–2	
1982 17 Nov	v Greece* (ECQ)	Salonika	3–0	
1982 15 Dec	v Luxembourg* (ECQ)	Wembley	9–0	
1983 1 June	v Scotland* (FR)	Wembley	2–0	1

1983–84

1983 12 Oct	v Hungary (ECQ)	Budapest	3–0	
1983 16 Nov	v Luxembourg* (ECQ)	Luxembourg	4–0	2
1984 29 Feb	v France* (FR)	Paris	0–2	
1984 4 April	v Northern Ireland* (FR)	Wembley	1–0	
1984 26 May	v Scotland* (FR)	Glasgow	1–1	
1984 2 June	v USSR* (FR)	Wembley	0–2	
1984 10 June	v Brazil* (FR)	Rio de Janeiro	2–0	
1984 13 June	v Uruguay* (FR)	Montevideo	0–2	
1984 17 June	v Chile* (FR)	Santiago	0–0	

1984–85

1984 12 Sept	v East Germany* (FR)	Wembley	1–0	1
1984 17 Oct	v Finland* (WCQ)	Wembley	5–0	1
1984 14 Nov	v Turkey* (WCQ)	Istanbul	8–0	3
1985 26 March	v Republic of Ireland* (FR)	Wembley	2–1	
1985 1 May	v Romania* (WCQ)	Bucharest	0–0	
1985 22 May	v Finland* (WCQ)	Helsinki	1–1	
1985 25 May	v Scotland* (RC)	Glasgow	0–1	
1985 6 June	v Italy* (FR)	Mexico City	1–2	
1985 9 June	v Mexico* (FR)	Mexico City	0–1	
1985 12 June	v West Germany* (FR)	Mexico City	3–0	1
1985 16 June	v USA* (FR)	Los Angeles	5–0	

1985–86

1985 11 Sept	v Romania* (WCQ)	Wembley	1–1	
1985 16 Oct	v Turkey* (WCQ)	Wembley	5–0	1
1986 26 Feb	v Israel* (FR)	Tel Aviv	2–1	2
1986 17 May	v Mexico* (FR)	Los Angeles	3–0	
1986 3 June	v Portugal* (WCF)	Monterrey	0–1	
1986 6 June	v Morocco* (WCF)	Monterrey	0–0	

1986–87

1986 15 Oct	v Northern Ireland* (ECQ)	Wembley	3–0	
1987 18 Feb	v Spain* (FR)	Madrid	4–2	
1987 1 April	v Northern Ireland*(ECQ)	Belfast	2–0	1
1987 29 April	v Turkey* (ECQ)	Izmir	0–0	
1987 19 May	v Brazil* (RC)	Wembley	1–1	
1987 23 May	v Scotland* (RC)	Glasgow	0–0	

1987–88

1987 14 Oct	v Turkey* (ECQ)	Wembley	8–0	1
1987 11 Nov	v Yugoslavia*(ECQ)	Belgrade	4–1	1
1988 23 March	v Holland* (FR)	Wembley	2–2	
1988 27 April	v Hungary* (FR)	Budapest	0–0	
1988 21 May	v Scotland* (RC)	Wembley	1–0	
1988 24 May	v Colombia* (RC)	Wembley	1–1	

			Score	No of goals
1988 28 May	v Switzerland* (FR)	Lausanne	1–0	
1988 12 June	v Republic of Ireland* (ECF)	Stuttgart	0–1	
1988 15 June	v Holland* (ECF)	Düsseldorf	1–3	1
1988 18 June	v USSR* (ECF)	Frankfurt	1–3	

1988–89

1988 14 Sept	v Denmark* (FR)	Wembley	1–0	
1988 19 Oct	v Sweden* (WCQ)	Wembley	0–0	
1988 16 Nov	v Saudi Arabia* (FR)	Riyadh	1–1	
1989 8 Feb	v Greece* (FR)	Athens	2–1	1
1989 8 March	v Albania* (WCQ)	Tirana	2–0	1
1989 26 April	v Albania* (WCQ)	Wembley	5–0	
1989 23 May	v Chile* (RC)	Wembley	0–0	
1989 27 May	v Scotland* (RC)	Glasgow	2–0	
1989 3 June	v Poland* (WCQ)	Wembley	3–0	
1989 7 June	v Denmark* (FR)	Copenhagen	1–1	

1989–90

1989 11 Oct	v Poland* (WCQ)	Katowice	0–0	
1989 15 Nov	v Italy* (FR)	Wembley	0–0	
1989 13 Dec	v Yugoslavia* (FR)	Wembley	2–1	2

Bryan Robson, who announced his international retirement during the 1991–92 season, enters the record books as one of the country's most inspirational captains

			Score	No of goals
1990 25 April	v Czechoslovakia* (FR)	Wembley	4–2	
1990 22 May	v Uruguay* (FR)	Wembley	1–2	
1990 2 June	v Tunisia* (FR)	Tunis	1–1	
1990 11 June	v Republic of Ireland* (WCF)	Cagliari	1–1	
1990 16 June	v Holland* (WCF)	Cagliari	0–0	

1990–91
| 1991 6 Feb | v Cameroon* (FR) | Wembley | 2–0 | |
| 1991 27 March | v Republic of Ireland* (ECQ) | Wembley | 1–1 | |

1991–92
| 1991 16 Oct | v Turkey (ECQ) | Wembley | 1–0 | |

CHRIS WADDLE'S INTERNATIONAL CAREER RECORD

†Denotes sub   WCQ World Cup Qualifier   FR Friendly   RC Rous Cup   WCF World Cup Finals
ECQ European Championship Qualifier   ECF European Championship Finals

			Score	No of goals
1984–85 (as Newcastle United player)				
1985 26 March	v Republic of Ireland (FR)	Wembley	2–1	
1985 1 May	v Romania† (WCQ)	Bucharest	0–0	
1985 22 May	v Finland† (WCQ)	Helsinki	1–1	
1985 25 May	v Scotland† (RC)	Glasgow	0–1	
1985 6 June	v Italy (FR)	Mexico City	1–2	
1985 9 June	v Mexico† (FR)	Mexico City	0–1	
1985 12 June	v West Germany (FR)	Mexico City	3–0	
1985 16 June	v USA (FR)	Los Angeles	5–0	
1985–86 (as Tottenham Hotspur player)				
1985 11 Sept	v Romania (WCQ)	Wembley	1–1	
1985 16 Oct	v Turkey (WCQ)	Wembley	5–0	1
1985 13 Nov	v Northern Ireland (WCQ)	Wembley	0–0	
1986 26 Feb	v Israel (FR)	Tel Aviv	2–1	
1986 26 March	v USSR (FR)	Tbilisi	1–0	1
1986 23 April	v Scotland (RC)	Wembley	2–1	
1986 17 May	v Mexico (FR)	Los Angeles	3–0	
1986 24 May	v Canada (FR)	Vancouver	1–0	
1986 3 June	v Portugal (WCF)	Monterrey	0–1	
1986 6 June	v Morocco (WCF)	Monterrey	0–0	
1986 11 June	v Poland† (WCF)	Monterrey	3–0	
1986 22 June	v Argentina† (WCF)	Mexico City	1–2	
1986–87				
1986 10 Sept	v Sweden† (FR)	Stockholm	0–1	
1986 15 Oct	v Northern Ireland (ECQ)	Wembley	3–0	1
1986 12 Nov	v Yugoslavia (ECQ)	Wembley	2–0	
1987 18 Feb	v Spain (FR)	Madrid	4–2	
1987 1 April	v Northern Ireland (ECQ)	Belfast	2–0	1
1987 29 April	v Turkey (ECQ)	Izmir	0–0	
1987 19 May	v Brazil (RC)	Wembley	1–1	
1987 23 May	v Scotland (RC)	Glasgow	0–0	
1987–88				
1987 9 Sept	v West Germany (FR)	Düsseldorf	1–3	
1988 17 Feb	v Israel (FR)	Tel Aviv	0–0	
1988 27 April	v Hungary (FR)	Budapest	0–0	
1988 21 May	v Scotland† (RC)	Wembley	1–0	
1988 24 May	v Colombia (RC)	Wembley	1–1	
1988 28 May	v Switzerland† (FR)	Lausanne	1–0	
1988 12 June	v Republic of Ireland (ECF)	Stuttgart	0–1	
1988 15 June	v Holland† (ECF)	Düsseldorf	1–3	
1988–89				
1988 19 Oct	v Sweden (WCQ)	Wembley	0–0	
1988 16 Nov	v Saudi Arabia (FR)	Riyadh	1–1	

Chris Waddle whose last England game was against Turkey in October 1991. Here he demonstrates his exciting acceleration against Portugal in the 1986 World Cup

			Score	No of goals
1989 8 March	v Albania (WCQ)	Tirana	2–0	
1989 26 April	v Albania (WCQ)	Wembley	5–0	1
1989 23 May	v Chile (RC)	Wembley	0–0	
1989 27 May	v Scotland (RC)	Glasgow	2–0	1
1989 3 June	v Poland (WCQ)	Wembley	3–0	
1989 7 June	v Denmark† (FR)	Copenhagen	1–1	
1989–90 (as Marseille player)				
1989 6 Sept	v Sweden (WCQ)	Stockholm	0–0	
1989 11 Oct	v Poland (WCQ)	Katowice	0–0	
1989 15 Nov	v Italy (FR)	Wembley	0–0	
1989 13 Dec	v Yugoslavia (FR)	Wembley	2–1	
1990 28 March	v Brazil (FR)	Wembley	1–0	
1990 15 May	v Denmark (FR)	Wembley	1–0	
1990 22 May	v Uruguay (FR)	Wembley	1–2	
1990 2 June	v Tunisia (FR)	Tunis	1–1	
1990 11 June	v Republic of Ireland (WCF)	Cagliari	1–1	
1990 16 June	v Holland (WCF)	Cagliari	0–0	
1990 21 June	v Egypt (WCF)	Cagliari	1–0	
1990 26 June	v Belgium (WCF)	Bologna	1–0	
1990 1 July	v Cameroon (WCF)	Naples	3–2	
1990 4 July	v West Germany (WCF)	Turin	1–1	
1990 7 July	v Italy† (WCF)	Bari	1–2	
1990–91				
1990 12 Sept	v Hungary† (FR)	Wembley	1–0	
1990 17 Oct	v Poland† (ECQ)	Wembley	2–0	
1991–92				
1991 16 Oct	v Turkey (ECQ)	Wembley	1–0	

15

1 /EUROPEAN CHAMPIONSHIP

Euro '92: Match Facts

Sweden 1, France 1 *(Stockholm, 10 June, 1992. Att: 29,860)*

A draw against the host nation is traditionally regarded as an honourable result and the French emerged from the Rasunda Stadium considerably happier with the scoreline than with the standard of the football they offered to the 29,860 fans. Michel Platini's pre-tournament favourites only honoured their artistic manifesto during a bright opening spell when Pascal Vahirua, on the left, and Jocelyn Angloma, pushed into an advanced role on the right, tested the Swedish full-backs but failed to find the

The welcome to the European Championship may be high-tech but it lacks nothing in warmth and sincerity

decisive final ball. The pace and sharpness of Jean-Pierre Papin threatened to overawe centre-backs Jan Eriksson and Patrik Andersson and the French striker was aggrieved not to be awarded a penalty when bundled to the ground during a run to the far post in the opening half.

Much of the game, however, was one-way traffic towards the French goal with Jonas Thern and Stefan Schwarz laying impressively solid foundations in midfield; Klas Ingesson working effectively on the right; and Tomas Brolin showing touches of class in attack. Casting aside their initial inhibitions about throwing men forward, the hosts took the lead in the 24th minute when Eriksson, timing a late run to perfection, met a left-wing corner with a stunning header.

At half-time Platini withdrew Vahirua and sent on diminutive winger Christian Perez – a ploy which failed to improve play although it did produce an equaliser. The Swedes, convinced that the game was theirs for the taking, launched wave after wave of exuberant attacking football which left the French in disarray. But just before the hour-mark, a long cross by Perez from the left caught all four Swedish defenders ball-watching and allowed Papin in behind them. His cross-shot, bent inside Thomas Ravelli's far post with the outside of the right foot, bore the hallmark of the European Footballer of the Year.

For the Swedes, the shock was comparable to emerging from the sauna and plunging into an icy pool. Their earlier inhibitions returned and the French, with veteran Luis Fernandez brought on to shore up the midfield, belatedly produced enough coherent moves to have snatched an undeserved win. Platini, while satisfied with the point gained, emerged worried by a midfield which had been unable to supply Papin with ammunition. In the Swedish camp the yellow cards shown to Schwarz and Thern were significant blots on an otherwise impressive debut.

Denmark 0, England 0 *(Malmö, 11 June, 1992. Att: 26,385)*

England team: Woods; Curle (Daley), Pearce, Keown, Walker, Platt, Steven, Lineker, Palmer, Merson (Webb), Smith.

There had been nothing to suggest in the early stages of England's opening European Championship match that Graham Taylor's side would not make a winning start to their bid for success. Denmark's late summons to replace the outcast Yugoslavs had left them short on preparation, and Taylor's team was going into the game with just one defeat in his two years as national manager.

To the surprise of those people who had believed he would make his victory attempt with three centre-halves, England began the game with a 4–4–2 line-up. The loss of three right full-backs through injury had left the squad without a recognised right-back and Keith Curle was asked to fill an emergency and play there against the Danes. Alan Smith was chosen as striking partner to Gary Lineker with the manager clearly feeling the Danes might be vulnerable in the air.

England might have had the ideal start when Lineker's dash down the right flank and cross caught the Danes flat and shapeless. But David Platt, having anticipated the cross and made his run, arrived a yard ahead of the ball and was unable to adjust to finish off what would have been a wonderful opening move. This was to be one of several chances falling to England in the first half where there seemed no real cause for alarm, other than from the measured and finely weighted passes of Brian Laudrup. Platt could himself have had a hat-trick on another day, while Paul Merson engineered a wonderful chance for himself, only to drive the ball across the face of goal.

With Curle finding the right-back position uncomfortable after an early caution, the Danes were beginning to cause alarm with their quick acceleration. Bent Christensen might well have embarrassed England, but lifted a fine opportunity created by Laudrup over the crossbar and in the 66th minute John Jensen hit the England upright.

The introduction of Tony Daley for Curle in the 62nd minute brought a flicker of hope as Peter Schmeichel was forced into a tip-over save. But then the Danes had yet another glorious opportunity in the 77th minute when Laudrup was through on goal only to steer his shot wide of the target. What had started as an encouraging performance ended with some worrying aspects for the England management team who had anticipated getting off to a winning start against Denmark.

Manchester City skipper Keith Curle would like the shirt of Denmark's Henrik Andersen during England's opening game. All he got for this transgression of the rules was a yellow card

CIS 1, Germany 1 *(Norrköping, 12 June, 1992. Att: 17,410)*

Germany's debut in the finals came within a minute of proving a disaster. Then Thomas Hässler, the best player on show in the Idrottsparken, bent a masterly free kick over the CIS wall with such power that it beat goalkeeper Dimitri Kharin in the corner he was theoretically protecting. It salvaged a point from a game amply dominated by a German side which had, none the less, been ensnared in a defend-and-break web intelligently woven by CIS coach, Anatoly Bishovets.

The match had started on a poignant note with the unified Germany making its big tournament debut against a moribund CIS team greeted with a rendering of the Song of Joy for lack of a national anthem. But then, by perming six men into midfield and seemingly misusing two creative players, Shalimov and Kanchelskis, deep on the flanks, Bishovets rapidly confirmed Berti Vogts' suspicions that the Germans had yet to find the right blend in midfield, where Effenberg and Doll were subdued. When Völler was forced to depart at half-time with a broken forearm, Vogts opted to field Andreas Möller as an additional midfielder until an unnecessary challenge by Stefan Reuter on Igor Dobrovolski in the 62nd minute allowed the latter to put the CIS ahead from the penalty spot.

Vogts immediately withdrew Reuter and sent on the 1990 World Cup hero Jürgen Klinsmann, but 25 minutes of sustained onslaught had brought no result until Hässler produced his gem of a free-kick.

Holland 1, Scotland 0 *(Gothenburg, 12 June, 1992. Att: 35,720)*

Italy's manager Arrigo Sacchi was one of the most attentive observers of a Scotland side, drawn against his own team in the 1994 World Cup qualifiers, and he emerged from the Ullevi stadium anything but reassured. 'Scotland gave a brave and creditable performance,' Sacchi conceded, 'but I felt I was watching a team playing at the ceiling of its capabilities. At least I hope that is the case.'

Andy Roxburgh's men certainly deserved a fair share of credit for such stout resistance to a Dutch side which produced top-quality football throughout the first phase. Richard Gough warranted special mention for his marking of Marco van Basten.

Holland threatened to overrun the Scottish defence with Ruud Gullit, operating wide on the right, giving Maurice Malpas one of the most torrid half-hours of his international career. Yet Gullit squandered a series of clear chances and hid those famous dreadlocks between his hands.

A tally of nine shots to Scotland's one provided a clear indication of Holland's first-half domination. But after the break, the Scots midfield, superbly led by Paul McStay, helped to keep the outcome very much in the balance. Dennis Bergkamp's breaks from immediately behind Marco van Basten proved to be the major threat to Scotland, and it was Bergkamp who broke clear inside the Scottish box in the 77th minute to break down the underdogs' stubborn resistance.

After the defeat, Andy Roxburgh felt moved to hark back to Scotland's drab performance in the 1990 World Cup. 'In Italy,' he recalled, 'we were disappointed by our results and by the standard of our football. Now we are disappointed by the scoreline but not by the football we played.'

France 0, England 0 *(Malmö, 14 June, 1992. Att: 25,535)*

England team: Woods; Steven, Pearce, Keown, Walker, Palmer, Sinton, Platt, Batty, Lineker, Shearer.

Graham Taylor made several changes for the challenge of France, one of the strong favourites to win the Championship and considered to be the toughest opposition in England's group. Alan Shearer was brought in to play alongside Gary Lineker, with David Batty of Leeds introduced to stiffen the midfield. Andy Sinton was also introduced, with Keith Curle, Paul Merson and Alan Smith the men stepping down. It was a selection carefully thought out by Graham Taylor to counter the anticipated French strengths: he was not to know that the French would adopt the playing philosophy they did.

Their status as favourites with Holland and Germany was the result of three magnificent seasons of flowing football under Michel Platini, with a side that expressed itself in the way he himself had played the game. So it was to England's immense surprise that they decided to take a cowering, defensive stance, as if their policy was to move into the semi-final with a draw against England and by defeating Denmark in their final group match.

It does take two sides to make a match and it seemed that only England were going for the victory. The consequence was that England were continually frustrated by France's refusal to open up the match. Indeed, there was little threat from the twin French striking spearhead of Jean Pierre Papin and Eric Cantona. They were kept in their place by the excellence of Des Walker and Martin Keown. Once again the principle concern for England was a shortage of service into the penalty area, where Gary Lineker was not enjoying the easiest of contests with his marker, Basile Boli.

It was a barren match for goal chances, but in the 26th minute England were handed a great opening as a result of a mistake by Bernard Casoni. The man to profit was Shearer, who cut in for goal from the left. Lineker had made the perfect run to receive the ball, but sadly Shearer's cross lacked the quality needed to turn the chance into England's first goal of the Championship.

But the real frustration of the game came in the second half, when England won a free-kick 25 yards from goal for a foul by Boli on Lineker. It was the perfect striking range for Stuart Pearce, whose face now was bloodied by an earlier head butt from Frenchman Boli. However, it did not appear to affect Pearce's sighting. He drove a superb free-kick against the underside of the French crossbar, but as it thudded on down the wrong side of the line, England's victory chance had gone, leaving them in need of a win in their final game against the hosts to qualify for the last four.

Sweden 1, Denmark 0 *(Stockholm, 14 June, 1992. Att: 29,902)*

'I had two very clear chances,' said Tomas Brolin after the match. 'When the first one came I stuck out my foot and the ball went straight in. I had more time with the second one and perhaps I tried to elaborate too much. I gave the Danish defence time to block my shot.'

Brolin became the toast of the host nation thanks to his meeting a 59th-minute cross from the right which was deflected against his foot and ended, almost accidently, in the Danish net. He could have emphasised a famous victory had he not dallied with another cross supplied late in the game by Anders Limpar after a spectacular run on the left.

Brolin's skill and mobility may have stolen the headlines but this deserved Swedish victory over the 'auld enemies' from Denmark was, once again, down to great endeavour in midfield and the compactness of Tommy Svensson's formation. The Danes coped admirably with the Swedish pressure game until, in the last half-hour, their lack of physical preparation for the tournament took its toll, and the knee injury suffered by Bent Christensen in the 51st minute meant that the striker took no further part in the tournament.

The Swedish skipper Jonas Thern produced another sterling performance, organising and distributing play from his central midfield position. 'One of the problems in being the host nation,' he commented afterwards, 'is that you don't play competitive games and you begin the tournament without a clear idea of the real value of the side. People always look for personalities, but the important thing is that the matches against France and Denmark have given us confidence and the reassurance that we can work as a unit.' The result left Sweden needing only a point against England but gave Denmark the daunting task of having to beat France.

Germany 2, Scotland 0 *(Norrköping, 15 June, 1992. Att: 17,638)*

The bald statistics state that once again Scotland were the first team to be eliminated mathematically. But a scoreline which suggests a comfortable German victory is grossly misleading, to the extent that Andy Roxburgh and his players were called back on to the pitch 15 minutes after the final whistle to receive the acclamation of the Scottish fans.

It is no exaggeration to say that the Scots, against both Holland and Germany, contributed to the best matches played thus far in the competition. The first 11 minutes produced many scoring chances and the lion's share belonged to the Scots. That the final scoreline was not vastly different was due to exceptional generosity by the Scots in front of goal and a combination of good fortune and outstanding goalkeeping from Bodo Illgner.

Far right: David Platt shows just how it feels to record England's first goal of the Championship, which came in the fourth minute of the third game against Sweden in Stockholm

Right: Gary Lineker was subjected to this kind of close attention from France's Basile Boli throughout the game against France as England were continually frustrated by negative French football

While Andy Roxburgh remained faithful to the team which had battled bravely against the Dutch, Berti Vogts sacrificed Stefan Reuter and Thomas Doll to make room for Matthias Sammer and Andreas Möller, while Jürgen Klinsmann replaced the injured Rudi Völler in attack. The result was a side which, although Jurgen Kohler and Guido Buchwald contained Ally McCoist and Gordon Durie, experienced great difficulty in finding antidotes to runs from deeper positions which created clear chances for, notably, Gary McAllister, Brian McClair and Richard Gough.

Germany, however, scored the goals in this thrilling end-to-end match. The first came when Klinsmann received a pass from Sammer and, with his back to goal, simply teed-up the shot from Karl-Heinz Riedle which beat Andy Goram to his right. The second, straight after the interval, owed a great deal to luck with Maurice Malpas deflecting a cross from Stefan Effenberg over Andy Goram and into the top corner of the Scottish net.

Holland 0, CIS 0 *(Gothenburg, 15 June, 1992. Att: 34,400)*

CIS manager Anatoli Byshovets once again opted for blotting paper tactics to absorb the flowing attacking football produced by Rinus Michels's Dutch team. Even though Ruud Gullit failed to reproduce the scintillating form shown against the Scots and had to swap wings with Brian Roy in a fruitless search for space, Holland asked so many questions that the CIS side was frequently stumped for answers.

With Marco van Basten shrewdly pulling his marker Oleg Kuznetsov into wide positions, Dennis Bergkamp found room for manoeuvre and enjoyed three clear chances, among them a clear run into the CIS box culminating in a shot against the legs of 'keeper Dimitri Kharin. Frank Rijkaard also surged forward and forced a magnificent save from Kharin with a point-blank header. Ronald Koeman failed to beat Kharin from dead-ball situations, and Marco van Basten might have scored the goal of the tournament had his spectacular left-footed volley not rattled the crossbar. To round off an evening of precious little cheer for the Dutch, a triumphant header from Marco van Basten in the 80th minute was erroneously adjudged offside by the linesman.

As a repetition of the 1988 final, the standard of play had not lived up to expectations. Rinus Michels was left to field questions about his team's inability to convert attacking pressure into goals, while the CIS could qualify provided they beat the Scots, at the expense of the losers of the Holland v Germany match.

Sweden 2, England 1 *(Platt 4) (Stockholm, 17 June, 1992. Att: 30,126)*

England team: Woods; Batty, Pearce, Keown, Walker, Palmer, Platt, Webb, Sinton (Merson), Lineker (Smith), Daley.

England knew they had to win their final game against the host country, Sweden, in Stockholm to be sure of a place in the semi-finals. In pursuit of that victory the manager Graham Taylor again made changes introducing Tony Daley, Aston Villa's speedy winger, into his attack and Manchester United's Neil Webb into midfield in the hope of producing a better supply to his strikers. It was a sound enough intent against the Swedes, who had drawn with France 1–1 and defeated Denmark 1–0 in their earlier matches.

England could not have begun more encouragingly, taking the lead in only the fourth minute of the match with David Platt against the scorer. Platt, whose move from Bari to Juventus for over 6m had been finalised while he was in Sweden, had been England's only scorer in the four previous internationals, perhaps a pointer to the major problem the side encountered in Sweden. However, he was there to finish a move that had been begun by Webb, with David Batty heading the ball on and Gary Lineker providing the centre.

The goal stunned the Swedes and it was England's opportunity to take advantage; but once again the second goal that would surely have finished the Swedes didn't come. There was a wonderful chance in the 34th minute when Daley was freed down the right flank by Platt. It seemed all he had to do was roll the ball into Lineker's path, but yet again the final ball was a poor one. The chances came, Daley wasting a header and Andy Sinton shooting wide, but at half-time England still held that slenderest of advantages. The fears were confirmed in the second half when the Swedes came out a transformed side.

Jan Eriksson, who had been a Tottenham trialist earlier in the year, headed his second goal of the tournament, almost a replica of his first against France. It was now the Swedes who gained in strength and they used that physical edge to overwhelm England. A winner threatened, and when it came it was a fine sweeping move between Martin Dahlin and Thomas Brolin with Parma's Brolin supplying the final touch. There was no coming back for England who seemed mentally and physically drained. The Swedes, who are fed a weekly diet of English soccer, had beaten the country they learned from at their own game.

France 1, Denmark 2 *(Malmö, 17 June, 1992. Att: 25,763)*

The French team, which had celebrated the draw with England as if it had guaranteed a semi-final place, was made to pay dearly for their over-confidence by a Danish side which was clearly improving by the game. If the final scoreline consituted a major surprise, few would claim that Richard Möller-Nielsen's team was not worth its victory.

The chances of Danish dynamite exploding on cue seemed all the more remote following the absences of the injured Bent Christensen and Kim Vilfort who had travelled home to be with his seriously ill seven-year-old daughter. Yet Denmark produced a memorable first half in which they overpowered a French side that earned itself four yellow cards. Two penalty claims were waved aside by the Austrian referee Hubert Forstinger and the Danes had to settle for a scant 1–0 half-time lead established in the seventh minute when Flemming Povlsen, emerging as one of the tournament's success stories, outjumped Manuel Amorós and headed the ball across the French area into the path of Henrik Larsen who beat Bruno Martini with a splendid left-footed volley.

Michel Platini, who had chosen both Pascal Vahirua and Christian Perez in his starting line-up, again withdrew the former at half-time and sent Luis Fernandez into the fray with a view to shoring up a midfield amply dominated by the Danes. The ploy seemed to have worked when Jean-Pierre Papin – as he had done against Sweden – equalised in the 59th minute, after Durand had superbly chested-down and back-heeled a cross from Eric Cantona.

At this stage the Danes seemed once again to be running short on stamina and Michel Platini's men, although struggling to build coherent attacks, looked favourites to win. But the French squandered a series of chances and then

Gary Lineker is substituted in the game against Sweden after 63 minutes, hardly an ideal end to his distinguished career for his country

Leeds United's French striker Eric Cantona has to accept second best in this duel as England's Martin Keown gets a leg up from his team-mate Andy Sinton

committed a fatal defensive error with only 12 minutes remaining. Central defender Basile Boli was left to cope with Torben Frank and Flemming Povlsen and the latter's low cross was missed by three defenders, allowing substitute Lars Elstrup to poke the ball home from the edge of the six-yard box.

The French, with Michel Platini announcing his resignation, limped home as the major disappointment of the tournament while Denmark, the underdogs of the first phase, went on to become the underdogs of the semi-finals.

Scotland 3, CIS 0 *(Norrköping, 18 June, 1992. Att: 14,660)*

Bookmakers who had accepted large bets that Scotland would return home without scoring a goal were relieved when Andy Roxburgh's side provided two in the opening 17 minutes of this match. Both, it has to be said, contained that element of luck which had deserted the Scots in their two previous fixtures. The fans in the Idrottsparken had barely settled in their seats when Paul McStay earned a measure of recompense for an excellent tournament. Having won possession some 30 yards out, he hit a fierce low shot which rebounded off the post and hit Dimitri Kharin on the back of the neck before rolling into the net. Ten minutes later an equally venomous shot from Brian McClair was deflected by Khakaber Tchadadze past a wrong-footed Kharin, and the CIS, who badly missed the suspended Akhrik Tsveiba in defence, were left with their semi-final hopes shattered.

Roxburgh had brought Tom Boyd into the defence for Maurice Malpas and Kevin Gallacher into attack for Gordon Durie, and relied once again on a well-organised and industrious four-man midfield to lay the foundations for another creditable performance. The CIS, on the other hand, rarely showed the bite and ambition necessary to overturn the early deficit, and star striker Sergei Yuran was sadly out of touch. When the Swiss referee awarded Scotland a late penalty for a push on Pat Nevin, Gary McAllister added a third goal and put an end to the brief international career of a CIS side considerably better at stifling opponents than creating opportunities.

The Scots, once again cheered off the pitch by their fans, returned home amid praise from the intenational pundits who applauded them for living up to their anthem of 'Scotland the Brave'.

Holland 3, Germany 1 *(Gothenburg, 18 June, 1992. Att: 37,725)*

Confrontations between these two countries in the 1988 European Championship and the 1990 World Cup had produced tension, spectacular football and a victory apiece. Nobody could have predicted that within 15 minutes Germany would be trailing to two Dutch goals from set pieces. The protagonists had yet to work up a sweat when Ronald Koeman curled a free-kick into the German penalty area and Frank Rijkaard outjumped Stefan Effenberg to send a looping header over Bodo Illgner into the far corner of the net.

Just over ten minutes later, Koeman touched another free-kick sideways for Rob Witschge to beat Illgner again with a low left-footed drive from almost 30 yards.

With Stefan Reuter and Guido Buchwald nursing the head injuries sustained against Scotland, Berti Vogts drafted Michael Fronzeck and Thomas Helmer into the side which had been outrun and out-thought during the first half. In the dressing-room at half-time Vogts reportedly told his men that the only positive thing to emerge from the opening 45 minutes had been the scoreline from the Scotland v CIS match and he pointedly enquired whether they thought they were participating in a playground kick-around or a crucial European Championship match. The immediate scapegoat – sweeper Manfred Binz – was withdrawn and not subsequently fielded, and Germany started the second half as if they really meant business. When Thomas Hässler's corner was headed home by Jürgen Klinsmann, the Dutch showed clear signs of disintegration and, for a while, a German equaliser seemed inevitable.

But Dutch substitute Aron Winter was then allowed to break free on the right flank and his cross was impeccably headed home by Dennis Bergkamp to put Holland's victory beyond doubt.

GROUP 1

Sweden (1) 1, France (1) 1 *(Stockholm, 10 June)*
Denmark 0, England 0 *(Malmö, 11 June)*
France 0, England 0 *(Malmö, 14 June)*
Sweden (0) 1, Demark (0) 0 *(Stockholm, 14 June)*
France (0) 1, Denmark (1) 2 *(Malmö, 17 June)*
Sweden (0) 2, England (1) 1 *(Stockholm, 17 June)*

	P	W	D	L	F	A	Pts
Sweden	3	2	1	0	4	2	5
Denmark	3	1	1	1	2	2	3
France	3	0	2	1	2	3	2
England	3	0	2	1	1	2	2

GROUP 2

Holland (0) 1, Scotland (0) 0 *(Gothenburg, 12 June)*
CIS (0) 1, Germany (0) 1 *(Norrköping, 15 June)*
Holland 0, CIS 0 *(Gothenburg, 15 June)*
Scotland (0) 0, Germany (1) 2 *(Norrköping, 15 June)*
Holland (2) 3, Germany (0) 1 *(Gothenburg, 18 June)*
Scotland (2) 3, CIS (0) 0 *(Norrköping, 18 June)*

	P	W	D	L	F	A	Pts
Holland	3	2	1	0	4	1	5
Germany	3	1	1	1	4	4	3
Scotland	3	1	0	2	3	3	2
CIS	3	0	2	1	1	4	2

SEMI-FINALS

Sweden 2 *(Brolin, Andersson)*, **Germany 3** *(Riedle 2, Hassler)* *(Rasunda Stadium, Stockholm, 21 June, 1992. Att: 27,827)*

Sweden: Ravelli; Nilsson R, Eriksson, Bjorklund, Ingesson, Thern, Brolin, Andersson, Dahlin (Ekstrom), Ljung, Nilsson J (Limpar).

Germany: Illgner; Reuter, Brehme, Kohler, Buchwald, Hassler, Riedle, Helmer, Sammer, Effenberg, Klinsmann (Doll).

Ref: Tullio Lanese (Italy)

The scoreline is a deceptive reflection of a one-sided match in which the Germans, although not rescaling the heights of their 1990 World Cup performances, finally played with cohesion and self-assurance against a Swedish side which, as Anders Limpar reflected afterwards, 'relaxed, feeling that reaching the semi-finals was a mission completed'.

Limpar was the controversial absentee from a Swedish line-up which caused much pre-match pessimism on the terraces of the Rasunda Sadium and some fans felt that Tommy Svensson, having guided his men brilliantly thus far, had ultimately taken a wrong turning. Although he later tried to cover his tracks, Svensson had told the press after the England match that Limpar had been substituted 'because he was afraid of the English', and against the Germans his place on the left flank was taken by Joakim Nilsson. Svensson's major dilemma, however, was to find the right replacement in the team's engine room for the suspended Stefan Schwarz. He opted for the lanky striker Kennet Andersson, while left-back Joachim Bjorklund was moved into the centre of the defence to replace Patrik Andersson, also suspended, with Roger Ljung coming in on the left. The changes in each department seriously damaged Sweden's compactness as a unit and, as early as the 17th minute, Tommy Svensson was calling his skipper Jonas Thern to the touchline to give advice on how to break the German stranglehold in midfield.

By this time the Germans were in front thanks to another gem of a free-kick by the diminutive Thomas Hässler bent way past Thomas Ravelli's right hand from the spot just outside the penalty area where Riedle had been fouled by Eriksson. Germany then went close with two more free-kicks superbly struck by Andreas Brehme. First he rattled the Swedish bar and then forced a great save from Ravelli during a first half impressively dominated by the Germans, with the midfield trio of Matthias

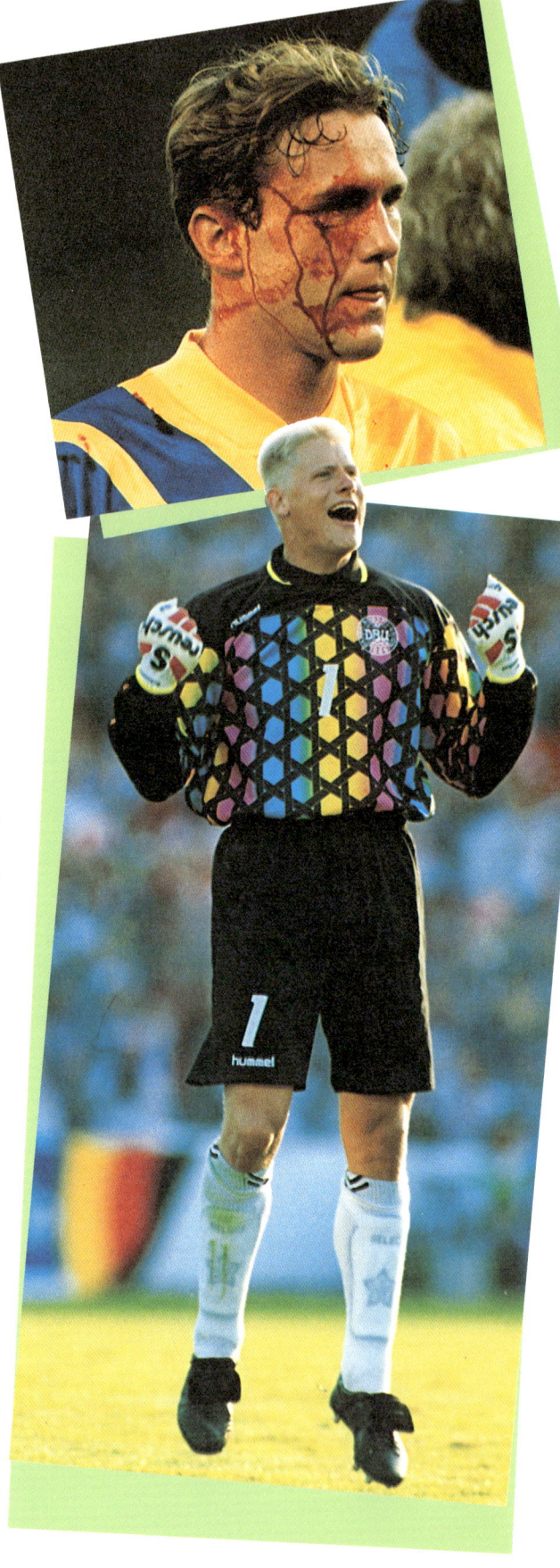

Left: Defeat can be painful – and very bloody – as Sweden's Jan Eriksson discovered during the host nation's semi-final exit against the superior Germans

Below left: Denmark's Manchester United goalkeeper Peter Schmeichel won the vote as the most colourful personality of the tournament. And his jersey was psychedelic too!

Sammer, Stefan Effenberg and Thomas Hässler over-running the improvised Swedish midfield.

The match looked to be over when Sammer reached the Swedish bye-line on the left after 59 minutes and, with Bjorklund failing to cut out his low cross, Karl-Heinz Riedle side-footed home a second goal for the Germans. But, as they had done against the CIS, the Germans made life complicated for themselves by conceding an unnecessary penalty six minutes later. This time it was Thomas Helmer, preferred to Manfred Binz for the role of sweeper, who brought down Klas Ingesson and the Italian referee, who was perhaps excessive with six yellow cards, pointed to the spot. Tomas Brolin duly scored his third goal of the tournament.

Helmer made amends in spectacular fashion during the closing minutes when he picked up the ball midway into the Swedish half, made his way past two opponents to the touchline, brilliantly turned inside and fed a peach of a pass to Riedle who beat Ravelli with a low cross-shot. The German fans were still cheering when their goalkeeper Bodo Illgner was too casual in going for an Ingesson cross from the right and allowed Kennet Andersson to take advantage with a simple nodded header.

The final flurry produced a scoreline which suggested a closely-fought contest. But the clear message from this semi-final was that the Germans were now looking capable of becoming the first nation to win the European Championship two years after winning the World Cup.

Denmark 2 *(Larsen 2)*, **Holland 2** *(Bergkamp, Rijkaard)* *(aet; 2–2 at 90 mins; Denmark won 5–4 on pens)* *(Ullevi Stadium, Gothenburg, 22 June, 1992. Att: 37,450)*

Denmark: Schmeichel; Sivebaek, Olsen, Andersen (Christiansen), Christofte, Jensen, Povlsen, Laudrup (Elstrup), Piechnik, Larsen, Vilfort.

Holland: van Breukelen; van Tiggelen, Koeman, Wouters, Bergkamp, Rijkaard, van Basten, Gullit, Witschge, de Boer (Kieft), Roy (van't Schip).

Ref: E. Soriano Aladren (Spain)

'The Dutch players,' said Danish coach Richard Möller-Nielsen before this match, 'have had time to pick up the papers and read how easily they are going to beat us. Maybe they will be over-confident.' He could hardly have been nearer the mark. The first to show signs of over-indulgence with the sports pages was Frank de Boer, drafted into the left side of the Dutch defence to replace the injured Berry van Aerle. When the ball first arrived at his feet he looked as though he could barely stifle a yawn as he languidly turned it 30 metres back to Hans van Breukelen. When he tried to treat his second spell of possession with similar lethargy, the ball was rapidly whipped away by Brian Laudrup and brilliantly centred to the far post where Henrik Larsen headed into the net. Five minutes gone and the unthinkable had happened. The tired, under-prepared, injury-plagued Danes, written off as underdogs *par excellence*, were 1–0 up against the Dutch side which had produced the best football of the tournament.

When Dennis Bergkamp's 23rd-minute shot bounced under Peter Schmeichel's dive to put the Dutch level, normal service seemed to have been resumed. But the Danes, with front-runners Brian Laudrup and Flemming Povlsen outstanding, were operating the counter-attack with such panache that their second goal after 33 minutes was richly deserved and passionately applauded by the 10,000 Danish 'roligans' who had travelled to Gothenburg to support their team. Povlsen broke free on the left and his deep cross was headed back across the area by Kim Vilfort who, after visiting his daughter who suffers from leukaemia, had been persuaded by his family to return to Sweden on the day before the game. Laudrup's goal-bound header struck the Dutch sweeper Ronald Koeman on the forehead and bounced to the edge of the penalty area where Henrik Larsen jubilantly shot home his third goal of the tournament.

The Dutch coach, Rinus Michels, withdrew the luckless de Boer at half-time and sent on Wim Kieft as an extra striker. But the path towards their expected place in the final was not opened by improved football but by the injuries and tiredness which sapped the speed so crucial to the Danish game in the first half. Brian Laudrup and Henrik Andersen, the best left-back of the tournament, both suffered injuries and when Frank Rijkaard stabbed home an 85th-minute equaliser from a corner, the only foreseeable outcome of extra-time was a Dutch victory over a Danish side forced to play the injured right-back John Sivebaek as centre-forward and to use striker Flemming Povlsen as sweeper. Survival during the extra half-hour was a story of grit, courage and a willingness to run long after they should have dropped.

The Danish goalkeeper Peter Schmeichel, responsible for some crucial saves during normal play, was to emerge as the hero of the penalty shoot-out. Ronald Koeman had already converted the first spot kick for the Dutch, but when penalty expert Marco van Basten struck the second, Schmeichel launched his six-foot frame smartly to his left to bring off a magnificent save. While the Dutch were converting their three remaining penalties, their goalkeeper Hans van Breukelen was resorting to the extremes of gamesmanship in a bid to distract the Danes. But when he had been beaten by Larsen, Povlsen, Elstrup and Vilfort, it was all down to Kim Christofte to convert the final kick. 'I thought van Breukelen had

Germany's Matthias Sammer makes short work of this challenge on Jan Eriksson but the Swede was determined there would be no naked aggression

been out of order,' he said afterwards, 'so I thought I would get my own back. I stopped to have a few words with the referee and then I moved the ball a bit. I thought that if he got nervous he would maybe move a little early. He did.' The Dutch keeper flung himself to his right; Christofte, with only a two-pace run-up, calmly shot left-footed into the other corner and, in a match worth a place in soccer history, Denmark had, against all the odds, qualified for their first-ever final.

FINAL

Denmark 2 *(Jensen, Vilfort)*, **Germany 0** *(Ullevi Stadium, Gothenburg, 26 June, 1992. Att: 37,800)*

Denmark: Schmeichel; Sivebaek (Christiansen), Nielsen, Olsen, Christofte, Jensen, Povlsen, Laudrup, Piechnik, Larsen, Vilfort.

Germany: Illgner; Reuter, Brehme, Kohler, Buchwald, Hassler, Riedle, Helmer, Sammer (Doll), Effenberg (Thom), Klinsmann.

Ref: Bruno Galler (Switzerland)

Nobody could find any logical reason for suspecting a Danish win. Pelé, in Gothenburg for the final, pronounced the Germans 'too serious, too strong and too efficient' for the Danes. Franz Beckenbauer, while admitting that Berti Vogts' side was not as strong as the team he had led to victory in the 1990 World Cup, maintained 'the Germans are mentally and physically stronger than the Danish team and, unlike the Dutch, they do not underestimate the opposition. Even the Danish coach, Richard Möller-Nielsen, admitted 'they are the world champions and they believe, just as I do, that nothing comes without effort. That is why they are more dangerous opponents than the others.'

Yet the Danes, in their harbour hide-out at Stenungsbaden, prepared for the final in good heart and humour. They even joked about an injury list which obliged them to fly in an additional physio from Copenhagen. Admitting that logic pointed to a German win, they invoked superstition. Denmark had beaten Sweden three times in the Ullevi Stadium, they pointed out. Club side Brondby, with over half the national squad in its ranks, had overcome IFK Gothenburg there in the 1987 UEFA Cup when the Swedish club were champions of the competition. And, of course, there was the epic semi-final win against Holland.

In the event, Möller-Nielsen headed for the 'lucky' stadium with all his players available except Bent Christensen and Henrik Andersen, both of whom had undergone surgery. Deciding how to replace the latter at left-back was his major headache and he gambled on moving Kim Christofte, one of the central pillars of the side, out to the flank. With Lars Olsen sweeping, he fielded Kent Nielsen and Torben Piechnik as markers. Berti Vogts, believing he had found the right mix, had long since announced the side which had beaten Sweden in Stockholm.

The final started as if to confirm fears of a no-contest. The Danes passed the ball back to Peter Schmeichel four times in the opening 110 seconds and didn't venture a shot at goal for 14 minutes. By that time the Germans, shrewdly calculating that the severest tests of Danish fitness would be long runs by midfielders and defenders, had already forced Schmeichel to make two superb saves from Karl-Heinz Riedle and Stefan Reuter. The Manchester United goalkeeper had been the butt of jokes by his team-mates. 'It is said that Denmark have the best keeper in the world,' Flemming Povlsen had announced. 'So it's a pity we didn't bring him with us.' Schmeichel went on to make six crucial saves and when he was finally beaten in the 74th minute there was Kent Nielsen to preserve the blank sheet with a spectacular volleyed clearance.

The match changed abruptly in the 19th minute. Jürgen Köhler took the ball cleanly away from Flemming Povlsen, but when Andreas Brehme tried to play his way out of the left-hand corner a sharp tackle by Kim Vilfort allowed the ball to break to Povlsen. He intelligently laid it back to the edge of the box where John Jensen, not the world's best finisher, hit a drive which beat Bodo Illgner, more through power than placement.

At this point, Germany's hitherto orderly game began to fall apart and, as early as the 33rd minute, the thousands of Danish fans began to chant 'Auf Wiedersehen'. The men especially responsible for plotting the German demise were John Jensen, Kim Vilfort and Henrik Larsen. While in-form strikers Brian Laudrup and Flemming Povlsen were fighting thrilling battles with Guido Buchwald and Jürgen Köhler, the Danish midfield trio were industriously and enthusiastically confirming that Germany's problems stemmed from lack of dominance in midfield. It is not irrelevant to point out that, of the eight goals conceded by Germany in the tournament, none were scored by opposing strikers but came from players operating from deeper positions.

Vogts, realising the problem, sent on Thomas Doll for Matthias Sammer after the interval and when Danish legs began to flag midway through the second half, a German equaliser seemed inevitable. Karl-Heinz Riedle squandered two clear chances in the 76th minute, but four minutes later a Danish counter-attack decided the title. Kim Vilfort, who had missed a great chance seven minutes earlier, latched on to a pass from Povlsen with a little unwitting help from his forearm and, when his run seemed to have been halted by the German sweeper Thomas Helmer, he suddenly emerged with the ball and beat Illgner at the near post with a low left-footed drive.

The rest of the story was a sequence of jubilant celebrations by players, fans and an entire nation. The players who had failed to qualify for the European Championship finals and who had broken off their holidays to travel to Sweden were now the champions, proving that, even in the world of super-professionalised football, there is still a place for romance.

European champions Denmark may have entered the finals through the back door but they emerged through the front carrying the trophy

Denmark are Champions

It was the most unlikely success story. The boys from Denmark had been scattered around Europe, their minds switched off from football, when the United Nations decided that Yugoslavia should have sanctions imposed that would leave UEFA no alternative but to kick them out of the European Championship. They had less than two weeks to absorb the relevance of their back-door entry into the competition – that they would be kicking off against England, a side with just one defeat in two seasons.

Denmark had been having their own problems with two of their more distinguished players, Liverpool's Jan Molby and Barcelona's Michael Laudrup, omitted from the squad because of disagreements with manager Richard Moller Nielsen. It hardly seemed the ideal preparation and nobody gave Denmark much more than a dismissive glance in predicting the eventual winners from the eight finalists.

The relief at scoring the final, decisive penalty of a dramatic semi-final shoot-out against Holland shows in this victory leap from Denmark's ice-cool Kim Christofte

Frankly, there was no reason to change that belief on the evidence of their first game against England, for as Denmark tried to sort out their tactics in the early stages, Graham Taylor's men might easily have been two goals ahead. How different it might have been then. But Denmark were to emerge from that goalless game with their confidence intact.

That was to be dented in their second match against Sweden, the local derby so to speak. Sweden have enjoyed considerable success against the Danes and when Thomas Brolin stroked home the 58th-minute goal there was no reason to believe that Denmark would not be heading for an early ferry home.

But shrewder observers had noted that the Danes were playing with fire and spirit, and perhaps the French management should have heeded that and seen it as a warning beacon. They went into that game expecting victory in Malmö but with their countrymen taking the short ferry journey from Copenhagen to lend them support, the Danes lifted their game to create something of a sensation with their 2–1 victory.

With England falling to Sweden the same night in Stockholm it was Denmark and Sweden who moved into the semi-finals, with England taking the next plane back to Luton, their morale shattered.

With Holland to face in the semi-final and their leading scorer Bent Christensen back home with a serious knee injury, it seemed that Denmark had reached the summit of their achievement. But in what was to be a memorable semi-final they stood up splendidly to the challenge of a Dutch side that appeared to think they needed only to stroll out on Gothenburg's Ullevi Stadium to win the match.

It was decided in nail-biting fashion by a penalty shoot-out after extra-time had finished 2–2, with Peter Schmeichel saving a Marco van Basten penalty and Kim Christofte converting Denmark's last kick to put them in the final.

That was a victory achieved at huge physical toll, however, and when the players limped into their headquarters, the delightful Stenungsbaden Yacht Club

31

north of Gothenburg, you wondered if they would even get a team out for the final match against a German side that had beaten Sweden comfortably in the other semi-final.

But the Danes flew in an additional physiotherapist and by intensive treatment and sheer will-power they got their side out for the final game, some players less than 100 per cent fit. You sensed that team spirit was going to be their greatest strength.

It was a valiant effort, conjuring up the Viking qualities that had made their forebears such fearful warriors. The Germans, at first arrogant then cautious and finally resorting to dramatic over-reaction, could not match the Danes for determination and will to win.

John Jensen, soon to become an Arsenal player and a wonderfully competitive midfielder, scored Denmark's first goal with a stunning shot from the edge of the area. And the heroics of the giant Manchester United goalkeeper Peter Schmeichel then kept the Danes in the match until Kim Vilfort steered home the decisive second goal in the 78th minute of a memorable climax to the competition.

Denmark might have been the champions who came in through the back door but they marched out of it through the front with the trophy held on high.

Below left: John Jensen, later to be signed by Arsenal, is almost suffocated by a pack of Great Danes after he puts Denmark ahead in the Gothenburg final

Below: For Brian Laudrup, amongst the most sophisticated players of the Championship, a hold on football's second-most coveted trophy is perhaps nothing less than he deserves

2/THE ROAD TO SWEDEN

England's Match Details

QUALIFICATION FOR EURO '92

England 2 *(Lineker pen 39, Beardsley 88),* **Poland 0**
(Wembley, 17 October, 1990. Att: 77,040)

England team: Woods; Dixon, Pearce, Parker, Walker, Wright, Platt, Gascoigne, Bull (Beardsley), Lineker (Waddle), Barnes.

There was a particularly healthy Wembley turn-out for England's opening qualifying international, the euphoria from the glorious summer of Italia '90 still a stimulant to expectant England fans.

Earlier in the day Jack Charlton's Republic of Ireland side had started their bid for a place in Sweden with a rousing 5–0 victory over Turkey in Dublin, thus gently applying pressure on England. Poland, of course, were a different proposition and they frustrated the home side successfully, getting players behind the ball and closing England down in midfield. Jozef Wandzik proved an obstinate goalkeeper, evoking memories of Jan Tomaszewski, who cost England a World Cup place with his heroics in 1974.

Gary Lineker eased England's concern in the 39th minute, however, converting a penalty after Piotr Czachowski had handled his shot on the line following a corner. But the England captain was forced to leave the pitch in the 53rd minute after his face had been badly cut by Dariusz Wdowczyk's boot as he stooped to head the ball. Chris Waddle came on for Lineker with Peter Beardsley replacing Steve Bull, and it was Beardsley with a superb swerving 25-yard shot in the 88th minute, who doubled England's margin of victory.

Republic of Ireland 1, England 1 *(Platt 67) (Dublin, 14 November, 1990. Att: 45,000)*

England team: Woods; Dixon, Pearce, Adams, Walker, Wright, Platt, Cowans, Beardsley, Lineker, Steve McMahon.

Graham Taylor had created a surprise on the day of the game when he dropped Paul Gascoigne, the hero in Italy and by now regarded as a player of world stature. Instead, the England manager elected to play his former Aston Villa player Gordon Cowans in the belief that it would not be the kind of game in which Gascoigne's talent would flourish. The match he anticipated could be judged from his defensive selection with three centre-backs in Des Walker, Tony Adams and Mark Wright.

It was an unkind afternoon with a swirling, difficult wind and squally showers, but there was nothing to suggest the manager's team selection would not be vindicated. And when Lee Dixon went on an overlapping run in the 67th minute and crossed to the far post David Platt was on hand to score his first goal since the World Cup.

Jack Charlton's side had been beaten only once at home (in his very first international), but that sequence of 21 home games without defeat now seemed in serious danger.

Taylor must have believed that he had outwitted Big Jack with only 11 minutes remaining one lapse of concentration in the England defence allowed Tony Cascarino to grab the equaliser.

England 1 *(Dixon 9)*, **Republic of Ireland 1** *(Wembley, 27 March, 1991. Att: 77,758)*

England team: Seaman; Dixon, Pearce, Adams (Sharpe), Walker, Wright M, Robson, Platt, Beardsley, Lineker (Wright I), Barnes.

This was the night that every Englishman anticipated Jack Charlton's Irish side would at last be put in its place. It was the third meeting between the countries in the space of ten months, but like the previous two it was to end as a draw.

Wembley was once again almost full and this time the Irish, who had never won at Wembley, had an enormous partisan backing. It was to be a traumatic night for England, the onus being on them to win the two points and so give themselves breathing space in the Group 7 table.

The night started well enough for England, the early pressure culminating in an opening goal in the ninth minute. A cross from Stuart Pearce was cleared by Steve Staunton but only as far as Lee Dixon who then drove it back at goal. The shot clipped Staunton on the knee, wrong footing Packie Bonner and enabling Dixon to claim his first goal for his country.

That should have been the launch pad for victory but instead it served to lift the Irish to produce a concerted bombardment of England's goalmouth – most of it predictably aerial. It was all hands to the pump and even Peter Beardsley turned up on his own goal-line to make a clearance from Paul McGrath. Inevitably, this pressure led to an Irish equaliser in the 27th minute. McGrath lofted one more ball into the heart of the English area and Niall Quinn got behind his old Arsenal team mate Tony Adams to guide home a header.

At half-time Graham Taylor decided to abandon his three centre-backs formation and gave Lee Sharpe his debut as substitute, (the first teenager to wear the England shirt since John Barnes in 1983). Still the deadlock could not be broken, although the Irish had the better of the second-half chances with first Kevin Sheedy and then Ray Houghton missing what were good opportunities.

Taylor went so far as to substitute his own skipper Gary Lineker with Ian Wright in the final 15 minutes, but to no avail. So the two games against the Irish had cancelled each other out.

Turkey 0, England 1 *(Wise 32) (Izmir, 1 May, 1991. Att: 20,000)*

England team: Seaman; Dixon, Pearce, Wise, Walker, Pallister, Platt, Thomas (Hodge), Smith, Lineker, Barnes.

With Poland and Ireland having drawn earlier in the day, it was critical that England should win this match. But it was never going to be a walkover, for although England had won 8–0 in Istanbul in the first international between the countries in 1984, a truer guide to the current form of the Turkish side was the 0–0 result in Izmir prior to the 1988 European Championship.

Graham Taylor used the occasion to present first caps to two London players, Geoff Thomas and Dennis Wise, reforged the old Leicester club partnership of Gary Lineker and Alan Smith and selected Gary Pallister for the injured Mark Wright who had played for the England B side four days earlier at Watford.

Yet the Turks played some surprisingly good football. In midfield Sepp Piontek had effective players in Mehmet and Muhammet. Colak Tanju, the most experienced of the Turkish players ought to have scored, but mis-hit his shot after David Seaman, making his fourth start for England, had only been able to block a shot from Dilmen Ridvan.

It was Chelsea's Wise who scored the decisive goal for England in the 32nd minute after they had been under some heavy attacks from a side who had not scored against England in five meetings stretching back to 1984. A Stuart Pearce free-kick was headed down by Pallister and Wise reacted quickly to the loose ball to steer it beyond Turkish keeper Hayrettin.

So England's superiority in the air had proved decisive and an important victory had been achieved after the two draws against the Irish. The result put England in a most advantageous position in the group table, with a home game to follow against Turkey later in the year.

England 1 *(Smith 21)*, **Turkey 0** *(Wembley, 16 October, 1991. Att: 50,896)*

England team: Woods; Dixon, Pearce, Batty, Walker, Mabbutt, Robson, Platt, Smith, Lineker, Waddle

This was a critical European Championship qualifier for England and one where they might have hoped to improve their goal differential over the other three teams in the group. That was not to be the case as a swirling wind around Wembley made it difficult for England to assert their clear superiority.

Bryan Robson was back at the heart of England's midfield but it was to be a comfortable passage against a Turkey side that had not come to Wembley to have its neck wrung.

The Turks broke at England from midfield and caused Chris Woods just a few problems. Chris Waddle, on what was to be his final England appearance, had difficulty making any impression on the match.

And it was Stuart Pearce who set up the decisive goal, surging past defender Riza and placing his cross perfectly on to the target, which happened to be Alan Smith's forehead.

From three yards the Arsenal striker could hardly miss, underlining his ability in the air and for once showing his old Leicester team-mate Gary Lineker the route to goal.

Poland 1, England 1 *(Lineker 77) (Poznan, 13 November, 1991. Att: 15,000)*

England team: Woods; Dixon, Pearce, Gray (Smith), Walker, Mabbutt, Platt, Thomas, Rocastle, Lineker, Sinton (Daley)

This was the match where England needed a point to ensure a place in the final eight of the European Championship and they got there courtesy of a goal from, perhaps inevitably, Gary Lineker.

When the history of English soccer is written there can be no doubt Lineker will merit a chapter all on his own for his scoring exploits in the hour of need. European exit was staring England in the face for part of this night in Poznan.

The Poles, playing sweet, slick football, had taken the lead in the 40th minute when Gary Mabbutt deflected a long free-kick past the unsuspecting Chris Woods.

English fans were left in suspense until David Rocastle, one of the heroes of the night, swung over a 77th minute corner which Mabbutt got his head to and Lineker hooked into the net.

The strains of 'Swing Low, Sweet Chariot' drifted across the night air since a draw was enough to see Taylor over his first major hurdle as manager, qualification for the European finals, a feat which eluded Bobby Robson in his early career.

FRIENDLIES

England 0, Germany 1 *(Wembley, 11 September, 1991)*

England team: Woods; Dixon, Dorigo, Batty, Pallister, Parker, Platt, Steven (Stewart), Smith, Lineker, Salako (Merson).

It was perhaps the toughest of games with which to open a new season, the world champions arriving at Wembley with just about their strongest line-up as Taylor sought revenge for the World Cup semi-final defeat.

This was Taylor's thirteenth game in charge – and it was to prove unlucky thirteen. Without Mark Wright and John Barnes this was a depleted England side, with only Gary Lineker, David Platt, Trevor Steven and Paul Parker in the team from that which had lost the penalty shoot-out in Turin.

Having weathered the early pressure England responded encouragingly, with Bodo Illgner making an acrobatic save to an Alan Smith header and David Platt heading against the bar.

There was special treatment reserved for Lineker and both Andreas Brehme and Jurgen Kohler were cautioned for their tough treatment of the England skipper. It was Karl-Heinz Riedle who won the game for the Germans with a goal just before half-time from which England, despite their second-half persistence, could not recover.

England 2 *(Shearer, Lineker)*, **France 0** *(Wembley, 19 February, 1992)*

England team: Woods; Jones, Pearce, Keown, Walker, Wright, Webb, Thomas, Clough, Shearer, Hirst (Lineker).

This was the first visit of a French side to Wembley for twenty-three years, when Geoff Hurst had scored a hat-trick in a 5–0 win. But the new generation under Michel Platini's management had not been beaten for three years.

That was to change as Des Walker stifled the threat of French hero Jean-Pierre Papin, the devastating striker from Marseille.

There had been half-chances at either end before Alan Shearer marked his full debut with a 44th-minute goal on the turn when Nigel Clough's corner was headed down to him.

Gary Lineker, who had not been selected in the starting line-up, came on for David Hirst in the second half and the effectiveness of England's attack improved. The skipper was never far from the penalty-area action and in the 72nd minute he was on hand to score his 47th goal for England when Clough's shot was only blocked by Rousset.

England 2 *(Merson, Keown)*, **Czechoslovakia 2** *(Prague, 25 March, 1992)*

England team: Seaman; Keown, Pearce, Rocastle (Dixon), Walker, Mabbutt (Lineker), Platt, Merson, Clough (Stewart), Hateley, Barnes (Dorigo).

It was against the Czechs in 1990 that Paul Gascoigne first gave notice that he was about to explode on to the international arena, and England were still searching for a player of his craft. The latest combination in midfield as Graham Taylor continued to experiment with potential players saw David Platt and Nigel Clough as a pairing.

It was a night, too, when Mark Hateley was recalled to the colours as a tribute to the form he had been showing with Rangers in the Scottish Premier Division, with Gary Lineker again not selected in the starting line-up.

The wonderfully gifted Tomas Skuhravy gave the Czechs the lead but it was Paul Merson, promoted to senior level, who snatched the equaliser.

Vaclav Nemecek restored the Czech lead after 58 minutes and it was Martin

John Barnes receives anxious treatment from England physios Fred Street and Norman Medhurst during the final build-up game to the Championship against Finland in Helsinki. But it is to no avail, a ruptured Achilles' tendon ruling out the Liverpool winger

Keown foraging forward from his defensive position who claimed the 66th-minute equaliser that put the sides level.

England 2 *(Lineker, Steven)*, **CIS 2** *(Moscow, 29 April, 1992)*

England team: Woods (Martyn); Stevens, Sinton (Curle), Palmer, Walker, Keown, Platt, Steven (Stewart), Shearer (Clough), Lineker, Daley.

At last England found a playmaker in Moscow as Trevor Steven blossomed in a central midfield role, orchestrating quite superbly.

The man from Marseille relished his new role in a side that again showed changes, QPR's Andy Sinton being given his chance on the left and the leggy Carlton Palmer taking a midfield role.

It was Gary Lineker who opened the scoring for England fifteen minutes into the match after a neat build-up which involved the pace of Tony Daley, Graham Taylor's 'secret weapon'.

Certainly the darting winger caused problems for the CIS side, though they did equalise just before half-time and then took the lead in the 55th minute. But it was fitting after his fine performance that it should be Steven who kept Taylor's unbeaten away record intact with a finely struck goal in the 72nd minute.

England 1 *(Webb)*, **Hungary 0** *(Budapest, 12 May, 1992)*

England team: Martyn (Seaman); Stevens, Dorigo, Curle (Sinton), Walker, Keown, Webb (Batty), Palmer, Merson (Smith), Lineker (Wright), Daley.

This was a flattering success for England but one, even so, that had allowed Graham Taylor to continue making his various experiments.

There were some very anxious moments in the first 20 minutes as the Hungarians ran at England from deep positions, and the chances of Gary Lineker equalling Bobby Charlton's record with a goal looked remote indeed.

As it was, England secured victory with a 57th-minute goal with Lineker acting as provider. There was some dispute as to whether Webb should be credited after the ball took a big deflection. But England were giving it to Webb and the Manchester United man, having a fine match, was happy to claim it.

Taylor made five substitutions in the match as he again made sure that he could examine all his options before deciding on his final twenty for Sweden.

England 1 *(Platt)*, **Brazil 1** *(Wembley, 17 May, 1992)*

England team: Woods; Stevens, Dorigo (Pearce), Palmer, Walker, Keown, Daley (Merson), Steven (Webb), Platt, Lineker, Sinton (Rocastle).

This was the day everyone was asking whether Graham Taylor was playing the team with which he intended to begin the European Championship. The answer was a definite 'No' for two of the players: Gary Stevens and Andy Sinton were not in the original final squad, though Sinton was cover for John Barnes.

Stevens, of course, came in as a late replacement for the injured Lee Dixon. Few players came out of the game with distinction for it was the Brazilians who held control. They played some wonderful touch football and a mistake by Stevens let in Bebeto for a 26th-minute goal few at Wembley would deny the Brazilians deserved.

But once again a Graham Taylor side stuck to their task, showing there is no lack of spirit or fight in the England ranks, and in the 49th minute came the reward.

It was Webb who chipped in the ball and Brazilian defender Charles headed it back across his own goal where David Platt was waiting to drive home his eighth international goal.

England 2 *(Platt 2)*, **Finland 1** *(Helsinki, 3 June, 1992)*

England team: Woods; Stevens (Palmer), Pearce, Keown, Walker, Wright, Platt, Steven (Daley), Webb, Lineker, Barnes (Merson).

England's final warm-up game before the European Championship was to prove a costly one in terms of injuries, for after only ten minutes John Barnes collapsed with a ruptured Achilles' tendon.

Though England were not to know at the time, it was a game that also put Rangers' Gary Stevens and Liverpool's Mark Wright out of the Swedish competition, all of them injuries that were disruptive to Graham Taylor's meticulous planning.

On the other hand, victory extended Graham Taylor's fine record of only one defeat in two seasons, a run of 21 matches. The England manager used the match to try a form of sweeper system, though Wright was encouraged to break from defence.

Unfortunately all three of England's centre-halves were caught too far forward in the 27th minute and on the break Finland won a penalty as Trevor Steven brought down Jari Litmanen. Ari Hjelm scored the penalty.

That was when David Platt took over, having missed a couple of chances earlier in the match. He strode purposefully on to a through-ball from Stevens to slide home the equaliser.

The winner was a fine goal, with Carlton Palmer taking a long throw-in down the right which was headed back by Wright. Platt had made the run down the blind side and fiercely volleyed home his shot.

3 / WORLD CUP 1994

US as Hosts

by Alan Rothenberg
Chairman and Chief Executive, World Cup USA 1994

The venues have been selected, the qualifying competition around the globe is under way and World Cup USA 1994 is running right on schedule.

We are delighted with the number of cities that have shown an interest in participating in this historic event because at the outset there were cynics who thought we would be lucky if we had even seven or eight cities wanting to be part of it. There turned out to be 26 putting in bona fide bids, all of them enthusiastically supporting the US decision to stage the World Cup.

I have always said that we want to put on the best World Cup in history and I am still expecting we will do that. But we also want to use the event to push the game to a higher position in the USA once the tournament is over, including the setting up of a new professional league to match those around the world.

It is this lack of an established league which tends to obscure just what interest there is in soccer in our country. At present there are 16 million regular players in the United States. You need only drive out to suburbia any weekend to see how many parents and volunteers there are out there with the kids, and it is our estimate that as many as 50 million are involved at the grass roots.

It was the excitement created in the mid 1970s by the importation of men like Cruyff, Beckenbauer and Pelé that was the bedrock for the creation of the youth leagues that flourish now and which we believe can be the base of the pyramid for the future.

A generation of kids has grown up playing the game and now we have this great jewel, the World Cup, which we hope will build a market for the sport.

Our national team made it to the World Cup in Italy and are enjoying some success at competitive level. We have the incentive for the young to say, 'Wow, I could be a worldwide sporting hero.' They know that their country is about to stage the world's biggest single-sport event. The total US stadium audience for the 52 games will be nearly 3.5 million. The Final alone will be telecast live in America and worldwide to an audience of 2 billion.

We want to make sure that all of those people can say they have witnessed the most spectacular World Cup ever, that those present can say they have attended the most enjoyable event in their lifetime. We will wrap the games with a lot of good old-fashioned American pazzazz, with a lot of side entertainment, street activity and cultural programmes, and make it the most enjoyable experience of a lifetime.

But also, when the Final has been played in the Pasadena Rose Bowl on 17 July 1994, we want there to be another legacy within the United States. We want our people to say, 'Now I realise why soccer is the number one sport in the world. Let's start our own professional league, and where do I get the tickets?'

We want to develop a national side that has the rest of the world quaking in its boots. We want the talented 16-year-old coming out of school to have somewhere to develop those talents at a competitive level.

I remain optimistic that the World Cup in America is going to be a smashing success. We are going to sell every seat in the house. We will create the interest

Graham Taylor's expression shows only determination as he looks forward to the World Cup in the United States in 1994

and the excitement to make sure we break a few records in attendances. I think the decision by FIFA to select the United States as the venue for World Cup 1994 will prove to be an inspired one, however much they have been criticised.

And I hope that you will be along for the ride.

THE STADIA AND SCHEDULE FOR THE FINALS

Giants Stadium
Venue: New York/New Jersey
Location: East Rutherford, New Jersey
Capacity: 76,891
Record attendance: 77,691 (New York Cosmos v Fort Lauderdale, 1977)

Robert F. Kennedy Memorial Stadium
Venue: Washington DC
Location: Washington, near the Capitol
Capacity: 56,500
Record attendance: 56,500 (home games of American football team Washington Redskins)

The Citrus Bowl
Venue: Orlando, Florida
Location: Orlando, one mile west of town centre
Capacity: 70,188
Record attendance: 70,000 (Citrus Bowl Final, annually)

Foxboro Stadium
Venue: Boston, Massachusetts
Location: Between Boston and Providence
Capacity: 61,000
Record attendance: 59,828 (American Football game between New England Patriots and Houston, October 1989)

Pontiac Silverdome
Venue: Detroit, Michigan
Location: Pontiac, 30km from Detroit
Capacity: 72,794
Record attendance: 82,000 (American Super Bowl, January 1982)

Soldier Field
Venue: Chicago, Illinois
Location: Michigan Lake
Capacity: 66,814
Record attendance: 67,475 (American Football, Chicago Bears v Minnesota Vikings, August 1989)

The Cotton Bowl
Venue: Dallas, Texas
Location: In centre of Dallas's historic Fair Park
Capacity: 72,000
Record attendance: 72,000 (American collegiate football)

The Rose Bowl
Venue: Los Angeles, California
Location: Pasadena, 11km from Los Angeles city centre
Capacity: 102,083
Record attendance: 101,799 (Olympic football tournament final, France v Brazil, August 1984)

Stanford Stadium
Venue: San Francisco, California
Location: Palo Alto, 43km south of San Francisco
Capacity: 86,019
Record attendance: 84,059 (American Super Bowl, January 1985)

The Opening Ceremony and first game of the World Cup finals will be staged at Chicago's Soldier Field, home to the Chicago Bears, on 17 June, 1994.
Chicago, with a population of 2.8 million, is the third-largest city in the United States, a hub of rail, air and road networks and still a transport town.
Each of the selected stadia will host four first-round matches between 17 and 30 June. The final 16 teams will then play a second round between 2 and 5 July with the venues selected as Boston, Chicago, Dallas, Los Angeles, New York/New Jersey, Orlando, San Francisco and Washington DC.

The quarter-finals will be held in Boston, Dallas, New York/New Jersey and San Francisco between 8 and 10 July.

The semi-finals will be staged in the Rose Bowl, Los Angeles, and the Giants Stadium, New Jersey, on 12 and 13 July with the third place play off at the Rose Bowl on 16 July and the World Cup Final at the same venue on 17 July.

England's World Cup Qualifiers

As soon as the European Championship finals in Sweden were over, Graham Taylor, the England manager, began planning for the 1994 World Cup qualifying campaign.

There were some familiar faces in England's group when the draw was made on 8 December, 1991 at the Paramount Theater, in New York's Madison Square Garden (more famous for the great heavyweight boxing contests of the 1960s and 70s, it is now to be the venue for the opening blows of the 1994 World Cup).

It was to be the biggest entry for the European qualifying section and history was made with the inclusion, for the first time, of the three Baltic states Latvia, Lithuania and Estonia. They were accepted by FIFA just two days before the draw, after the break-up of the old Soviet Union, although applications from Georgia, Ukraine and the Yugoslav republics of Croatia and Slovenia were not approved.

In September 1992 the FIFA Executive Committee decided that Yugoslavia should not compete in the preliminary competition of the 1994 World Cup, and they were omitted from the Preliminary Group 5 of the European Zone, with no replacement being sought.

A total of 37 nations went into the draw – Liechtenstein had withdrawn on the eve of the draw – which meant that, for the first time, there would be six teams in five European groups and seven in one group. The England manager was keen to avoid the seven-team group because of the 12 qualifying matches that would have to be fitted into the next 18 months.

Seeded first after finishing fourth in the 1990 World Cup, England were automatically placed in Group 2 and were soon joined by some old adversaries. In both the 1990 World Cup qualifying group and the 1992 European Championship section, England had found themselves up against Poland. On both occasions England had travelled to Poland needing a point to proceed to the finals. On both occasions – in Katowice and Poznan – England succeeded.

Now, as third seeds, Poland were in England's group yet again. Turkey, who were opponents in the 1986 World Cup qualifying tournament, as well as the 1988 and 1992 European Championship qualifying groups, were fifth seeds for England.

Norway, who acquitted themselves well in a strong group including the then Soviet Union (now the Commonwealth of Independent States) and Italy, were the 'dark horses' of the section according to Graham Taylor.

While England and Holland, who were the dangerous second seeds allocated to Group 2, are expected to qualify, Graham Taylor was concerned that the Norwegians, a big, powerful side, might be the team to cause the greatest upsets.

Holland, of course, had played England in the 1988 European Championship, winning 3–1 in Düsseldorf and then again in the World Cup finals in 1990. That match, in Cagliari, had ended in a goalless draw.

The new name in England's group was San Marino. Scotland had played San Marino in the Scots' successful qualification for the European Championship in Sweden and Andy Roxburgh, the Scottish manager, promised to brief Graham Taylor on the strengths and many weaknesses of the San Marino side. England have never played San Marino at any level before. At the fixture meeting held in Amsterdam on 14 February, 1992, the two countries agreed that the first ever match would be played at Wembley on 17 February, 1993.

Here is Graham Taylor's assessment of the teams in England's qualifying group.

HOLLAND

The Dutch are one of the strongest teams in Europe but it is difficult to know just who will remain from their current side. It seemed to me that the European Championship was likely to be the last major tournament for players such as Ruud Gullit, Marco van Basten and some of the more experienced members of the Dutch squad.

The Holland that we face may be very different from the one that played in Sweden. I am sure, though, that both countries will see the matches as great crowd-pullers – the glamour matches of the group.

Record in World Cup final stages
P20, W8, D6, L6, F35, A23.
Played in 1934 (9th), 1938 (14th), 1974 (runners-up), 1978 (runners-up), 1990 (15th).
Overall ranking: 16th.

POLAND

There is no doubt that there was an air of disappointment when we drew Poland and, of course, Turkey again. But I know that things change over two years and Poland will be just as worried about facing England.

The last two qualifying competitions have gone to the last match and on both occasions we faced Poland in Poland. Fortunately we got the point we needed but it shows just how close these things can be.

Record in World Cup final stages
P25, W13, D5, L7, F39, A29.
Played in 1938 (11th), 1974 (3rd), 1978 (5th), 1982 (3rd), 1986 (14th).
Overall ranking: 12th.

NORWAY

Norway were in a strong European Championship qualifying group and although they did not reach the finals in Sweden they had a very strong say in who did. They beat Italy, who after all finished third in the 1990 World Cup.

I have seen Norway play a couple of times and they are physically a big side who are well organised and I am sure they will have a big part to play in who qualifies for the World Cup in the United States. It would be wrong to underestimate them.

Record in World Cup final stages
P1, W0, D0, L1, F1, A2.
Played in 1938 (12th – eliminated first round).

TURKEY

Like Poland, we played Turkey in the 1992 European Championship qualifying competition. At least the majority of the England players will not be going into the unknown since they will have met them before.

There will not be much that our team does not know about Turkey by the time that the qualifying matches begin. At the same time they will know all our strengths and the Turks, in Sepp Piontek, have an experienced manager.

Record in World Cup final stages
P3, W1, D0, L2, F10, A11.
Played in 1954 (10th).

SAN MARINO

San Marino are obviously an unknown quantity. We have never played them before but they did play against Scotland in the European Championship qualifiers and we will study the videos of those performances. They did not win a game in the qualifiers but they will be better for the experience. Andy Roxburgh has promised his assistance which we will be happy to accept.

Record in World Cup final stages
Never played. This is San Marino's first World Cup qualifying competition.

ENGLAND'S FIXTURE SCHEDULE

The first contest of the qualifying group was at that fixture meeting in Amsterdam's Hilton Hotel. Graham Taylor, briefed on the performances of England's opponents in previous qualifying campaigns, met managers from the other five nations. They emerged four hours later with a good spread of fixtures. 'I have given the England team the best chance to qualify,' said Graham Taylor. 'It is up to them now.'

Not only did Taylor manage to produce an attractive fixture list, but he also avoided playing a competitive fixture in the first month of the next campaign. Instead England will play a friendly international.

He also managed to preserve England's hopes of taking part in a World Cup acclimatisation tour to the United States in the summer of 1993. 'I think that would be a vital part of our preparation for the World Cup,' he said. But to achieve that Taylor had to make compromises. England will fly to Poland and then to Norway to play two World Cup ties in five days at the end of May and the start of June 1993. 'There had to be compromises somewhere and this was obviously one of the areas. At least our League season will have finished three weeks earlier,' said Taylor. 'The squad will have good preparation time for the games. We will be hoping that we can also fit in a friendly or two before we fly to Poland. The only concern would be if an English team were to reach the European Cup final which is scheduled for May 26.'

The prospect of a tour to Canada and then one to Los Angeles means an intense period of international football for England but Graham Taylor is excited by the prospect. 'There could be seven or eight internationals in that four-week period, so we would be facing the same routine as a European Championship or a World Cup finals. It is ideal preparation for the following year.'

GROUP 2 FIXTURES

England, Holland, Poland, Norway, Turkey, San Marino

9 Sept, 1992: Norway 10, San Marino 0; 23 Sept, 1992: Norway v Holland, Poland v Turkey; 7 Oct, 1992: San Marino v Norway; 14 Oct, 1992: ENGLAND v Norway, Holland v Poland; 28 Oct, 1992: Turkey v San Marino; 18 Nov, 1992: ENGLAND v Turkey; 16 Dec, 1992: Turkey v Holland; 17 Feb, 1993: ENGLAND v San Marino; 24 Feb, 1993: Holland v Turkey; 10 March, 1993: San Marino v Turkey; 24 March, 1993: Holland v San Marino; 31 March, 1993: Turkey v ENGLAND; 28 April, 1993: ENGLAND v Holland, Norway v Turkey, Poland v San Marino; 19 May, 1993: San Marino v Poland; 29 May, 1993: Poland v ENGLAND; 2 June, 1993: Norway v ENGLAND; 9 June, 1993: Holland v Norway; 8 Sept, 1993: ENGLAND v Poland; 22 Sept, 1993: Norway v Poland, San Marino v Holland; 13 Oct, 1993: Holland v ENGLAND, Poland v Norway; 27 Oct, 1993: Turkey v Poland; 10 Nov, 1993: Turkey v Norway; 16 Nov, 1993: San Marino v ENGLAND; 17 Nov, 1993: Poland v Holland.

The Other British Countries' Qualifiers

SCOTLAND'S OPPONENTS AND FIXTURES

Andy Roxburgh, the Scotland manager, wanted an 'attractive fixture list' for his country's fans after what he described as 'an uninspiring group' for the European Championship.

Scotland, who hold the record of qualifying for the last five World Cup finals, avoided their usual Eastern European opponents. Instead they found themselves in what promises to be another tight group with Italy (third in 1990), Portugal and Switzerland (who came so close to reaching Euro '92 in Sweden).

GROUP 1 FIXTURES

Scotland, Italy, Portugal, Switzerland, Malta, Estonia

16 Aug, 1992: Estonia 0, Switzerland 6; 9 Sept, 1992: Switzerland 3 SCOTLAND 1; 14 Oct, 1992: Italy v Switzerland, SCOTLAND v Portugal; 25 Oct, 1992: Malta v Estonia; 18 Nov, 1992: SCOTLAND v Italy, Switzerland v Malta; 19 Dec, 1992: Malta v Italy; 24 Jan, 1993: Malta v Portugal; 17 Feb, 1993: SCOTLAND v Malta; 24 Feb, 1993: Portugal v Italy; 24 March, 1993: Italy v Malta; 31 March, 1993: Switzerland v Portugal; 14 April, 1993: Malta v Switzerland; 28 April, 1993: Portugal v SCOTLAND; 1 May, 1993: Switzerland v Italy; 12 May, 1993: Estonia v Malta; 19 May,1993: Estonia v SCOTLAND; 2 June, 1993: SCOTLAND v Estonia; 19 June, 1993: Portugal v Malta; 5 Sept, 1993: Estonia v Portugal; 8 Sept, 1993: SCOTLAND v Switzerland; 22 Sept, 1993: Estonia v Italy; 13 Oct, 1993: Portugal v Switzerland, Italy v SCOTLAND; 10 Nov, 1993: Portugal v Estonia; 17 Nov, 1993: Italy v Portugal, Malta v SCOTLAND, Switzerland v Estonia.

NORTHERN IRELAND'S AND THE REPUBLIC OF IRELAND'S OPPONENTS AND FIXTURES

GROUP 3 FIXTURES

Northern Ireland, Republic of Ireland, Spain, Denmark, Albania, Lithuania, Latvia

22 April, 1992: Spain 3, Albania 0; 28 April, 1992: NORTHERN IRELAND 2, Lithuania 2; 26 May, 1992: REPUBLIC OF IRELAND 2, Albania 0; 3 June, 1992: Albania 1, Lithuania 0; 12 Aug, 1992: Latvia 2, Lithuania 0; 26, Aug, 1992: Latvia 0, Denmark 0; 9 Sept, 1992: REPUBLIC OF IRELAND 4, NORTHERN IRELAND v Albania; 23 Sept, 1992: Latvia v Spain, Lithuania v Denmark; 14 Oct, 1992: Denmark v REPUBLIC OF IRELAND, NORTHERN IRELAND v Spain; 28 Oct, 1992: Lithuania v Latvia; 11 Nov, 1992: Albania v Latvia; 18 Nov, 1992: NORTHERN IRELAND v Denmark, Spain v REPUBLIC OF IRELAND; 16 Dec, 1992: Spain v Latvia; 17 Feb, 1993: Albania v NORTHERN IRELAND; 24 Feb, 1993: Spain v Lithuania; 31 March, 1993: Denmark v Spain, REPUBLIC OF IRELAND v NORTHERN IRELAND; 14 April, 1993: Denmark v Latvia, Lithuania v Albania; 28 April, 1993: Spain v NORTHERN IRELAND; 15 May, 1993: Latvia v Albania; 25 May, 1993: Lithuania v NORTHERN IRELAND; 26 May, 1993: Albania v REPUBLIC OF IRELAND; 2 June, 1993: Denmark v Albania, Latvia v NORTHERN IRELAND, Lithuania v Spain; 9 June, 1993: Latvia v REPUBLIC OF IRELAND; 16 June, 1993: Lithuania v REPUBLIC OF IRELAND; 25 Aug, 1993: Denmark v Lithuania; 8 Sept, 1993: Albania v Denmark, REPUBLIC OF IRELAND v Lithuania, NORTHERN IRELAND v Latvia; 22 Sept, 1993: Albania v Spain; 13 Oct, 1993: Denmark v NORTHERN IRELAND, REPUBLIC OF IRELAND v Spain; 17 Nov, 1993: NORTHERN IRELAND v REPUBLIC OF IRELAND, Spain v Denmark.

WALES' OPPONENTS AND FIXTURES

GROUP 4 FIXTURES

Wales, Belgium, Cyprus, Romania, Czechoslovakia, Faroe Islands

22 April, 1992: Belgium 1, Cyprus 0; 6 May, 1992: Romania 7, Faroe Islands 0; 20 May, 1992: Romania 5 WALES 1; 3 June, 1992: Faroe Islands 0, Belgium 3; 18 June, 1992: Faroe Islands 0, Cyprus 2; 2 Sept, 1992: Czechoslovakia 1, Belgium 2; 9 Sept, 1992: WALES 6, Faroe Islands 0; 23 Sept, 1992: Czechoslovakia v Faroe Islands; 14 Oct, 1992: Belgium v Romania, Cyprus v WALES; 14 Nov, 1992: Romania v Czechoslovakia; 18 Nov, 1992: WALES v Belgium; 29 Nov, 1992: Cyprus v Romania; 2 Jan, 1993: Cyprus v Belgium; 24 March, 1993: Cyprus v Czechoslovakia; 31 March, 1993: Belgium v WALES; 14 April, 1993: Romania v Cyprus; 25 April, 1993: Cyprus v Faroe Islands; 28 April, 1993: Czechoslovakia v WALES; 22 May, 1993:

Belgium v Faroe Islands; 2 June 2, 1993: Czechoslovakia v Romania; 6 June, 1993: Faroe Islands v WALES; 16 June, 1993: Faroe Islands v Czechoslovakia; 8 Sept, 1993: WALES v Czechoslovakia, Faroe Islands v Romania; 13 Oct, 1993: Romania v Belgium, WALES v Cyprus; 27 Oct, 1993: Czechoslovakia v Cyprus; 17 Nov, 1993: WALES v Romania, Belgium v Czechoslovakia.

Other Fixtures in Europe

GROUP 5 FIXTURES

CIS, Hungary, Greece, Iceland, Luxembourg

13 May, 1992: Greece 1, Iceland 0; 3 June, 1992: Hungary 1, Iceland 2; 9 Sept, 1992: Luxembourg 0, Hungary 3; 7 Oct, 1992: Iceland v Greece; 14 Oct, 1992: CIS v Iceland; 28 Oct, 1992: CIS v Luxembourg; 11 Nov, 1992: Greece v Hungary; 17 Feb, 1993: Greece v Luxembourg; 31 March, 1993: Hungary v Greece; 14 April, 1993: Luxembourg v CIS; 28 April, 1993: CIS v Hungary; 20 May, 1993: CIS v Greece, Luxembourg v Iceland; 2 June, 1993: Iceland v CIS; 16 June, 1993: Iceland v Hungary; 8 Sept, 1993: Hungary v CIS, Iceland v Luxembourg; 12 Oct, 1993: Luxembourg v Greece; 27 Oct, 1993: Hungary v Luxembourg; 17 Nov, 1993: Greece v CIS.

GROUP 6 FIXTURES

France, Austria, Sweden, Bulgaria, Finland, Israel

14 May, 1992: Finland 0, Bulgaria 3; 9 Sept,1992: Bulgaria 2, France 0, Finland 0, Sweden 1; 7 Oct, 1992: Sweden v Bulgaria; 14 Oct, 1992: France v Austria; 28 Oct, 1992: Austria v Israel; 11 Nov, 1992: Israel v Sweden; 14 Nov, 1992: France v Finland; 2 Dec, 1992: Israel v Bulgaria; 17 Feb, 1993: Israel v France; 27 March,1993: Austria v France; 14 April, 1993: Austria v Bulgaria; 28 April, 1993: France v Sweden, Bulgaria v Finland; 12 May, 1993: Bulgaria v Israel; 13 May, 1993: Finland v Austria; 19 May, 1993: Sweden v Austria; 2 June, 1993: Sweden v Israel; 16 June, 1993: Finland v Israel; 22 Aug, 1993: Sweden v France; 25 Aug: 1993: Austria v Finland; 8 Sept, 1993: Finland v France, Bulgaria v Sweden; 13 Oct, 1993: France v Israel, Bulgaria v Austria, Sweden v Finland; 27 Oct, 1993: Israel v Austria; 10 Nov, 1993: Austria v Sweden, Israel v Finland; 17 Nov, 1993: France v Bulgaria.

Argentina's bid to retain the World Cup in Italy in 1990 is foiled by the sheer power of the West Germans exemplified by their skipper Lothar Matthäus, seen here proudly holding the prize

45

4 /B INTERNATIONAL YEAR

Match Reports 1991–92

England B 1 *(Merson)*, **Spain B 0** *(Castellon de la Plana, 18 December, 1991)* (Friendly)

England team: Seaman; Barrett, Winterburn, Webb, Keown, Curle, Rocastle, Campbell (Slater), Hirst, Palmer, Merson (Deane).

This was the match that Paul Merson might look back on as the one that earned him a place in the European Championship squad, for he blossomed on this mild winter night in Castellon de la Plana.

His was a fine goal against a Spanish side being brought together as the country's team to bid for the Olympic soccer title in Barcelona. Merson's intelligent use of space was a critical factor in a splendid victory, even though he had been a doubtful starter for the match because of a tummy bug.

This was the night, too, when Carlton Palmer further pressed his claim for international consideration and was prominent in midfield where Neil Webb supplied some imaginative passing.

It was a significant night also for Martin Keown, one on which he was to further his credibility, eventually leading to senior recognition.

England B 3 *(Merson, Stewart, Dumas o.g.)*, **France B 0** *(Queen's Park Rangers, 18 February, 1992)* (Friendly)

England team: Seaman (Coton); Curle, Dorigo, Stewart, Mabbutt, Pallister, Ince (Le Tissier), Merson, Wright (White), Palmer, Sinton.

This was another good night for Paul Merson as he intensified his bid for senior status with a wonderfully struck free-kick after his Arsenal colleague Ian Wright had been fouled. England played with three centre-halves and the full-backs pushing forward, the style manager Graham Taylor appeared to be developing in all international selections. Frank Dumas, the Frenchman who had conceded the foul that led to Merson's goal, then put through his own goal and Tottenham's Paul Stewart made it a convincing scoreline for England.

England B 1 (*Smith*), **Czechoslovakia B 0** *(Ceske Budejovice, 24 March, 1992)* (Friendly)

England team: Martyn; Barrett, Dicks, Batty, Jobson, Palmer, Sinton, Thomas, Smith (Dorigo), Shearer (Hirst), Le Tissier.

This was a particularly satisfying night for Arsenal's tall centre-forward Alan Smith who the previous weekend

Far left: Matthew Le Tissier, Southampton's highly talented winger, accelerates away from a French defender during the England B game against France at Queen's Park Rangers in February 1992

Left: The England B line-up that drew 1–1 with CIS in Moscow in April. Back row from left to right: Mabbutt, Smith, Thomas, Rocastle, Webb, Jobson. Front row left to right: Dixon, Sharpe, Seaman, Dicks, Beardsley

had been dropped by his manager George Graham. He scored the 75th-minute winner, his third B team goal in as many appearances at this level and enough to keep his name in the frame for the European Championship.

It was a good night, too, for Sheffield Wednesday's Carlton Palmer whose consistency in these matches was certainly capturing the attention of manager Graham Taylor. England, indeed, might have had a healthier victory margin than Smith's tap-in after a shot from Matthew Le Tissier had been blocked.

England B 1 *(Smith)*, **CIS B 1** *(Moscow, 28 April, 1992)* (Friendly)

England team: Seaman; Dixon, Dicks, Webb, Mabbutt, Jobson, Rocastle, Beardsley (Le Saux), Smith, Thomas, Sharpe (Le Tissier).

This was really an uninspired performance by the England second string, but as usual there was some value in it for England manager Graham Taylor. It came with the passing from Neil Webb, the Manchester United midfield player who had finished the season out of favour at his club. But here, against a young CIS side, he was the pass master, though England's opener was scored by Alan Smith, one which probably secured his place in the Sweden squad.

Peter Beardsley was replaced by Chelsea's Graeme Le Saux in the second half and it is possible that the little Everton man was making his last-ever appearance in an England shirt.

5 / UNDER-21 INTERNATIONALS

Match Reports 1991–92

England 2 *(Johnson, Ebbrell)*, **Germany 1** *(Scunthorpe, 10 September, 1991)*
(Friendly)

England team: James; Dodd, Vinnicombe, Ebbrell, Tiler, Warhurst, Johnson, Draper (Matthew), Shearer, Williams, Campbell.

For the first time, an Under-21 international was taken to Scunthorpe, the club where manager Graham Taylor began his career as a 16-year-old apprentice. His return to his roots proved a successful evening thanks to the inspirational captaincy of Everton's John Ebbrell, a graduate of the FA National School at Lilleshall.

It was Notts County's Tommy Johnson, though, who gave England the lead in the 35th minute after he had already forced a fine save from the German goalkeeper. The Germans equalised early in the second half through a Carl Tiler own goal but it was Ebbrell who had the last, telling contribution with a winning volley from 35 yards.

England 2 *(Shearer 2)*, **Turkey 0** *(Reading, 15 October, 1991)*
(UEFA Under-21 Championship)

England team: James; Charles, Vinnicombe, Ebbrell, Tiler, Atherton, Johnson, Matthew (Blake), Shearer, Williams, Campbell.

The match had started with disappointment since Poland's victory over the Irish Republic earlier in the day had ensured that they would qualify for the later stages of the UEFA Under-21 competition. This knowledge made self-motivation difficult at Reading, but England went in search of goals and Chelsea's promising young midfield player Damien Matthew hit the post from a Tommy Johnson cross.

Yet it was only in the second half that England at last made their superior strength really apparent, and then it was Southampton's young Geordie striker who did the business. He scored a typical, opportunistic goal when the Turkish keeper could only block a shot from Gary Charles, and then added a second to put the issue beyond dispute with three minutes remaining.

England 1 *(Kitson)*, **Poland 2** *(Pila, 12 November, 1991)*
(UEFA Under-21 Championship)

England team: James; Dodd, Vinnicombe (Atkinson), Blake (Olney), Cundy, Lee, Kitson, Draper, Shearer, Williams, Johnson.

Without their formerly ever-present skipper John Ebbrell, England went down to qualifiers Poland in Pula in what was a disappointing performance and result. Mark Blake, a substitute in the opening two Under-21 games of the season, started the match, but England were not decisive at the back. The one consolation from the defeat was that Southampton's Alan Shearer again suggested he might be ready for a higher level of football.

England 2 *(Allen, Cole)*, **Hungary 2** *(Vac, 12 May, 1992)*
(Friendly)

England team: Walker; Jackson (Ashcroft), Minto, Sutch, Ehiogu, Hendon (Bazeley), Sheron, Parlour, Cole (Hall), Allen, Heaney.

Right: Dean Blackwell climbs superbly above a Turkish defender but England's Under-21 side did not finish high enough to gain European Under-21 Championship semi-final qualification

Far right: David James' exemplary goalkeeping performances for the England Under-21 side not only brought him to the threshold of senior squad selection, but also helped earn him a move from Watford to Liverpool

There was an exciting debut in this match for the latest off the assembly line of the Allen family, Clive's younger brother Bradley from QPR. He and Arsenal's equally promising Andrew Cole provided the goals against a talented Hungarian side. There was promise in plenty from the young side Lawrie McMenemy is building for the 1992-94 European Under-21 Championship.

But there were two second-half goals from the home side as England's defence was at last exposed for its lack of experience. Even so, it had been an encouraging performance since many of the side were enjoying their first taste of international football.

PROGRAMME FOR 1992–93

8 Sept, 1992	Spain v England in Burgos, Spain
13 Oct, 1992	England v Norway at Peterborough United FC
17 Nov, 1992	England v Turkey at Leyton Orient FC
16 Feb, 1993	England v San Marino *Venue:* TBA
30 March, 1993	Turkey v England in Turkey
27 April, 1993	England v Holland *Venue:* TBA
28 May, 1993	Poland v England in Poland
1 June, 1993	Norway v England in Norway
4-13 June, 1993	Under-21 Tournament in Toulon, France

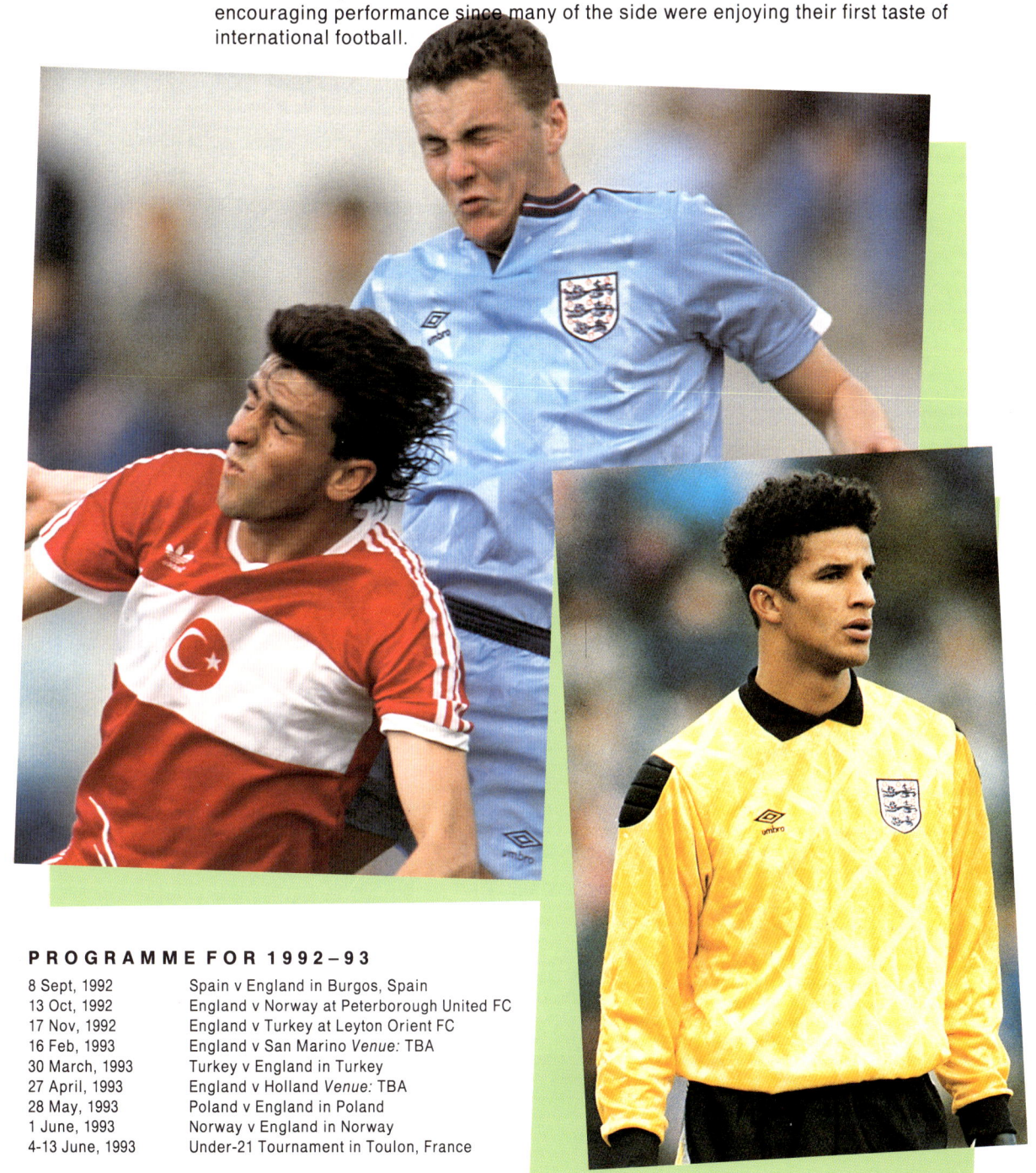

Toulon Tournament

In England's group it was the hosts France and Mexico who eventually qualified for the semi-finals of the competition.

For France, the pre-tournament favourites, there had been two wins and a draw to celebrate in their first three group matches, including a 4–0 thrashing of Mexico who for the second year running had three players dismissed in one single match.

But the Mexicans had proved that they could play football too, drawing with England and beating the promising Czechs 3–1 to secure a semi-final berth.

In Group B it was Portugal and Yugoslavia, fielding perhaps the last national representative sporting team as their country slid into chaos, who slipped quietly through to the semi-finals. Portugal, fielding several players who had triumphed so stylishly in the World Youth Championship in Portugal the previous year, swept to victory in the first semi-final with a 5–1 drubbing of Mexico.

Somewhat surprisingly, it was Yugoslavia who went through to the final at the expense of France when they won 4–3 on penalties following a 0–0 draw.

In the final the superior skill and technique of the Portuguese eventually swayed the outcome of the contest. Despite going behind to an early goal, the Portuguese came back to complete a magnificent fightback with a 2–1 victory.

ENGLAND MATCH DETAILS

England 1, Mexico 1 *(Six-Fours, 24 May, 1992)*

England team: Marriott; Jackson, Hendon, Ehiogu, Minto, Sutch, Parlour, Heaney, Johnson, Kitson, Allen.

England 1, Czechoslovakia 2 *(La Seyne, 26 May, 1992)*

England team: Walker; Jackson, Hendon, Ehiogu, Minto (Johnson), Parlour, Sutch (Cole), Clark, Kitson, Allen, Heaney.

England 0, France 0 *(Aubagne, 28 May, 1992)*

England team: Walker; Jackson, Hendon, Hall, Ehiogu, Sheron, Parlour (Ramage), Clark, Kitson (Cole), Allen, Heaney.

RESULTS

GROUP A

England 1, Mexico 1 *(Six-Fours, 24 May, 1992)*
France 1, Czechoslovakia 2 *(Arles, 26 May, 1992)*
England 1, Czechoslovakia 2 *(La Seyne, 26 May, 1992)*
France 4, Mexico 0 *(La Ciotat, 26 May, 1992)*
France 0, England 0 *(Aubagne, 28 May, 1992)*
Mexico 3, Czechoslovakia 1 *(Brignoles, 28 May, 1992)*

GROUP B

Scotland 0, USA 5 *(Sainte-Maxime, 25 May, 1992)*
Portugal 1, Yugoslavia 0 *(St Cyr, 25 May, 1992)*
Portugal 1, Scotland 0 *(Vitrolles, 27 May, 1992)*
USA 0, Yugoslavia 3 *(Bormes, 27 May, 1992)*
Scotland 0, Yugoslavia 1 *(Fréjus, 29 May, 1992)*
Portugal 2, USA 0 *(Miramas, 29 May, 1992)*

SEMI-FINALS

1st in Group A played 2nd in Group B; 1st in Group B played 2nd in Group A
Yugoslavia 0, France 0 *(Nice, 31 May, 1992)* (aet; Yugoslavia won 4–3 on pens)
Portugal 5, Mexico 1 *(Toulon, 31 May, 1992)*

FINAL

Portugal 2, Yugoslavia 1 *(Toulon, 2 June, 1992)*

6/ENGLAND YOUTH YEAR

The future of English football may not be as bleak as has been widely predicted in recent months, if the opinion of current England Youth Team manager David Burnside is to be believed. The 50-year-old coach, who has spent 11 years as an FA Regional coach, and the last four in charge of the England Youth side, is convinced that English football is not languishing in the doldrums, rather it is undergoing an important transitional period.

'I've always believed that English players have got just as much technical ability as continental players, it's just the understanding to combine as effectively as a team that lets them down.

'The foreign players are always aware of the supporting positions available to them and as a result can string their passes together extremely fluently, which is why people always think that they possess superior technical ability. But the basic difference between them and English players is that continental players have been taught to do that and encouraged to play that way for several consecutive years. English football is a very different type of game in which our players use their technique in different ways.'

Burnside was in charge of the England Youth team which narrowly failed to qualify for the quarter-finals of the 1990 World Youth Championship, but still gave a creditable account of themselves, with several players showing enormous promise for the future.

'We have a number of players who played in the European Youth Cup this summer who have almost certainly got big futures in the game. Stephen Watson from Newcastle United and Chris Bart-Williams from Sheffield Wednesday both came to the World Youth Championship in Portugal last year because they were outstanding prospects for their age.

'They have both come on extremely well, as have Andy Myers from Chelsea and Nicky Barmby (Tottenham). I would say that these players have all got a big future in the Premier League. But we have a lot of fine players in the current youth squad, all of whom have shown great potential.

'In players of their age you like to look for enthusiasm, natural athleticism, a single-minded determination, and a willingness to run for others on the football field as well as the training pitch. All of my players have displayed that so far and that can only augur well for the future.'

Burnside believes that English youth football is among the best in Europe, with only Portugal and the CIS showing greater consistency.

'People always fear having to play English teams. At the moment I would say that we are right up there with the best and if we can make up the small

Alan Shearer, the man tipped as long-term successor to Gary Lineker in the England side, enjoys the company of Martin Keown (left), John Barnes and Tony Daley on his promotion to senior grade

deficiencies which separate our game from that of the continentals, there is no limit to what we can achieve.

'It's such a fine line between winning and losing that if we can adapt our system a little, our record would be even better than it is already.

'My objective now is quite simple. I look to produce one world-class player a season. Already in my four years in charge I have seen the likes of Ian Walker, the Tottenham goalkeeper, and Andy Awford from Portsmouth impress me immensely at this level. They have gone on to attract attention at U-21 level and again I think they will be top-class players. That is what I spend all my time and energy working towards and I am delighted to say that I am just as encouraged now by the wealth of talent coming through as I have always been.'

Under-18

EUROPEAN YOUTH CHAMPIONSHIP

RESULTS

QUARTER-FINALS

Portugal Youth (1) 4, Germany Youth (0) 0 *(Nurnberg, 20 July, 1992)*
Turkey Youth (1) 3, Hungary Youth (0) 0 *(Nordlinge, 20 July, 1992)*
England Youth (2) 6, Poland Youth (1) 1 *(Regensburg, 20 July, 1992)*
CIS Youth (2) 4, Norway Youth (1) 4 *(Hassfurt, 20 July, 1992) (aet; Norway Youth won on pens)*

PLAY-OFFS

Germany Youth (1) 3, Poland Youth (0) 2 *(Bamberg, 22 July, 1992)*
Hungary Youth (0) 1, CIS Youth (1) 3 *(Vestenberg, 22 July, 1992)*

SEMI-FINALS

Portugal Youth (0) 1, England Youth (0) 1 *(Schweinfurt, 22 July, 1992) (aet; Portugal Youth won 12–11 on pens)*
Norway Youth (1) 1, Turkey Youth (2) 2 *(Schwandorf, 22 July, 1992)*

THIRD PLACE PLAY-OFF

England Youth (1) 1, Norway Youth (1) 1 *(Amberg, 24 July, 1992) (aet; Norway Youth won 8–7 on pens)*

FINAL

Portugal Youth (1) 1, Turkey Youth (1) 2 *(Bayreuth, 25 July, 1992) (aet; 1–1 at 90 mins)*

ENGLAND MATCH DETAILS

QUALIFYING COMPETITION

England Youth 2 *(Bart-Williams, Myers)*, **Iceland Youth 1** *(Crystal Palace, 12 September, 1991)*

England team: Stephenson; Watson S (Watson D), Unsworth, Harriott, Basham, Thompson, Bart-Williams, Caskey, Hodges (Marlowe), Myers, Howe.

Belgium Youth 1, England Youth 0 *(SK Eernegem, 16 October, 1991)*

England team: Sheppard; Watson S, Unsworth (Marlowe), Pearce, Jackson, Thompson, Bart-Williams (Elliot), Caskey, Shaw, Myers, Howe.

FINALS

England Youth (2) 6 *(Watson S, Myers 2, Barmby, Thompson, Bart-Williams)*, **Poland Youth (1) 1** *(Regensberg, 20 July, 1992)*

England team: Watson D; Watson S, Unsworth, Harriott, Pearce, Myers, Pollock (Marlow), Caskey, Barmby (Howe), Thompson, Bart-Williams.

Portugal Youth (0) 1, England Youth (0) 1 *(Pollock) (Schweinfurt, 22 July, 1992) (aet; 1–1 at 90 mins; Portugal Youth won 12–11 on pens)*

England team: Watson D; Watson S, Unsworth, Harriott, Pearce, Myers, Pollock, Caskey, Barmby, Thompson, Bart-Williams.

England Youth (1) 1 *(Bart-Williams)*, **Norway Youth (1) 1** *(Amberg, 24 July, 1992) (aet: 1–1 at 90 mins; Norway Youth won 8–7 on pens)*

England team: Watson D; Watson S, Unsworth (Marlowe), Harriott, Pearce, Myers, Pollock, Caskey, Barmby, Hughes, Bart-Williams.

TOUR TO SWEDEN

England 1 *(Barmby)*, **Halmstads Bollklubb 1**
(Halmstad, 7 July, 1992)
(Friendly)

England team: Sheppard; Watson S, Unsworth, Harriott, Pearce, Myers, Pollock, Caskey, Barmby (Berry), Thompson, Bart-Williams.

England 2 *(Myers, Barmby)*, **iFK Goteborg 0**
(Rambergsvallen, 10 July, 1992)
(Friendly)

England team: Watson D; Watson S, Unsworth, Marlowe, Pearce, Myers, Pollock, Caskey, Barmby, Thompson, Bart-Williams.

Under-16

NORDIC CUP

England 1 *(Walker)*, **Denmark 4** *(Tysvollur, 7 August, 1991)*

England team: Hopper; Frost (Smith), Thatcher, Hinshelwood, Faulkner (Holland), Murray, Worrall, Irving, Beech, Walker, Challis.

England 2 *(Murray, Faulkner)*, **Sweden 0**
(Porsvollur, 8 August, 1991)

England team: Hopper; Faulkner, Challis, Hinshelwood, Holland, Murray, Worrall, Irving (Feltham), Beech (Smith), Walker, Serrant.

England 3 *(Irving 2, Beech)*, **Iceland 2** *(Tysvollur, 10 August, 1991)*

England team: Woods; Holland (Frost), Challis (Thatcher), Hinshelwood, Faulkner, Murray, Worrall, Irving (Smith), Beech (Feltham), Walker, Serrant.

England 2 *(Serrant, Hinshelwood)*, **Norway 1**
(Haesteinvolluk, 11 August, 1991)

England team: Hopper; Frost (Thatcher), Challis, Hinshelwood, Faulkner, Murray, Worrall, Irving (Feltham), Beech, Walker, Serrant.

England 3 *(Worrall 2, Hinshelwood)*, **Finland 2**
(Porsvollur, 12 August, 1991)

England team: Hopper; Holland, Challis, Hinshelwood, Faulkner, Murray, Worrall, Feltham (Woods), Beech, Walker, Serrant.

FRIENDLY INTERNATIONALS

England 1 *(Murray)*, **Denmark 1** *(Lilleshall Sports Centre, 1 October, 1991)*

England team: Hopper; Hinshelwood, Challis, Feltham, Murray, Worrall, Holland (Tierney), Walker, Irving (Smith), Beech (Frost), Serrant.

England 0, Denmark 1 *(Lilleshall Sports Centre, 3 October, 1991)*

England team: Hopper (Woods); Hinshelwood (Holland), Challis, Feltham (Vaughan), Murray, Worrall, Frost (Tierney), Irving (Beech), Smith, Walker, Serrant (Strong).

GENOA TOURNAMENT

England 1 *(Irving)*, **Scotland 3** *(Com. Alassi, 15 October, 1992)*

England team: Woods; Holland (Tierney), Challis, Hinshelwood, Faulkner, Murray, Worrall, Walker, Beech, Irving, Serrant.

England 0, Italy 3 *(Cairo Montenotte, 16 October, 1992)*

England team: Pettinger; Holland, Challis, Hinshelwood, Faulkner, Murray (Feltham), Worrall, Walker, Beech (Smith), Irving, Serrant (Frost).

England 3 *(Irving 2, Tierney)*, **Austria 1** *(Cairo Montenotte, 17 October, 1992)*

England team: Woods (Pettinger); Frost (Holland), Hinshelwood (Serrant), Murray, Feltham, Walker, Worrall, Challis, Irving, Smith (Beech), Tierney.

TOUR TO QATAR AND OMAN

Qatar 3, England 3 *(Worrall, Challis, Beech)*
(Doha, Qatar, 25 February, 1992)

England team: Hopper (Woods); Hinshelwood, Challis (Thatcher), Murray, Faulkner (Feltham), Worrall (Frost), Holland, Walker, Beech, Irving (Smith), Serrant.

Oman 2, England 1 *(Frost)* *(Sultan Qaboos Stadium, Muscat, Oman, 28 February, 1992)*

England team: Hopper; Hinshelwood, Challis, Murray, Faulkner, Worrall (Frost), Holland, Walker, Beech, Irving, Serrant.

53

7 / WOMEN'S FOOTBALL

The season of 1991–92 will go down as arguably the most historic in the development of organised women's football in this country. Under the leadership of chairman Tim Stearn and secretary Linda Whitehead, the women's game demonstrated its ability to sustain a thriving new National League comprising three divisions of eight clubs. Closely following the guidelines established by clubs outside the Football League, women's football now has its own pyramid, with promotion from the grass roots through to a Premier Division organised on a national basis.

In the Premier Division there was little deviation from the norm, with the Doncaster Belles, who once again formed the nucleus of the England team, completing a unique League and Cup double. The South Yorkshire club, who clinched the League Championship with a 100% record, added the Mycil WFA Cup to their list of honours by defeating Red Star Southampton 4–0 in the final, which was televised for the fourth year running by Channel 4. Top scorer and England international Karen Walker captured 36 goals in the League and confirmed her status as the game's premier markswomen with a further 22 goals in the Mycil WFA Cup. She collected a hat-trick in every round of the competition, including the final.

The success of the new competition has led to an expansion of the League structure to 30 clubs in season 1992–93, as women's football aims to consolidate its position as Britain's fastest growing participation sport.

On the international front, England warmed up for the UEFA Women's International Championship in 1993 with two qualifying victories over Scotland and Iceland.

Women's World Cup, China 1991

The huge success of the first FIFA World Championship for women's teams held in China in November 1991 was a clear indication of the progress made in the sport by female players. There were 12 nations competing in the finals, won by the United States where women's football is immensely popular in high schools and colleges. The Chinese success has been warmly welcomed by those tireless people who have worked so hard to give the women's game some status in Britain. In recognition of their efforts we record the milestones of the development of women's football.

GROUP A

Played in Canton, Foshan and Punya
China PR (1) 4, Norway (0) 0 *(16 November, 1991)*
Denmark (2) 3, New Zealand (1) 2 *(17 November, 1991)*
China (1) 2, Denmark (1) 2 *(19 November, 1991)*
Norway (3) 4, New Zealand (0) 0 *(19 November, 1991)*
China (3) 4, New Zealand (0) 1 *(21 November, 1991)*
Norway (1) 2, Denmark (0) 1 *(21 November, 1991)*

	P	W	D	L	F	A	Pts
China	3	2	1	0	10	3	5
Norway	3	2	0	1	6	5	4
Denmark	3	1	1	1	6	4	3
New Zealand	3	0	0	3	1	11	0

GROUP B

Played in Foshan and Punya
Japan (0) 0, Brazil (1) 1 *(17 November, 1991)*
Sweden (0) 2, USA (1) 3 *(17 November, 1991)*
Japan (0) 0, Sweden (6) 8 *(19 November, 1991)*
Brazil (0) 0, USA (4) 5 *(19 November, 1991)*
Japan (0) 0, USA (3) 3 *(21 November, 1991)*
Brazil (0) 0, Sweden (0) 2 *(21 November, 1991)*

	P	W	D	L	F	A	Pts
USA	3	3	0	0	11	2	6
Sweden	3	2	0	1	12	3	4
Brazil	3	1	0	2	1	7	2
Japan	3	0	0	3	0	12	0

GROUP C

Played in Jiangmen and Zhongshan
Chinese Taipei (0) 0, Italy (3) 5 *(17 November, 1991)*
Germany (3) 4, Nigeria (0) 0 *(17 November, 1991)*
Chinese Taipei (0) 0, Germany (2) 3 *(19 November, 1991)*
Italy (0) 1, Nigeria (0) 0 *(19 November, 1991)*
Chinese Taipei (1) 2, Nigeria (0) 0 *(21 November, 1991)*
Italy (0) 0, Germany (0) 2 *(21 November, 1991)*

	P	W	D	L	F	A	Pts
Germany	3	3	0	0	9	0	6
Italy	3	2	0	1	6	2	4
Taiwan	3	1	0	2	2	8	2
Nigeria	3	0	0	3	0	7	0

QUARTER-FINALS

China (0) 0, Sweden (1) 1 *(24 November, 1991)*
Norway (1) 3, Italy (1) 2 *(aet; 2–2 at 90 mins) (24 November, 1991)*
Denmark (1) 1, Germany (1) 2 *aet (24 November, 1991)*
USA (4) 7, Chinese Taipei (0) 0 *(24 November, 1991)*

THIRD PLACE PLAY OFF

Sweden (3) 4, Germany (0) 0 *(29 November, 1991)*

SEMI-FINALS

Sweden (1) 1, Norway (1) 4 *(27 November, 1991)*

Sweden: Leidinge; Hansson, Lundgren, Karlsson, Zeikfalvy, Hedberg, Sundhage, Johansson, Ewielius, Videkull, Andelen.

Norway: Seth; Stoere, Espeseth, Svensson, Carlsen, Haugen, Zaborowski, Nyborg, Riise, Medalen, Hegstad.

Germany (1) 2, USA (3) 5 *(27 November, 1991)*

Germany: Isbert; Fitschen, Paul, Nardenbach, Austerrnühl, Kuhlmann, Bindl, Wiegmann, Gottschlich, Voss, Mohr.

USA: Harvey; Werden, Beifeld, Hamilton, Hamm, Higgins, Foudy, Lilly, Henrichs, Akers-Stahl, Jennings.

FINAL

Norway (1) 1, USA (1) 2 *(Guangzhou, 30 November, 1991)*

Norway: Seth; Stoere, Svensson, Espeseth, Nyborg, Haugen, Zaborowski, Carlsen, Riise, Medalen, Hegstad.

USA: Harvey; Werden, Beifeld, Hamilton, Hamm, Higgins, Foudy, Lilly, Henrichs, Akers-Stahl, Jennings.

UEFA International Championship

QUALIFYING ROUNDS

England 1 *(Walker)*, **Scotland 0** *(Bescot Stadium, Walsall, 18 April, 1992)*

England 4 *(Bampton 2, Murray, Walker)*, **Iceland 0** *(Huish Park, Yeovil, 17 May, 1992)*

International Matches 1972–1992

UQ UEFA Qualifying   US UEFA Semi-final   UF UEFA Final

1972
| v Scotland | W | 3–2 |

1973
v France	W	3–0
v Scotland	W	8–0
v Northern Ireland	W	5–1
v Holland	W	1–0

1974
v Wales	W	5–0
v Holland	W	3–0
v France	W	2–0

1975
v Switzerland	W	3–1
v Sweden	L	0–2
v Sweden	L	1–3

1976
v Holland	W	2–1
v Wales	W	4–0
v Scotland	W	5–1
v Italy	L	0–2
v Italy	L	1–2
v Wales	L	0–1

1977
v France	D	0–0
v Switzerland	W	9–1
v Scotland	L	1–2
v Wales	W	5–0
v Italy	W	1–0

1978
v Republic of Ireland	W	6–1
v Holland	L	1–3
v Belgium	W	3–0

1979
v Denmark	L	1–3
v Finland	W	3–1
v Switzerland	W	2–0
v Italy	L	1–3
v Sweden	L	0–0
(Sweden won 4–3 on pens)
| v Denmark | D | 2–2 |

1980
| v Belgium | L | 1–2 |
| v Wales | W | 6–1 |
| v Sweden | D | 1–1 | 1981
| v Republic of Ireland | W | 5–0 |

v Japan	W	4–0
v Denmark	L	0–1
v Norway	L	0–3

1982
v Sweden	D	1–1
v Italy	L	0–2
v Northern Ireland	W	7–1 (UQ)
v Scotland	W	4–0 (UQ)
v Republic of Ireland	W	1–0 (UQ)

1983
v Northern Ireland	W	4–0 (UQ)
v Scotland	W	2–0 (UQ)
v Republic of Ireland	W	6–0 (UQ)
v Sweden	D	2–2

1984
v Denmark	W	2–1 (US)
v Denmark	W	1–0 (US)
v Sweden	L	0–1 (UF)
v Sweden	W	1–0 (UF)
(Sweden won on pens)

Competition in Italy
| v Belgium | D | 1–1 |

v West Germany	L	0–2
v Italy	D	1–1
v Belgium	W	2–1
v Italy	W	3–1

1985
v Scotland	W	4–0 (UQ)
v Northern Ireland	W	7–1 (UQ)
v Republic of Ireland	W	7–0 (UQ)
v Wales	W	6–0

Competition in Italy
v Denmark	L	0–1
v Italy	D	1–1
v USA	W	3–1
v Italy	W	3–2

1986
v Northern Ireland	W	10–0 (UQ)
v Republic of Ireland	W	4–0 (UQ)
v Scotland	W	3–1 (UQ)

1987
v Republic of Ireland	W	1–0
v Northern Ireland	W	6–0
v Sweden	L	2–3 (US)
(aet; 2–2 at 90 mins)		
v Italy	L	1–2
v Finland	W	2–1 (UQ)
v Denmark	W	2–1 (UQ)

1988
Competition in Italy
| v Italy | W | 3–0 |
| v France | D | 1–1 |

v USA	W	2–0
v Italy	W	2–1
v Norway	L	0–2 (UQ)
v Finland	D	1–1 (UQ)
v Norway	L	1–3 (UQ)
v Denmark	L	0–2 (UQ)

1989
v Scotland	W	3–0
v Sweden	L	0–2
v Finland	D	0–0 (UQ)
v Italy	D	1–1

1990
v Belgium	W	3–0 (UQ)
v Belgium	W	1–0 (UQ)
v Scotland	W	4–0
v Norway	L	0–2 (UQ)

USA Tour
v West Germany	L	1–3
v USA	L	0–3
v USSR	D	1–1
v Norway	D	0–0 (UQ)
v Finland	D	0–0 (UQ)
v Germany	L	1–4 (US)
v Germany	L	0–2 (US)

1991
v Scotland	W	5–0
v USA	L	1–3
v Denmark	D	0–0
v Denmark	D	3–3
v USSR	W	2–1

v USSR	W	2–0
v USSR	W	2–0
v USSR	L	1–3

1992
v Scotland	W	1–0 (UQ)
v Iceland	W	4–0 (UQ)
v Iceland	W	2–1 (UQ)
v Scotland	W	2–0 (UQ)

P108, W61, D17, L30, F248, A107

The England Women's soccer squad, prior to their game against Iceland in Yeovil last May. The squad is, top left to right: Samantha Britton (Huddersfield), Michelle Jackson (Doncaster Belles), Marianne Spacey (Wimbledon), Jan Murray (Doncaster Belles), Lesley Shipp (Arsenal), Shirley Garnham (Sheffield Wednesday), Debbie Bampton (Wimbledon), Jackie Sherrard (Doncaster Belles), Clare Taylor (Brent), Gail Borman (Doncaster Belles), Karen Burke (Knowsley United), Samantha Hayward (Knowsley United), Louise Walker (Millwall Lionesses), Gillian Coultard (Doncaster Belles), Sue Law (Bromley Borough), Karen Walker (Doncaster Belles)

RECORD SECTION

England

Full International Line-ups 1946-1992

* after extra time † World Cup Finals

1946 N Ireland
Swift
Scott
Hardwick
Wright W
Franklin
Cockburn
Finney
Carter
Lawton
Mannion
Langton
Belfast 28 Sept: 7–2
Carter, Mannion 3,
Finney, Lawton,
Langton

1946 Rep of Ireland
Swift
Scott
Hardwick
Wright W
Franklin
Cockburn
Finney
Carter
Lawton
Mannion
Langton
Dublin 30 Sept: 1–0
Finney

1946 Wales
Swift
Scott
Hardwick
Wright W
Franklin
Cockburn
Finney
Carter
Lawton
Mannion
Langton
Maine Road 19 Oct:
3–0 Mannion 2, Lawton

1946 Netherlands
Swift
Scott
Hardwick
Wright W
Franklin
Johnston
Finney
Carter
Lawton
Mannion
Langton
Huddersfield 27 Nov:
8–2 Lawton 4, Carter 2,
Mannion, Finney

1947 Scotland
Swift
Scott
Hardwick
Wright W
Franklin
Johnston
Matthews S
Carter
Lawton
Mannion
Mullen
Wembley 12 April: 1–1
Carter

1947 France
Swift
Scott
Hardwick
Wright W
Franklin
Lowe
Finney
Carter
Lawton
Mannion
Langton
Highbury 3 May: 3–0
Finney, Mannion,
Carter

1947 Switzerland
Swift
Scott
Hardwick
Wright W
Franklin
Lowe
Matthews S
Carter
Lawton
Mannion
Langton
Zurich 18 May: 0–1

1947 Portugal
Swift
Scott
Hardwick
Wright W
Franklin
Lowe
Matthews S
Mortensen
Lawton
Mannion
Finney
Lisbon 27 May: 10–0
Lawton 4, Mortensen 4,
Finney, Matthews

1947 Belgium
Swift
Scott
Hardwick
Ward
Franklin
Wright W
Matthews S
Mortensen
Lawton
Mannion
Finney
Brussels 21 Sept: 5–2
Lawton 2, Mortensen,
Finney 2

1947 Wales
Swift
Scott
Hardwick
Taylor P
Franklin
Wright W
Matthews S
Mortensen
Lawton
Mannion
Finney
Cardiff 18 Oct: 3–0
Finney, Mortensen,
Lawton

1947 N Ireland
Swift
Scott
Hardwick
Taylor P
Franklin
Wright W
Matthews S
Mortensen
Lawton
Mannion
Finney
Everton 5 Nov: 2–2
Mannion, Lawton

1947 Sweden
Swift
Scott
Hardwick
Taylor P
Franklin
Wright W
Finney
Mortensen
Lawton
Mannion
Langton
Highbury 19 Nov: 4–2
Mortensen 3, Lawton
pen

1948 Scotland
Swift
Scott
Hardwick
Wright W
Franklin
Cockburn
Matthews S
Mortensen
Lawton
Pearson
Finney
Glasgow 10 April: 2–0
Finney, Mortensen

1948 Italy
Swift
Scott
Howe J
Wright W
Franklin
Cockburn
Matthews S
Mortensen
Lawton
Mannion
Finney
Turin 16 May: 4–0
Mortensen, Lawton,
Finney 2

1948 Denmark
Swift
Scott
Aston
Wright W
Franklin
Cockburn
Matthews S
Hagan
Lawton
Shackleton
Langton
Copenhagen 26 Sept:
0–0

1948 N Ireland
Swift
Scott
Howe J
Wright W
Franklin
Cockburn
Matthews S
Mortensen
Milburn
Pearson
Finney
Belfast 9 Oct: 6–2
Matthews S, Mortensen
3, Milburn, Pearson

1948 Wales
Swift
Scott
Aston
Ward
Franklin
Wright W
Matthews S
Mortensen
Milburn
Shackleton

57

Finney
Villa Park 10 Nov: 1–0
Finney

1948 Switzerland
Ditchburn
Ramsey
Aston
Wright W
Franklin
Cockburn
Matthews S
Rowley J
Milburn
Haines
Hancocks
Highbury 1 Dec: 6–0
Haines 2, Hancocks 2,
Rowley, Milburn

1948 Scotland
Swift
Aston
Howe J
Wright W
Franklin
Cockburn
Matthews S
Mortensen
Milburn
Pearson
Finney
Wembley 9 April: 1–3
Milburn

1949 Sweden
Ditchburn
Shinwell
Aston
Wright W
Franklin
Cockburn
Finney
Mortensen
Bentley
Rowley J
Langton
Stockholm 13 May: 1–3
Finney

1949 Norway
Swift
Ellerington
Aston
Wright W
Franklin
Dickinson
Finney
Morris
Mortensen
Mannion
Mullen
Oslo 18 May: 4–1
Mullen, Finney,
Spydevolde o.g., Morris

1949 France
Williams
Ellerington
Aston
Wright W
Franklin
Dickinson
Finney
Morris
Rowley J
Mannion
Mullen
Paris 22 May: 3–1
Morris 2, Wright

1949 Rep of Ireland
Williams
Mozley
Aston
Wright W
Franklin
Dickinson
Harris P
Morris
Pye
Mannion
Finney
Goodison Park 21 Sept:
0–2

1949 Wales
Williams
Mozley
Aston
Wright W
Franklin
Dickinson
Finney
Mortensen
Milburn
Shackleton
Hancocks
Cardiff 15 Oct: 4–1
Mortensen, Milburn 3

1949 N Ireland
Streten
Mozley
Aston
Watson
Franklin
Wright W
Finney
Mortensen
Rowley J
Pearson
Froggatt J
Maine Road 16 Nov: 9–2
Rowley 4, Froggatt,
Pearson 2, Mortensen 2

1949 Italy
Williams
Ramsey
Aston
Watson
Franklin
Wright W
Finney
Mortensen
Rowley J
Pearson
Froggatt J
Tottenham 30 Nov: 2–0
Rowley, Wright

1950 Scotland
Williams
Ramsey
Aston
Wright W
Franklin
Dickinson
Finney
Mannion
Mortensen
Bentley
Langton
Glasgow 15 April: 1–0
Bentley

1950 Portugal
Williams
Ramsey
Aston
Wright W
Jones WH
Dickinson
Milburn
Mortensen
Bentley
Mannion
Finney
Lisbon 14 May: 5–3
Finney 4 (2 pens),
Mortensen

1950 Belgium
Williams
Ramsey
Aston
Wright W
Jones WH
Dickinson
Milburn
(Mullen)
Mortensen
Bentley
Mannion
Finney
Brussels 18 May: 4–1
Mullen, Mortensen,
Mannion, Bentley

1950 Chile†
Williams
Ramsey
Aston
Wright W
Hughes L
Dickinson
Finney
Mannion
Bentley
Mortensen
Mullen
Rio de Janeiro 25 June:
2–0 Mortensen,
Mannion

1950 USA†
Williams
Ramsey
Aston
Wright W
Hughes L
Dickinson
Finney
Mannion
Bentley
Mortensen
Mullen
Belo Horizonte 29 June:
0–1

1950 Spain†
Williams
Ramsey
Eckersley
Wright W
Hughes L
Dickinson
Matthews S
Mortensen
Milburn
Baily E
Finney
Rio de Janeiro 2 July:
0–1

1950 N Ireland
Williams
Ramsey
Aston
Wright W
Chilton
Dickinson
Matthews S
Mannion
Lee J
Baily E
Langton
Belfast 7 Oct: 4–1 Baily
2, Lee, Wright

1950 Wales
Williams
Ramsey
Smith L
Watson
Compton L
Dickinson
Finney
Mannion
Milburn
Baily E
Medley
Sunderland 15 Nov:
4–2 Baily 2, Mannion,
Milburn

1950 Yugoslavia
Williams
Ramsey
Eckersley
Watson
Compton L
Dickinson
Hancocks
Mannion
Lofthouse
Baily E
Medley
Highbury 22 Nov: 2–2
Lofthouse 2

1951 Scotland
Williams
Ramsey
Eckersley
Johnston
Froggatt J
Wright W
Matthews S
Mannion
Mortensen
Hassall
Finney
Wembley 14 April: 2–3
Hassall, Finney

1951 Argentina
Williams
Ramsey
Eckersley
Wright W
Taylor J
Cockburn
Finney
Mortensen
Milburn
Hassall
Metcalfe
Wembley 9 May: 2–1
Mortensen 2

1951 Portugal
Williams
Ramsey
Eckersley
Nicholson
Taylor J
Cockburn
Finney
Pearson
Milburn
Hassall
Metcalfe
Goodison Park 19 May:
5–2 Nicholson, Milburn
2, Finney, Hassall

1951 France
Williams
Ramsey

Willis
Wright W
Chilton
Cockburn
Finney
Mannion
Milburn
Hassall
Medley
Highbury 3 Oct: 2–2
Firoud o.g., Medley

1951 Wales
Williams
Ramsey
Smith L
Wright W
Barrass
Dickinson
Finney
Thompson T
Lofthouse
Baily E
Medley
Cardiff 20 Oct: 1–1 Baily

1951 N Ireland
Merrick
Ramsey
Smith L
Wright W
Barrass
Dickinson
Finney
Sewell
Lofthouse
Phillips
Medley
Villa Park 14 Nov: 2–0
Lofthouse 2

1951 Austria
Merrick
Ramsey
Eckersley
Wright W
Froggatt J
Dickinson
Milton
Broadis
Lofthouse
Baily E
Medley
Wembley 28 Nov: 2–2
Ramsey pen, Lofthouse

1952 Scotland
Merrick
Ramsey
Garrett
Wright W
Froggatt J
Dickinson
Finney
Broadis
Lofthouse

Pearson
Rowley J
Glasgow 5 April: 2–1
Pearson 2

1952 Italy
Merrick
Ramsey
Garrett
Wright W
Froggatt J
Dickinson
Finney
Broadis
Lofthouse
Pearson
Elliott
Florence 18 May: 1–1
Broadis

1952 Austria
Merrick
Ramsey
Eckersley
Wright W
Froggatt J
Dickinson
Finney
Sewell
Lofthouse
Baily E
Elliott
Vienna 25 May: 3–2
Lofthouse 2, Sewell

1952 Switzerland
Merrick
Ramsey
Eckersley
Wright W
Froggatt J
Dickinson
Allen R
Sewell
Lofthouse
Baily E
Finney
Zurich 28 May: 3–0
Sewell, Lofthouse 2

1952 N Ireland
Merrick
Ramsey
Eckersley
Wright W
Froggatt J
Dickinson
Finney
Sewell
Lofthouse
Baily E
Elliott
Belfast 4 Oct: 2–2
Lofthouse, Elliott

1952 Wales
Merrick

Ramsey
Smith L
Wright W
Froggatt J
Dickinson
Finney
Froggatt R
Lofthouse
Bentley
Elliott
Wembley 12 Nov: 5–2
Finney, Lofthouse 2,
Froggatt J, Bentley

1952 Belgium
Merrick
Ramsey
Smith L
Wright W
Froggatt J
Dickinson
Finney
Bentley
Lofthouse
Froggatt R
Elliott
Wembley 26 Nov: 5–0
Elliott 2, Lofthouse 2,
Froggatt R

1953 Scotland
Merrick
Ramsey
Smith L
Wright W
Barrass
Dickinson
Finney
Broadis
Lofthouse
Froggatt R
Froggatt J
Wembley 18 April: 2–2
Broadis 2

1953 Argentina
Merrick
Ramsey
Eckersley
Wright W
Johnston
Dickinson
Finney
Broadis
Lofthouse
Taylor T
Berry
Buenos Aires 17 May:
0–0 (abandoned after 23
mins.)

1953 Chile
Merrick
Ramsey
Eckersley
Wright W

Johnston
Dickinson
Finney
Broadis
Lofthouse
Taylor T
Berry
Santiago 24 May: 2–1
Taylor, Lofthouse

1953 Uruguay
Merrick
Ramsey
Eckersley
Wright W
Johnston
Dickinson
Finney
Broadis
Lofthouse
Taylor T
Berry
Montevideo 31 May: 1–2
Taylor

1953 USA
Ditchburn
Ramsey
Eckersley
Wright W
Johnston
Dickinson
Finney
Broadis
Lofthouse
Froggatt R
Froggatt J
New York 8 June: 6–3
Broadis, Finney 2,
Lofthouse 2, Froggatt R

1953 Wales
Merrick
Garrett
Eckersley
Wright W
Johnston
Dickinson
Finney
Quixall
Lofthouse
Wilshaw
Mullen
Cardiff 10 Oct: 4–1
Wilshaw 2, Lofthouse 2

1953 FIFA
Merrick
Ramsey
Eckersley
Wright W
Ufton
Dickinson
Matthews S
Mortensen
Lofthouse

Quixall
Mullen
Wembley 21 Oct: 4–4
Mullen 2, Mortensen,
Ramsey pen

1953 N Ireland
Merrick
Rickaby
Eckersley
Wright W
Johnston
Dickinson
Matthews S
Quixall
Lofthouse
Hassall
Mullen
Goodison Park 11 Nov:
3–1 Hassall 2,
Lofthouse

1953 Hungary
Merrick
Ramsey
Eckersley
Wright W
Johnston
Dickinson
Matthews S
Taylor E
Mortensen
Sewell
Robb
Wembley 25 Nov: 3–6
Sewell, Mortensen,
Ramsey pen

1954 Scotland
Merrick
Staniforth
Byrne R
Wright W
Clarke H
Dickinson
Finney
Broadis
Allen R
Nicholls
Mullen
Glasgow 3 April: 4–2
Broadis, Nicholls,
Allen, Mullen

1954 Yugoslavia
Merrick
Staniforth
Byrne R
Wright W
Owen
Dickinson
Finney
Broadis
Allen R
Nicholls

59

Mullen
Belgrade 16 May: 0–1

1954 Hungary
Merrick
Staniforth
Byrne R
Wright W
Owen
Dickinson
Harris P
Sewell
Jezzard
Broadis
Finney
Budapest 23 May: 1–7
Broadis

1954 Belgium†
Merrick
Staniforth
Byrne R
Wright W
Owen
Dickinson
Matthews S
Broadis
Lofthouse
Taylor T
Finney
Basle 17 June: 4–4†
Broadis 2, Lofthouse 2

1954 Switzerland†
Merrick
Staniforth
Byrne R
McGarry
Wright W
Dickinson
Finney
Broadis
Taylor T
Wilshaw
Mullen
Berne 20 June: 2–0
Wilshaw, Mullen

1954 Uruguay†
Merrick
Staniforth
Byrne R
McGarry
Wright W
Dickinson
Matthews S
Broadis
Lofthouse
Wilshaw
Finney
Basle 26 June: 2–4
Lofthouse, Finney

1954 N Ireland
Wood
Foulkes
Byrne R
Wheeler
Wright W
Barlow
Matthews S
Revie
Lofthouse
Haynes
Pilkington
Belfast 2 Oct: 2–0
Haynes, Revie

1954 Wales
Wood
Staniforth
Byrne R
Phillips
Wright W
Slater
Matthews S
Bentley
Allen R
Shackleton
Blunstone
Wembley 10 Nov: 3–2
Bentley 3

1954 W Germany
Williams
Staniforth
Byrne R
Phillips
Wright W
Slater
Matthews S
Bentley
Allen R
Shackleton
Finney
Wembley 1 Dec: 3–1
Bentley, Allen,
Shackleton

1955 Scotland
Williams
Meadows
Byrne R
Armstrong
Wright W
Edwards
Matthews S
Revie
Lofthouse
Wilshaw
Blunstone
Wembley 2 April: 7–2
Wilshaw 4, Lofthouse 2,
Revie

1955 France
Williams
Sillett P
Byrne R
Flowers
Wright W
Edwards
Matthews S
Revie
Lofthouse
Wilshaw
Blunstone
Paris 18 May: 0–1

1955 Spain
Williams
Sillett P
Byrne R
Dickinson
Wright W
Edwards
Matthews S
Bentley
Lofthouse
Quixall
Wilshaw
Madrid 18 May: 1–1
Bentley

1955 Portugal
Williams
Sillett P
Byrne R
Dickinson
Wright W
Edwards
Matthews S
Bentley
Lofthouse
(Quixall)
Wilshaw
Blunstone
Oporto 22 May: 1–3
Bentley

1955 Denmark
Baynham
Hall
Byrne R
McGarry
Wright W
Dickinson
Milburn
Revie
Lofthouse
Bradford
Finney
Copenhagen 2 Oct: 5–1
Revie 2 (1 pen),
Lofthouse 2, Bradford

1955 Wales
Williams
Hall
Byrne R
McGarry
Wright W
Dickinson
Matthews S
Revie
Lofthouse
Wilshaw
Finney
Cardiff 22 Oct: 1–2
Charles J o.g.

1955 N Ireland
Baynham
Hall
Byrne R
Clayton
Wright W
Dickinson
Finney
Haynes
Jezzard
Wilshaw
Perry
Wembley 2 Nov: 3–0
Wilshaw 2, Finney

1955 Spain
Baynham
Hall
Byrne R
Clayton
Wright W
Dickinson
Finney
Atyeo
Lofthouse
Haynes
Perry
Wembley 30 Nov: 4–1
Atyeo, Perry 2, Finney

1956 Scotland
Matthews R
Hall
Byrne R
Dickinson
Wright W
Edwards
Finney
Taylor T
Lofthouse
Haynes
Perry
Glasgow 14 April: 1–1
Haynes

1956 Brazil
Matthews R
Hall
Byrne R
Clayton
Wright S
Edwards
Matthews S
Atyeo
Taylor T
Haynes
Grainger
Wembley 9 May: 4–2
Taylor 2, Grainger 2

1956 Sweden
Matthews R
Hall
Byrne R
Clayton
Wright W
Edwards
Berry
Atyeo
Taylor T
Haynes
Grainger
Stockholm 16 May: 0–0

1956 Finland
Wood
Hall
Byrne R
Clayton
Wright W
Edwards
Astall
Haynes
Taylor T
(Lofthouse)
Wilshaw
Grainger
Helsinki 20 May: 5–1
Wilshaw, Haynes,
Astall, Lofthouse 2

1956 W Germany
Matthews R
Hall
Byrne R
Clayton
Wright W
Edwards
Astall
Haynes
Taylor T
Wilshaw
Grainger
Berlin 26 May: 3–1
Edwards, Grainger,
Haynes

1956 N Ireland
Matthews R
Hall
Byrne R
Clayton
Wright W
Edwards
Matthews S
Revie
Taylor T
Wilshaw
Grainger
Belfast 6 Oct: 1–1
Matthews S

1956 Wales
Ditchburn
Hall
Byrne R
Clayton
Wright W
Dickinson
Matthews S

Right: Stanley Matthews, one of the game's outstanding legends, shows the grace that made him world famous in this game against Brazil at Wembley in 1956

Below: Billy Wright, who was to win 105 England caps, and his defensive partner Bill McGarry in World Cup action against Uruguay in Basle in 1954

Brooks
Finney
Haynes
Grainger
Wembley 14 Nov: 3–1
Haynes, Brooks, Finney

1956 Yugoslavia
Ditchburn
Hall
Byrne R
Clayton
Wright W
Dickinson
Matthews S
Brooks
Finney
Haynes
(Taylor T)
Blunstone
Wembley 28 Nov: 3–0
Brooks, Taylor 2

1956 Denmark
Ditchburn
Hall
Byrne R
Clayton
Wright W
Dickinson
Matthews S
Brooks
Taylor T
Edwards
Finney
Wolverhampton 5 Dec:
5–2 Taylor 3, Edwards 2

1957 Scotland
Hodgkinson
Hall
Byrne R
Clayton
Wright W
Edwards
Matthews S
Thompson T
Finney
Kevan
Grainger
Wembley 6 April: 2–1
Kevan, Edwards

1957 Rep of Ireland
Hodgkinson
Hall
Byrne R
Clayton
Wright W
Edwards
Matthews S
Atyeo
Taylor T
Haynes
Finney

Wembley 8 May: 5–1
Taylor 3, Atyeo 2

1957 Denmark
Hodgkinson
Hall
Byrne R
Clayton
Wright W
Edwards
Matthews S
Atyeo
Taylor T
Haynes
Finney
Copenhagen 15 May:
4–1 Haynes, Taylor 2,
Atyeo

1957 Rep of Ireland
Hodgkinson
Hall
Byrne R
Clayton
Wright W
Edwards
Finney
Atyeo
Taylor T
Haynes
Pegg
Dublin 19 May: 1–1
Atyeo

1957 Wales
Hopkinson
Howe D
Byrne R
Clayton
Wright W
Edwards
Douglas
Kevan
Taylor T
Haynes
Finney
Cardiff 19 Oct: 4–0
Hopkins o.g., Haynes 2,
Finney

1957 N Ireland
Hopkinson
Howe D
Byrne R
Clayton
Wright W
Edwards
Douglas
Kevan
Taylor T
Haynes
A'Court
Wembley 6 Nov: 2–3
A'Court, Edwards

1957 France
Hopkinson

Howe D
Byrne R
Clayton
Wright W
Edwards
Douglas
Robson R
Taylor T
Haynes
Finney
Wembley 27 Nov: 4–0
Taylor 2, Robson 2

1958 Scotland
Hopkinson
Howe D
Langley
Clayton
Wright W
Slater
Douglas
Charlton R
Kevan
Haynes
Finney
Glasgow 19 April: 4–0
Douglas, Kevan 2,
Charlton

1958 Portugal
Hopkinson
Howe D
Langley
Clayton
Wright W
Slater
Douglas
Charlton R
Kevan
Haynes
Finney
Wembley 7 May: 2–1
Charlton 2

1958 Yugoslavia
Hopkinson
Howe D
Langley
Clayton
Wright W
Slater
Douglas
Charlton R
Kevan
Haynes
Finney
Belgrade 11 May: 0–5

1958 USSR
McDonald
Howe D
Banks T
Clamp
Wright W
Slater
Douglas

Robson R
Kevan
Haynes
Finney
Moscow 18 May: 1–1
Kevan

1958 USSR†
McDonald
Howe D
Banks T
Clamp
Wright W
Slater
Douglas
Robson R
Kevan
Haynes
Finney
Gothenburg 8 June: 2–2
Kevan, Finney pen

1958 Brazil†
McDonald
Howe D
Banks T
Clamp
Wright W
Slater
Douglas
Robson R
Kevan
Haynes
A'Court
Gothenburg 11 June:
0–0

1958 Austria†
McDonald
Howe D
Banks T
Clamp
Wright W
Slater
Douglas
Robson R
Kevan
Haynes
A'Court
Boras 15 June: 2–2
Haynes, Kevan

1958 USSR†
McDonald
Howe D
Banks T
Clayton
Wright W
Slater
Brabrook
Broadbent
Kevan
Haynes
A'Court
Gothenburg 17 June:
0–1

1958 N Ireland
McDonald
Howe D
Banks T
Clayton
Wright W
McGuinness
Brabrook
Broadbent
Charlton R
Haynes
Finney
Belfast 4 Oct: 3–3
Charlton 2, Finney

1958 USSR
McDonald
Howe D
Shaw G
Clayton
Wright W
Slater
Douglas
Charlton R
Lofthouse
Haynes
Finney
Wembley 22 Oct: 5–0
Haynes 3, Charlton pen,
Lofthouse

1958 Wales
McDonald
Howe D
Shaw G
Clayton
Wright W
Flowers
Clapton
Broadbent
Lofthouse
Haynes
A'Court
Villa Park 26 Nov: 2–2
Broadbent 2

1959 Scotland
Hopkinson
Howe D
Shaw G
Clayton
Wright W
Flowers
Douglas
Broadbent
Charlton R
Haynes
Holden
Wembley 11 April: 1–0
Charlton

1959 Italy
Hopkinson
Howe D
Shaw G
Clayton

Wright W
Flowers
Bradley
Broadbent
Charlton R
Haynes
Holden
Wembley 6 May: 2–2
Charlton, Bradley

1959 Brazil
Hopkinson
Howe D
Armfield
Clayton
Wright W
Flowers
Deeley
Broadbent
Charlton R
Haynes
Holden
Rio de Janeiro 13 May: 0–2

1959 Peru
Hopkinson
Howe D
Armfield
Clayton
Wright W
Flowers
Deeley
Greaves
Charlton R
Haynes
Holden
Lima 17 May: 1–4
Greaves

1959 Mexico
Hopkinson
Howe D
Armfield
Clayton
Wright W
McGuinness
(Flowers)
Holden
(Bradley)
Greaves
Kevan
Haynes
Charlton R
Mexico City 24 May: 1–2
Kevan

1959 USA
Hopkinson
Howe D
Armfield
Clayton
Wright W
Flowers
Bradley
Greaves

Kevan
Haynes
Charlton R
Los Angeles 28 May:
8–1 Charlton 3, Flowers 2, Bradley, Kevan, Haynes

1959 Wales
Hopkinson
Howe D
Allen A
Clayton
Smith T
Flowers
Connelly
Greaves
Clough
Charlton R
Holliday
Cardiff 17 Oct: 1–1
Greaves

1959 Sweden
Hopkinson
Howe D
Allen A
Clayton
Smith T
Flowers
Connelly
Greaves
Clough
Charlton R
Holliday
Wembley 28 Oct: 2–3
Connelly, Charlton

1959 N Ireland
Springett R
Howe D
Allen A
Clayton
Brown
Flowers
Connelly
Haynes
Baker
Parry
Holliday
Wembley 18 Nov: 2–1
Baker, Parry

1960 Scotland
Springett R
Armfield
Wilson
Clayton
Slater
Flowers
Connelly
Broadbent
Baker
Parry
Charlton R

Glasgow 19 April: 1–1
Charlton pen

1960 Yugoslavia
Springett R
Armfield
Wilson
Clayton
Swan
Flowers
Douglas
Haynes
Baker
Greaves
Charlton R
Wembley 11 May: 3–3
Douglas, Greaves, Haynes

1960 Spain
Springett R
Armfield
Wilson
Robson R
Swan
Flowers
Brabrook
Haynes
Baker
Greaves
Charlton R
Madrid 15 May: 0–3

1960 Hungary
Springett R
Armfield
Wilson
Robson R
Swan
Flowers
Douglas
Haynes
Baker
Viollet
Charlton R
Budapest 22 May: 0–2

1960 N Ireland
Springett R
Armfield
McNeil
Robson R
Swan
Flowers
Douglas
Greaves
Smith R
Haynes
Charlton R
Belfast 8 Oct: 5–2
Smith, Greaves 2, Charlton, Douglas

1960 Luxembourg
Springett R
Armfield
McNeil

Robson R
Swan
Flowers
Douglas
Greaves
Smith R
Haynes
Charlton R
Luxembourg 19 Oct: 9–0
Greaves 3, Charlton 3, Smith 2, Haynes

1960 Spain
Springett R
Armfield
McNeil
Robson R
Swan
Flowers
Douglas
Greaves
Smith R
Haynes
Charlton R
Wembley 26 Oct: 4–2
Greaves, Douglas, Smith 2

1960 Wales
Hodgkinson
Armfield
McNeil
Robson R
Swan
Flowers
Douglas
Greaves
Smith R
Haynes
Charlton R
Wembley 23 Nov: 5–1
Greaves 2, Charlton, Smith, Haynes

1961 Scotland
Springett R
Armfield
McNeil
Robson R
Swan
Flowers
Douglas
Greaves
Smith R
Haynes
Charlton R
Wembley 15 April: 9–3
Robson, Greaves 3, Douglas, Smith 2, Haynes 2

1961 Mexico
Springett R
Armfield
McNeil
Robson R

Swan
Flowers
Douglas
Kevan
Hitchens
Haynes
Charlton R
Wembley 10 May: 8–0
Hitchens, Charlton 3, Robson, Douglas 2, Flowers pen

1961 Portugal
Springett R
Armfield
McNeil
Robson R
Swan
Flowers
Douglas
Greaves
Smith R
Haynes
Charlton R
Lisbon 21 May: 1–1
Flowers

1961 Italy
Springett R
Armfield
McNeil
Robson R
Swan
Flowers
Douglas
Greaves
Hitchens
Haynes
Charlton R
Rome 24 May: 3–2
Hitchens 2, Greaves

1961 Austria
Springett R
Armfield
Angus
Miller
Swan
Flowers
Douglas
Greaves
Hitchens
Haynes
Charlton R
Vienna 27 May: 1–3
Greaves

1961 Luxembourg
Springett R
Armfield
McNeil
Robson R
Swan
Flowers
Douglas
Fantham

Pointer
Viollet
Charlton R
Highbury 28 Sept: 4–1
Pointer, Viollet,
Charlton 2

1961 Wales
Springett R
Armfield
Wilson
Robson R
Swan
Flowers
Connelly
Douglas
Pointer
Haynes
Charlton R
Cardiff 14 Oct: 1–1
Douglas

1961 Portugal
Springett R
Armfield
Wilson
Robson R
Swan
Flowers
Connelly
Douglas
Pointer
Haynes
Charlton R
Wembley 25 Oct: 2–0
Connelly, Pointer

1961 N Ireland
Springett R
Armfield
Wilson
Robson R
Swan
Flowers
Douglas
Byrne J
Crawford
Haynes
Charlton R
Wembley 22 Nov: 1–1
Charlton

1962 Austria
Springett R
Armfield
Wilson
Anderson
Swan
Flowers
Connelly
Hunt
Crawford
Haynes
Charlton R
Wembley 4 April: 3–1

Crawford, Flowers pen,
Hunt

1962 Scotland
Springett R
Armfield
Wilson
Anderson
Swan
Flowers
Douglas
Greaves
Smith R
Haynes
Charlton R
Glasgow 14 April: 0–2

1962 Switzerland
Springett R
Armfield
Wilson
Robson R
Swan
Flowers
Connelly
Greaves
Hitchens
Haynes
Charlton R
Wembley 9 May: 3–1
Flowers, Hitchens,
Connelly

1962 Peru
Springett R
Armfield
Wilson
Moore
Norman
Flowers
Douglas
Greaves
Hitchens
Haynes
Charlton R
Lima 20 May: 4–0
Flowers pen, Greaves 3

1962 Hungary†
Springett R
Armfield
Wilson
Moore
Norman
Flowers
Douglas
Greaves
Hitchens
Haynes
Charlton R
Rancagua 31 May: 1–2
Flowers pen

1962 Argentina†
Springett R
Armfield
Wilson

Moore
Norman
Flowers
Douglas
Greaves
Peacock
Haynes
Charlton R
Rancagua 2 June: 3–1
Flowers pen, Charlton,
Greaves

1962 Bulgaria†
Springett R
Armfield
Wilson
Moore
Norman
Flowers
Douglas
Greaves
Peacock
Haynes
Charlton R
Rancagua 7 June: 0–0

1962 Brazil†
Springett R
Armfield
Wilson
Moore
Norman
Flowers
Douglas
Greaves
Hitchens
Haynes
Charlton R
Vina del Mar 10 June:
1–3 Hitchens

1962 France
Springett R
Armfield
Wilson
Moore
Norman
Flowers
Hellawell
Crowe
Charnley
Greaves
Hinton A
Hillsborough 3 Oct: 1–1
Flowers pen

1962 N Ireland
Springett R
Armfield
Wilson
Moore
Labone
Flowers
Hellawell
Hill F
Peacock

Greaves
O'Grady
Belfast 20 Oct: 3–1
Greaves, O'Grady 2

1962 Wales
Springett R
Armfield
Shaw G
Moore
Labone
Flowers
Connelly
Hill F
Peacock
Greaves
Tambling
Wembley 21 Nov: 4–0
Connelly, Peacock 2,
Greaves

1963 France
Springett R
Armfield
Henry
Moore
Labone
Flowers
Connelly
Tambling
Smith R
Greaves
Charlton R
Paris 27 Feb: 2–5 Smith,
Tambling

1963 Scotland
Banks G
Armfield
Byrne G
Moore
Norman
Flowers
Douglas
Greaves
Smith R
Melia
Charlton R
Wembley 6 April: 1–2
Douglas

1963 Brazil
Banks G
Armfield
Wilson
Milne
Norman
Moore
Douglas
Greaves
Smith R
Eastham
Charlton R
Wembley 8 May: 1–1
Douglas

1963 Czechoslovakia
Banks G
Shellito
Wilson
Milne
Norman
Moore
Paine
Greaves
Smith R
Eastham
Charlton R
Bratislava 20 May: 4–2
Greaves 2, Smith,
Charlton

1963 E Germany
Banks G
Armfield
Wilson
Milne
Norman
Moore
Paine
Hunt
Smith R
Eastham
Charlton R
Leipzig 2 June: 2–1
Hunt, Charlton

1963 Switzerland
Springett R
Armfield
Wilson
Kay
Moore
Flowers
Douglas
Greaves
Byrne J
Melia
Charlton R
Basle 5 June: 8–1
Charlton 3, Byrne 2,
Douglas, Kay, Melia

1963 Wales
Banks G
Armfield
Wilson
Milne
Norman
Moore
Paine
Greaves
Smith R
Eastham
Charlton R
Cardiff 12 Oct: 4–0
Smith 2, Greaves,
Charlton

1963 Rest of World
Banks G
Armfield

Wilson
Milne
Norman
Moore
Paine
Greaves
Smith R
Eastham
Charlton R
*Wembley 23 Oct: 2–1
Paine, Greaves*

1963 N Ireland
Banks G
Armfield
Thomson R
Milne
Norman
Moore
Paine
Greaves
Smith R
Eastham
Charlton R
*Wembley (first by floodlight) 20 Nov: 8–3
Greaves 4, Paine 3, Smith*

1964 Scotland
Banks G
Armfield
Wilson
Milne
Norman
Moore
Paine
Hunt
Byrne J
Eastham
Charlton R
Glasgow 11 April: 0–1

1964 Uruguay
Banks G
Cohen
Wilson
Milne
Norman
Moore
Paine
Greaves
Byrne J
Eastham
Charlton R
*Wembley 6 May: 2–1
Byrne 2*

1964 Portugal
Banks G
Cohen
Wilson
Milne
Norman
Moore
Thompson P

Greaves
Byrne J
Eastham
Charlton R
*Lisbon 17 May: 4–3
Byrne 3, Charlton*

1964 Rep of Ireland
Waiters
Cohen
Wilson
Milne
Flowers
Moore
Thompson P
Greaves
Byrne J
Eastham
Charlton R
*Dublin 24 May: 3–1
Eastham, Byrne, Greaves*

1964 USA
Banks G
Cohen
Thomson R
Bailey M
Norman
Flowers
Paine
Hunt
Pickering
Eastham
(Charlton R)
Thompson P
*New York 27 May: 10–0
Hunt 4, Pickering 3, Paine 2, Charlton*

1964 Brazil
Waiters
Cohen
Wilson
Milne
Norman
Moore
Thompson P
Greaves
Byrne J
Eastham
Charlton R
Rio de Janeiro 30 May: 1–5 Greaves

1964 Portugal
Banks G
Thomson R
Wilson
Flowers
Norman
Moore
Paine
Greaves
Byrne J
Hunt

Thompson P
*Sao Paolo 4 June: 1–1
Hunt*

1964 Argentina
Banks G
Thomson R
Wilson
Milne
Norman
Moore
Thompson P
Greaves
Byrne J
Eastham
Charlton R
Rio de Janeiro 6 June: 0–1

1964 N Ireland
Banks G
Cohen
Thomson R
Milne
Norman
Moore
Paine
Greaves
Pickering
Charlton R
Thompson P
*Belfast 3 Oct: 4–3
Pickering, Greaves 3*

1964 Belgium
Waiters
Cohen
Thomson R
Milne
Norman
Moore
Thompson P
Greaves
Pickering
Venables
Hinton A
*Wembley 21 Oct: 2–2
Pickering, Hinton*

1964 Wales
Waiters
Cohen
Thomson R
Bailey M
Flowers
Young
Thompson P
Hunt
Wignall
Byrne J
Hinton A
*Wembley 18 Nov: 2–1
Wignall 2*

1964 Netherlands
Waiters
Cohen

Thomson R
Mullery
Norman
Flowers
Thompson P
Greaves
Wignall
Venables
Charlton R
*Amsterdam 9 Dec: 1–1
Greaves*

1965 Scotland
Banks G
Cohen
Wilson
Stiles
Charlton J
Moore
Thompson P
Greaves
Bridges
Byrne J
Charlton R
*Wembley 10 April: 2–2
Charlton R, Greaves*

1965 Hungary
Banks G
Cohen
Wilson
Stiles
Charlton J
Moore
Paine
Greaves
Bridges
Eastham
Connelly
*Wembley 5 May: 1–0
Greaves*

1965 Yugoslavia
Banks G
Cohen
Wilson
Stiles
Charlton J
Moore
Paine
Greaves
Bridges
Ball
Connelly
*Belgrade 9 May: 1–1
Bridges*

1965 W Germany
Banks G
Cohen
Wilson
Flowers
Charlton J
Moore
Paine
Ball

Jones M
Eastham
Temple
Nuremberg 12 May: 1–0 Paine

1965 Sweden
Banks G
Cohen
Wilson
Stiles
Charlton J
Moore
Paine
Ball
Jones M
Eastham
Connelly
Gothenburg 16 May: 2–1 Ball, Connelly

1965 Wales
Springett R
Cohen
Wilson
Stiles
Charlton J
Moore
Paine
Greaves
Peacock
Charlton R
Connelly
Cardiff 2 Oct: 0–0

1965 Austria
Springett R
Cohen
Wilson
Stiles
Charlton J
Moore
Paine
Greaves
Bridges
Charlton R
Connelly
*Wembley 20 Oct: 2–3
Charlton R, Connelly*

1965 N Ireland
Banks G
Cohen
Wilson
Stiles
Charlton J
Moore
Thompson P
Baker
Peacock
Charlton R
Connelly
*Wembley 10 Nov: 2–1
Baker, Peacock*

1965 Spain
Banks G

Below: The most famous goal in World Cup history. West Germany can't believe it as Geoff Hurst's second goal for England at Wembley is judged to have hit the underside of the bar and crossed the line

Right: At the end of the match, Bobby Moore is held aloft by team-mates Geoff Hurst (left) and Ray Wilson as the England team celebrate the country's most outstanding soccer achievement – winning the World Cup in 1966

Cohen
Wilson
Stiles
Charlton J
Moore
Ball
Hunt
Baker
(Hunter)
Eastham
Charlton R
Madrid 8 Dec: 2–0
Baker, Hunt

1966 Poland
Banks G
Cohen
Wilson
Stiles
Charlton J
Moore
Ball
Hunt
Baker
Eastham
Harris G
Liverpool 5 Jan: 1–1
Moore

1966 W Germany
Banks G
Cohen
Newton K
(Wilson)
Moore
Charlton J
Hunter
Ball
Hunt
Stiles
Hurst G
Charlton R
Wembley 23 Feb: 1–0
Stiles

1966 Scotland
Banks G
Cohen
Newton K
Stiles
Charlton J
Moore
Ball
Hunt
Charlton R
Hurst G
Connelly
Glasgow 2 April: 4–3
Hurst, Hunt 2,
Charlton R

1966 Yugoslavia
Banks G
Armfield
Wilson
Peters
Charlton J
Hunter
Paine
Greaves
Charlton R
Hurst G
Tambling
Wembley 4 May: 2–0
Greaves, Charlton R

1966 Finland
Banks G
Armfield
Wilson
Peters
Charlton J
Hunter
Callaghan
Hunt
Charlton R
Hurst G
Ball
Helsinki 26 June: 3–0
Peters, Hunt, Charlton J

1966 Norway
Springett R
Cohen
Byrne G
Stiles
Flowers
Moore
Paine
Greaves
Charlton R
Hunt
Connelly
Oslo 29 June: 6–1
Greaves 4, Connelly,
Moore

1966 Denmark
Bonetti
Cohen
Wilson
Stiles
Charlton J
Moore
Ball
Greaves
Hurst G
Eastham
Connelly
Copenhagen 3 July: 2–0
Charlton J, Eastham

1966 Poland
Banks G
Cohen
Wilson
Stiles
Charlton J
Moore
Ball
Greaves
Charlton R
Hunt
Peters
Chorzow 5 July: 1–0
Hunt

1966 Uruguay†
Banks G
Cohen
Wilson
Stiles
Charlton J
Moore
Ball
Greaves
Charlton R
Hunt
Connelly
Wembley 11 July: 0–0

1966 Mexico†
Banks G
Cohen
Wilson
Stiles
Charlton J
Moore
Paine
Greaves
Charlton R
Hunt
Peters
Wembley 16 July: 2–0
Charlton R, Hunt

1966 France†
Banks G
Cohen
Wilson
Stiles
Charlton J
Moore
Callaghan
Greaves
Charlton R
Hunt
Peters
Wembley 20 July: 2–0
Hunt 2

1966 Argentina†
Banks G
Cohen
Wilson
Stiles
Charlton J
Moore
Ball
Hurst G
Charlton R
Hunt
Peters
Wembley 23 July: 1–0
Hurst

1966 Portugal†
Banks G
Cohen
Wilson
Stiles
Charlton J
Moore
Ball
Hurst G
Charlton R
Hunt
Peters
Wembley 26 July: 2–1
Charlton R 2

1966 W Germany†
Banks G
Cohen
Wilson
Stiles
Charlton J
Moore
Ball
Hurst G
Charlton R
Hunt
Peters
Wembley (World Cup Final) 30 July: 4–2*
Hurst 3, Peters

1966 N Ireland
Banks G
Cohen
Wilson
Stiles
Charlton J
Moore
Ball
Hurst G
Charlton R
Hunt
Peters
Belfast 22 Oct: 2–0
Hunt, Peters

1966 Czechoslovakia
Banks G
Cohen
Wilson
Stiles
Charlton J
Moore
Ball
Hurst G
Charlton R
Hunt
Peters
Wembley 2 Nov: 0–0

1966 Wales
Banks G
Cohen
Wilson
Stiles
Charlton J
Moore
Ball
Hurst G
Charlton R
Hunt
Peters
Wembley 16 Nov: 5–1
Hurst 2, Charlton R,
Charlton J, Hennessy
o.g.

1967 Scotland
Banks G
Cohen
Wilson
Stiles
Charlton J
Moore
Ball
Greaves
Charlton R
Hurst G
Peters
Wembley 15 April: 2–3
Charlton J, Hurst

1967 Spain
Bonetti
Cohen
Newton K
Mullery
Labone
Moore
Ball
Greaves
Hurst G
Hunt
Hollins
Wembley 24 May: 2–0
Greaves, Hunt

1967 Austria
Bonetti
Newton K
Wilson
Mullery
Labone
Moore
Ball
Greaves
Hurst G
Hunt
Hunter
Vienna 27 May: 1–0 Ball

1967 Wales
Banks G
Cohen
Newton K
Mullery
Charlton J
Moore
Ball
Hunt
Charlton R
Hurst G
Peters
Cardiff 21 Oct: 3–0
Peters, Charlton R, Ball

1967 N Ireland
Banks G
Cohen
Wilson
Mullery
Sadler
Moore
Thompson P
Hunt
Charlton R
Hurst G
Peters
Wembley 22 Nov: 2–0
Hurst, Charlton

1967 USSR
Banks G
Knowles C
Wilson
Mullery
Sadler
Moore
Ball
Hunt
Charlton R
Hurst G
Peters
Wembley 6 Dec: 2–2
Ball, Peters

1968 Scotland
Banks G
Newton K
Wilson
Mullery
Labone
Moore
Ball
Hurst G
Summerbee
Charlton R
Peters
Glasgow 24 Feb: 1–1
Peters

1968 Spain
Banks G
Knowles C
Wilson
Mullery
Charlton J
Moore
Ball
Hunt
Summerbee
Charlton R
Peters
Wembley 3 April: 1–0
Charlton R

1968 Spain
Bonetti
Newton K
Wilson
Mullery
Labone
Moore
Ball
Peters
Charlton R
Hunt
Hunter
Madrid 8 May: 2–1
Peters, Hunter

1968 Sweden
Stepney
Newton K
Knowles C
Mullery
Labone
Moore
Bell
Peters
Charlton R
(Hurst G)
Hunt
Hunter
Wembley 22 May: 3–1
Peters, Charlton, Hunt

1968 W Germany
Banks G
Newton K
Knowles C
Hunter
Labone
Moore
Ball
Bell
Summerbee
Hurst G
Thompson P
Hanover 1 June: 0–1

1968 Yugoslavia
Banks G
Newton K
Wilson
Mullery
Labone
Moore
Ball
Peters
Charlton R
Hunt
Hunter
Florence 5 June: 0–1

1968 USSR
Banks G
Wright T
Wilson
Stiles
Labone
Moore
Hunter
Hunt
Charlton R
Hurst G
Peters
Rome 8 June: 2–0
Charlton, Hurst

1968 Romania
Banks G
Wright T
(McNab)
Newton K
Mullery
Labone
Moore
Ball
Hunt
Charlton R
Hurst G
Peters
Bucharest 6 Nov: 0–0

1968 Bulgaria
West
Newton K
(Reaney)
McNab
Mullery
Labone
Moore
Lee F
Bell
Charlton R
Hurst G
Peters
Wembley 11 Dec: 1–1
Hurst

1969 Romania
Banks G
Wright T
McNab
Stiles
Charlton J
Hunter
Radford
Hunt
Charlton R
Hurst G
Ball
Wembley 15 Jan: 1–1
Charlton J

1969 France
Banks G
Newton K
Cooper
Mullery
Charlton J
Moore
Lee F
Bell
Hurst G
Peters
O'Grady
Wembley 12 Mar: 5–0
Hurst 3, O'Grady, Lee

1969 N Ireland
Banks G
Newton K
McNab
Mullery
Labone
Moore
Ball
Lee F
Charlton R
Hurst G
Peters
Belfast 3 May: 3–1
Peters, Lee, Hurst pen

1969 Wales
West
Newton K
Cooper
Moore
Charlton J
Hunter
Lee F
Bell
Astle
Charlton R
Ball
Wembley 7 May: 2–1
Charlton R, Lee

1969 Scotland
Banks G
Newton K
Cooper
Mullery
Labone
Moore
Lee F
Ball
Charlton R
Hurst G
Peters
Wembley 10 May: 4–1
Peters 2, Hurst 2 (1 pen)

1969 Mexico
West
Newton K
(Wright T)
Cooper
Mullery
Labone
Moore
Lee F
Ball
Charlton R
Hurst G
Peters
Mexico City 1 June: 0–0

1969 Uruguay
Banks G
Wright T
Newton K
Mullery
Labone
Moore
Lee F
Bell
Hurst G
Ball
Peters
Montevideo 8 June: 2–1
Lee, Hurst

1969 Brazil
Banks G
Wright T
Newton K
Mullery
Labone
Moore
Ball
Bell
Charlton R
Hurst G
Peters
Rio de Janeiro 12 June: 1–2 Bell

1969 Netherlands
Bonetti
Wright T
Hughes E
Mullery
Charlton J
Moore
Lee F
(Thompson P)
Bell
Charlton R
Hurst G
Peters
Amsterdam 5 Nov: 1–0
Bell

1969 Portugal
Bonetti
Reaney
Hughes E
Mullery
Charlton J
Moore
Lee F
Bell
(Peters)
Astle
Charlton R
Ball
Wembley 10 Dec: 1–0
Charlton J

1970 Netherlands
Banks G
Newton K
Cooper
Peters
Charlton J
Hunter
Lee F
(Mullery)
Bell
Jones M
(Hurst G)
Charlton R

Moore I
Wembley 14 Jan: 0–0

1970 Belgium
Banks G
Wright T
Cooper
Moore
Labone
Hughes E
Lee F
Ball
Osgood
Hurst G
Peters
*Brussels 25 Feb: 3–1
Ball 2, Hurst*

1970 Wales
Banks G
Wright T
Hughes E
Mullery
Labone
Moore
Lee F
Ball
Charlton R
Hurst G
Peters
Cardiff 18 April: 1–1 Lee

1970 N Ireland
Banks G
Newton K
(Bell)
Hughes E
Mullery
Moore
Stiles
Coates
Kidd
Charlton R
Hurst G
Peters
*Wembley 21 April: 3–1
Peters, Hurst, Charlton*

1970 Scotland
Banks G
Newton K
Hughes E
Stiles
Labone
Moore
Thompson P
(Mullery)
Ball
Astle
Hurst G
Peters
Glasgow 25 April: 0–0

1970 Colombia
Banks G
Newton K
Cooper

Mullery
Labone
Moore
Lee F
Ball
Charlton R
Hurst G
Peters
*Bogota 20 May: 4–0
Peters 2, Charlton, Ball*

1970 Ecuador
Banks G
Newton K
Cooper
Mullery
Labone
Moore
Lee F
(Kidd)
Ball
Charlton R
(Sadler)
Hurst G
Peters
*Quito 24 May: 2–0 Lee,
Kidd*

1970 Romania†
Banks G
Newton K
(Wright T)
Cooper
Mullery
Labone
Moore
Lee F
(Osgood)
Ball
Charlton R
Hurst G
Peters
*Guadalajara 2 June:
1–0 Hurst*

1970 Brazil†
Banks G
Wright T
Cooper
Mullery
Labone
Moore
Lee F
(Astle)
Ball
Charlton R
(Bell)
Hurst G
Peters
*Guadalajara 7 June:
0–1*

1970 Czechoslovakia†
Banks G
Newton K
Cooper

Mullery
Charlton J
Moore
Bell
Charlton R
(Ball)
Astle
(Osgood)
Clarke A
Peters
*Guadalajara 11 June:
1–0 Clarke pen*

1970 W Germany†
Bonetti
Newton K
Cooper
Mullery
Labone
Moore
Lee F
Ball
Charlton R
(Bell)
Hurst G
Peters
(Hunter)
Leon 14 June: 2–3
Mullery, Peters*

1970 E Germany
Shilton
Hughes
Cooper
Mullery
Sadler
Moore
Lee F
Ball
Hurst G
Clarke A
Peters
*Wembley 25 Nov: 3–1
Lee, Peters, Clarke*

1971 Malta
Banks G
Reaney
Hughes
Mullery
McFarland
Hunter
Ball
Chivers
Royle
Harvey
Peters
*Valletta 3 Feb: 1–0
Peters*

1971 Greece
Banks G
Storey
Hughes
Mullery
McFarland

Moore
Lee F
Ball
(Coates)
Chivers
Hurst G
Peters
*Wembley 21 April: 3–0
Chivers, Hurst, Lee*

1971 Malta
Banks G
Lawler
Cooper
Moore
McFarland
Hughes
Lee F
Coates
Chivers
Clarke
Peters
(Ball)
*Wembley 12 May: 5–0
Chivers 2, Lee, Clarke
pen, Lawler*

1971 N Ireland
Banks G
Madeley
Cooper
Storey
McFarland
Moore
Lee F
Ball
Chivers
Clarke
Peters
*Belfast 15 May: 1–0
Clarke*

1971 Wales
Shilton
Lawler
Cooper
Smith
Lloyd
Hughes
Lee F
Coates
(Clarke)
Hurst G
Brown A
Peters
Wembley 19 May: 0–0

1971 Scotland
Banks G
Lawler
Cooper
Storey
McFarland
Moore
Lee F
(Clarke)

Ball
Chivers
Hurst G
Peters
*Wembley 22 May: 3–1
Peters, Chivers 2*

1971 Switzerland
Banks G
Lawler
Cooper
Mullery
McFarland
Moore
Lee F
Madeley
Chivers
Hurst G
(Radford)
Peters
*Basle 13 Oct: 3–2 Hurst,
Chivers, Weibel o.g.*

1971 Switzerland
Shilton
Madeley
Cooper
Storey
Lloyd
Moore
Summerbee
(Chivers)
Ball
Hurst G
Lee F
(Marsh)
Hughes
*Wembley 10 Nov: 1–1
Summerbee*

1971 Greece
Banks G
Madeley
Hughes
Bell
McFarland
Moore
Lee F
Ball
Chivers
Hurst G
Peters
*Athens 1 Dec: 2–0
Hurst, Chivers*

1972 W Germany
Banks G
Madeley
Hughes
Bell
Moore
Hunter
Lee F
Ball
Chivers
Hurst G

69

(Marsh)
Peters
Wembley 29 April: 1–3
Lee

1972 W Germany
Banks G
Madeley
Hughes
Storey
McFarland
Moore
Ball
Bell
Chivers
Marsh
(Summerbee)
Hunter
(Peters)
Berlin 13 May: 0–0

1972 Wales
Banks G
Madeley
Hughes
Storey
McFarland
Moore
Summerbee
Bell
Macdonald
Marsh
Hunter
Cardiff 20 May: 3–0
Hughes, Bell, Marsh

1972 N Ireland
Shilton
Todd
Hughes
Storey
Lloyd
Hunter
Summerbee
Bell
Macdonald
(Chivers)
Marsh
Currie
(Peters)
Wembley 23 May: 0–1

1972 Scotland
Banks G
Madeley
Hughes
Storey
McFarland
Moore
Ball
Bell
Chivers
Marsh
(Macdonald)
Hunter

Glasgow 27 May: 1–0
Ball

1972 Yugoslavia
Shilton
Mills
Lampard
Storey
Blockley
Moore
Ball
Channon
Royle
Bell
Marsh
Wembley 11 Oct: 1–1
Royle

1972 Wales
Clemence
Storey
Hughes
Hunter
McFarland
Moore
Keegan
Chivers
Marsh
Bell
Ball
Cardiff 15 Nov: 1–0 Bell

1973 Wales
Clemence
Storey
Hughes
Hunter
McFarland
Moore
Keegan
Bell
Chivers
Marsh
Ball
Wembley 24 Jan: 1–1
Hunter

1973 Scotland
Shilton
Storey
Hughes
Bell
Madeley
Moore
Ball
Channon
Chivers
Clarke
Peters
Glasgow 14 Feb: 5–0
Lorimer o.g., Clarke 2,
Channon, Chivers

1973 N Ireland
Shilton
Storey
Nish

Bell
McFarland
Moore
Ball
Channon
Chivers
Richards
Peters
Goodison Park 12 May:
2–1 Chivers 2

1973 Wales
Shilton
Storey
Hughes
Bell
McFarland
Moore
Ball
Channon
Chivers
Clarke
Peters
Wembley 15 May: 3–0
Chivers, Channon,
Peters

1973 Scotland
Shilton
Storey
Hughes
Bell
McFarland
Moore
Ball
Channon
Chivers
Clarke
Peters
Wembley 19 May: 1–0
Peters

1973 Czechoslovakia
Shilton
Madeley
Storey
Bell
McFarland
Moore
Ball
Channon
Chivers
Clarke
Peters
Prague 27 May: 1–1
Clarke

1973 Poland
Shilton
Madeley
Hughes
Storey
McFarland
Moore
Ball
Bell

Chivers
Clarke
Peters
Chorzow 6 June: 0–2

1973 USSR
Shilton
Madeley
Hughes
Storey
McFarland
Moore
Currie
Channon
(Summerbee)
Chivers
Clarke
(Macdonald)
Peters
(Hunter)
Moscow 10 June: 2–1
Chivers, Khurtislava
o.g.

1973 Italy
Shilton
Madeley
Hughes
Storey
McFarland
Moore
Currie
Channon
Chivers
Clarke
Peters
Turin 14 June: 0–2

1973 Austria
Shilton
Madeley
Hughes
Bell
McFarland
Hunter
Currie
Channon
Chivers
Clarke
Peters
Wembley 26 Sept: 7–0
Channon, 2, Clarke 2,
Chivers, Currie, Bell

1973 Poland
Shilton
Madeley
Hughes
Bell
McFarland
Hunter
Currie
Channon
Chivers
(Hector)
Clarke

Peters
Wembley 17 Oct: 1–1
Clarke pen

1973 Italy
Shilton
Madeley
Hughes
Bell
McFarland
Moore
Currie
Channon
Osgood
Clarke
(Hector)
Peters
Wembley 14 Nov: 0–1

1974 Portugal
Parkes
Nish
Pejic
Dobson
Watson
Todd
Bowles
Channon
Macdonald
(Ball)
Brooking
Peters
Lisbon April 3: 0–0

1974 Wales
Shilton
Nish
Pejic
Hughes
McFarland
Todd
Keegan
Bell
Channon
Weller
Bowles
Cardiff 11 May: 2–0
Bowles, Keegan

1974 N Ireland
Shilton
Nish
Pejic
Hughes
McFarland
(Hunter)
Todd
Keegan
Weller
Channon
Bell
Bowles
(Worthington)
Wembley 15 May: 1–0
Weller

70

1974 Scotland
Shilton
Nish
Pejic
Hughes
Hunter
(Watson)
Todd
Channon
Bell
Worthington
(Macdonald)
Weller
Peters
Glasgow 18 May: 0–2

1974 Argentina
Shilton
Hughes
Lindsay
Todd
Watson
Bell
Keegan
Channon
Worthington
Weller
Brooking
Wembley 22 May: 2–2
Channon, Worthington

1974 E Germany
Clemence
Hughes
Lindsay
Todd
Watson
Dobson
Keegan
Channon
Worthington
Bell
Brooking
Leipzig 29 May: 1–1
Channon

1974 Bulgaria
Clemence
Hughes
Todd
Watson
Lindsay
Dobson
Brooking
Bell
Keegan
Channon
Worthington
Sofia 1 June: 1–0
Worthington

1974 Yugoslavia
Clemence
Hughes
Lindsay
Todd

Watson
Dobson
Keegan
Channon
Worthington
(Macdonald)
Bell
Brooking
Belgrade 5 June: 2–2
Channon, Keegan

1974 Czechoslovakia
Clemence
Madeley
Hughes
Dobson
(Brooking)
Watson
Hunter
Bell
Francis G
Worthington
(Thomas)
Channon
Keegan
Wembley 30 Oct: 3–0
Channon, Bell 2

1974 Portugal
Clemence
Madeley
Watson
Hughes
Cooper
(Todd)
Brooking
Francis G
Bell
Thomas
Channon
Clarke
(Worthington)
Wembley 20 Nov: 0–0

1975 W Germany
Clemence
Whitworth
Gillard
Bell
Watson
Todd
Ball
Macdonald
Channon
Hudson
Keegan
Wembley 12 Mar: 2–0
Bell, Macdonald

1975 Cyprus
Shilton
Madeley
Watson
Todd
Beattie
Bell

Ball
Hudson
Channon
(Thomas)
Macdonald
Keegan
Wembley 16 April: 5–0
Macdonald 5

1975 Cyprus
Clemence
Whitworth
Beattie
(Hughes)
Watson
Todd
Bell
Thomas
Ball
Channon
Macdonald
Keegan
(Tueart)
Limassol 11 May: 1–0
Keegan

1975 N Ireland
Clemence
Whitworth
Hughes
Bell
Watson
Todd
Ball
Viljoen
Macdonald
(Channon)
Keegan
Tueart
Belfast 17 May: 0–0

1975 Wales
Clemence
Whitworth
Gillard
Francis G
Watson
Todd
Ball
Channon
(Little)
Johnson
Viljoen
Thomas
Wembley 21 May: 2–2
Johnson 2

1975 Scotland
Clemence
Whitworth
Beattie
Bell
Watson
Todd
Ball
Channon

Johnson
Francis G
Keegan
(Thomas)
Wembley 24 May: 5–1
Francis 2, Beattie, Bell, Johnson

1975 Switzerland
Clemence
Whitworth
Todd
Watson
Beattie
Bell
Currie
Francis G
Channon
Johnson
(Macdonald)
Keegan
Basle 3 Sept: 2–1
Keegan, Channon

1975 Czechoslovakia
Clemence
Madeley
Gillard
Francis G
McFarland
(Watson)
Todd
Keegan
Channon
(Thomas)
Macdonald
Clarke
Bell
Bratislava 30 Oct: 1–2
Channon

1975 Portugal
Clemence
Whitworth
Beattie
Francis G
Watson
Todd
Keegan
Channon
Macdonald
(Thomas)
Brooking
Madeley
(Clarke)
Lisbon 19 Nov: 1–1
Channon

1976 Wales
Clemence
Cherry
(Clement)
Mills
Neal
Thompson
Doyle

Keegan
Channon
(Taylor)
Boyer
Brooking
Kennedy
Wrexham 24 Mar: 2–1
Kennedy, Taylor

1976 Wales
Clemence
Clement
Mills
Towers
Greenhoff
Thompson
Keegan
Francis G
Pearson
Kennedy
Taylor
Cardiff 8 May: 1–0
Taylor

1976 N Ireland
Clemence
Todd
Mills
Thompson
Greenhoff
Kennedy
Keegan
(Royle)
Francis G
Pearson
Channon
Taylor
(Towers)
Wembley 11 May: 4–0
Francis, Channon 2 (1 pen), Pearson

1976 Scotland
Clemence
Todd
Mills
Thompson
McFarland
(Doyle)
Kennedy
Keegan
Francis G
Pearson
(Cherry)
Channon
Taylor
Glasgow 15 May: 1–2
Channon

1976 Brazil
Clemence
Todd
Doyle
Thompson
Mills
Francis G

71

Cherry
Brooking
Keegan
Pearson
Channon
Los Angeles 23 May:
0–1

1976 Italy
Rimmer
(Corrigan)
Clements
Neal
(Mills)
Thompson
Doyle
Towers
Wilkins
Brooking
Royle
Channon
Hill
New York 28 May: 3–2
Channon 2, Thompson

1976 Finland
Clemence
Todd
Mills
Thompson
Madeley
Cherry
Keegan
Channon
Pearson
Brooking
Francis G
Helsinki 13 June: 4–1
Keegan 2, Channon,
Pearson

1976 Rep of Ireland
Clemence
Todd
Madeley
Cherry
McFarland
Greenhoff
Keegan
Wilkins
Pearson
Brooking
George
(Hill)
Wembley 8 Sept: 1–1
Pearson

1976 Finland
Clemence
Todd
Beattie
Thompson
Greenhoff
Wilkins
Keegan
Channon

Royle
Brooking
(Mills)
Tueart
(Hill)
Wembley 13 Oct: 2–1
Tueart, Royle

1976 Italy
Clemence
Clement
(Beattie)
Mills
Greenhoff
McFarland
Hughes
Keegan
Channon
Bowles
Cherry
Brooking
Rome 17 Nov: 0–2

1977 Netherlands
Clemence
Clement
Beattie
Doyle
Watson
Madeley
(Pearson)
Keegan
Greenhoff
(Todd)
Francis T
Bowles
Brooking
Wembley 9 Feb: 0–2

1977 Luxembourg
Clemence
Gidman
Cherry
Kennedy
Watson
Hughes
Keegan
Channon
Royle
(Mariner)
Francis T
Hill
Wembley 30 Mar: 5–0
Keegan, Francis,
Kennedy, Channon 2
(1 pen)

1977 N Ireland
Shilton
Cherry
Mills
Greenhoff
Watson
Todd
Wilkins
(Talbot)

Channon
Mariner
Brooking
Tueart
Belfast 28 May: 2–1
Channon, Tueart

1977 Wales
Shilton
Neal
Mills
Greenhoff
Watson
Hughes
Keegan
Channon
Pearson
Brooking
(Tueart)
Kennedy
Wembley 31 May: 0–1

1977 Scotland
Clemence
Neal
Mills
Greenhoff
(Cherry)
Watson
Hughes
Francis T
Channon
Pearson
Talbot
Kennedy
(Tueart)
Wembley 4 June: 1–2
Channon pen

1977 Brazil
Clemence
Neal
Cherry
Greenhoff
Watson
Hughes
Keegan
Francis T
Pearson
(Channon)
Wilkins
(Kennedy)
Talbot
Rio de Janeiro 8 June:
0–0

1977 Argentina
Clemence
Neal
Cherry
Greenhoff
(Kennedy)
Watson
Hughes
Keegan
Channon

Pearson
Wilkins
Talbot
Buenos Aires 12 June:
1–1 Pearson

1977 Uruguay
Clemence
Neal
Cherry
Greenhoff
Watson
Hughes
Keegan
Channon
Pearson
Wilkins
Talbot
Montevideo 15 June:
0–0

1977 Switzerland
Clemence
Neal
Cherry
McDermott
Watson
Hughes
Keegan
Channon
(Hill)
Francis T
Kennedy
Callaghan
(Wilkins)
Wembley 7 Sept: 0–0

1977 Luxembourg
Clemence
Cherry
Watson
(Beattie)
Hughes
Kennedy
Callaghan
McDermott
(Whymark)
Wilkins
Francis T
Mariner
Hill
Luxembourg 12 Oct: 2–0
Kennedy, Mariner

1977 Italy
Clemence
Neal
Cherry
Wilkins
Watson
Hughes
Keegan
(Francis T)
Coppell
Latchford
(Pearson)

Brooking
Barnes
Wembley 16 Nov: 2–0
Keegan, Brooking

1978 W Germany
Clemence
Neal
Mills
Wilkins
Watson
Hughes
Keegan
(Francis T)
Coppell
Pearson
Brooking
Barnes
Munich 22 Feb: 1–2
Pearson

1978 Brazil
Corrigan
Mills
Cherry
Greenhoff
Watson
Currie
Keegan
Coppell
Latchford
Francis T
Barnes
Wembley 19 April: 1–1
Keegan

1978 Wales
Shilton
Mills
Cherry
(Currie)
Greenhoff
Watson
Wilkins
Coppell
Francis T
Latchford
(Mariner)
Brooking
Barnes
Cardiff 13 May: 3–1
Latchford, Currie,
Barnes

1978 N Ireland
Clemence
Neal
Mills
Wilkins
Watson
Hughes
Currie
Coppell
Pearson
Woodcock
Greenhoff

Bryan Robson has his shoulder dislocated as a result of this challenge from Morocco's Mostafa El Bryas in the opening phase of the 1986 World Cup in Monterrey, Mexico

Wembley 16 May: 1–0
Neal

1978 Scotland
Clemence
Neal
Mills
Currie
Watson
Hughes
(Greenhoff)
Wilkins
Coppell
Mariner
(Brooking)
Francis T
Barnes
Glasgow 20 May: 1–0
Coppell

1978 Hungary
Shilton
Neal
Mills
Wilkins
Watson
(Greenhoff)
Hughes
Keegan
Coppell
(Currie)
Francis T
Brooking
Barnes
Wembley 24 May: 4–1
Barnes, Neal pen,
Francis, Currie

1978 Denmark
Clemence
Neal
Mills
Wilkins
Watson
Hughes
Keegan
Coppell
Latchford
Brooking
Barnes
Copenhagen 20 Sept:
4–3 Keegan 2,
Latchford, Neal

1978 Rep of Ireland
Clemence
Neal
Mills
Wilkins
Watson
(Thompson)
Hughes
Keegan
Coppell
Latchford
Brooking

Barnes
(Woodcock)
Dublin 25 Oct: 1–1
Latchford

1978 Czechoslovakia
Shilton
Anderson
Cherry
Thompson
Watson
Wilkins
Keegan
Coppell
Woodcock
(Latchford)
Currie
Barnes
Wembley 29 Nov: 1–0
Coppell

1979 N Ireland
Clemence
Neal
Mills
Currie
Watson
Hughes
Keegan
Coppell
Latchford
Brooking
Barnes
Wembley 7 Feb: 4–0
Keegan, Latchford 2,
Watson

1979 N Ireland
Clemence
Neal
Mills
Thompson
Watson
Wilkins
Coppell
McDermott
Latchford
Currie
Barnes
Belfast 19 May: 2–0
Watson, Coppell

1979 Wales
Corrigan
Cherry
Sansom
Wilkins
(Brooking)
Watson
Hughes
Keegan
Currie
Latchford
(Coppell)
McDermott

Cunningham
Wembley 23 May: 0–0

1979 Scotland
Clemence
Neal
Mills
Thompson
Watson
Wilkins
Keegan
Coppell
Latchford
Brooking
Barnes
Wembley 26 May: 3–1
Barnes, Coppell,
Keegan

1979 Bulgaria
Clemence
Neal
Mills
Thompson
Watson
Wilkins
Keegan
Coppell
Latchford
(Francis T)
Brooking
Barnes
(Woodcock)
Sofia 6 June: 3–0
Keegan, Watson,
Barnes

1979 Sweden
Shilton
Anderson
Cherry
McDermott
(Wilkins)
Watson
Hughes
Keegan
Currie
(Brooking)
Francis T
Woodcock
Cunningham
Stockholm 10 June: 0–0

1979 Austria
Shilton
(Clemence)
Neal
Mills
Thompson
Watson
Wilkins
Keegan
Coppell
Latchford
(Francis T)
Brooking

Barnes
(Cunningham)
Vienna 13 June: 3–4
Keegan, Coppell,
Wilkins

1979 Denmark
Clemence
Neal
Mills
Thompson
Watson
Wilkins
Coppell
McDermott
Keegan
Brooking
Barnes
Wembley 9 Sept: 1–0
Keegan

1979 N Ireland
Shilton
Neal
Mills
Thompson
Watson
Wilkins
Keegan
Coppell
Francis T
Brooking
(McDermott)
Woodcock
Belfast 17 Oct: 5–1
Francis 2, Woodcock 2
Nicholl o.g.

1979 Bulgaria
Clemence
Anderson
Sansom
Thompson
Watson
Wilkins
Reeves
Hoddle
Francis T
Kennedy
Woodcock
Wembley 22 Nov: 2–0
Watson, Hoddle

1980 Rep of Ireland
Clemence
Cherry
Sansom
Thompson
Watson
Robson
Keegan
McDermott
Johnson
(Coppell)
Woodcock

Cunningham
Wembley 6 Feb: 2–0
Keegan 2

1980 Spain
Shilton
Neal
(Hughes)
Mills
Thompson
Watson
Wilkins
Keegan
Coppell
Francis T
(Cunningham)
Kennedy
Woodcock
Barcelona 26 March:
2–0 Woodcock, Francis

1980 Argentina
Clemence
Neal
(Cherry)
Sansom
Thompson
Watson
Wilkins
Keegan
Coppell
Johnson
(Birtles)
Woodcock
Kennedy
(Brooking)
Wembley 13 May: 3–1
Johnson 2, Keegan

1980 Wales
Clemence
Neal
(Sansom)
Cherry
Thompson
Lloyd
(Wilkins)
Kennedy
Coppell
Hoddle
Mariner
Brooking
Barnes
Wrexham 17 May: 1–4
Mariner

1980 N Ireland
Corrigan
Cherry
Sansom
Hughes
Watson
Wilkins
Reeves
(Mariner)
McDermott

74

Johnson
Brooking
Devonshire
Wembley 20 May: 1–1
Johnson

1980 Scotland
Clemence
Cherry
Sansom
Thompson
Watson
Wilkins
Coppell
McDermott
Johnson
Mariner
(Hughes)
Brooking
Glasgow 24 May: 2–0
Brooking, Coppell

1980 Australia
Corrigan
Cherry
Lampard
Talbot
Osman
Butcher
Robson
(Greenhoff)
Sunderland
(Ward)
Mariner
Hoddle
Armstrong
(Devonshire)
Sydney 31 May: 2–1
Hoddle, Mariner

1980 Belgium
Clemence
Neal
Sansom
Thompson
Watson
Wilkins
Keegan
Coppell
(McDermott)
Johnson
(Kennedy)
Woodcock
Brooking
Turin 12 June: 1–1
Wilkins

1980 Italy
Shilton
Neal
Sansom
Thompson
Watson
Wilkins
Keegan
Coppell

Birtles
(Mariner)
Kennedy
Woodcock
Turin 15 June: 0–1

1980 Spain
Clemence
Anderson
(Cherry)
Mills
Thompson
Watson
Wilkins
McDermott
Hoddle
(Mariner)
Keegan
Woodcock
Brooking
Naples 18 June: 2–1
Brooking, Woodcock

1980 Norway
Shilton
Anderson
Sansom
Thompson
Watson
Robson
Gates
McDermott
Mariner
Woodcock
Rix
Wembley 10 Sept: 4–0
McDermott 2 (1 pen),
Woodcock, Mariner

1980 Romania
Clemence
Neal
Sansom
Thompson
Watson
Robson
Rix
McDermott
Birtles
(Cunningham)
Woodcock
Gates
(Coppell)
Bucharest 15 Oct: 1–2
Woodcock

1980 Switzerland
Shilton
Neal
Sansom
Robson
Watson
Mills
Coppell
McDermott
Mariner

Brooking
(Rix)
Woodcock
Wembley 19 Nov: 2–1
Tanner o.g., Mariner

1981 Spain
Clemence
Neal
Sansom
Robson
Butcher
Osman
Keegan
Francis
(Barnes)
Mariner
Brooking
(Wilkins)
Hoddle
Wembley 25 Mar: 1–2
Hoddle

1981 Romania
Shilton
Anderson
Sansom
Robson
Watson
Osman
Wilkins
Brooking
(McDermott)
Coppell
Francis
Woodcock
Wembley 29 April: 0–0

1981 Brazil
Clemence
Neal
Sansom
Robson
Martin
Wilkins
Coppell
McDermott
Withe
Rix
Barnes
Wembley 12 May: 0–1

1981 Wales
Corrigan
Anderson
Sansom
Robson
Watson
Wilkins
Coppell
Hoddle
Withe
(Woodcock)
Rix
Barnes
Wembley 20 May: 0–0

1981 Scotland
Corrigan
Anderson
Sansom
Wilkins
Watson
(Martin)
Robson
Coppell
Hoddle
Withe
Rix
Woodcock
(Francis)
Wembley 23 May: 0–1

1981 Switzerland
Clemence
Mills
Sansom
Wilkins
Watson
(Barnes)
Osman
Coppell
Robson
Keegan
Mariner
Francis
(McDermott)
Basle 30 May: 1–2
McDermott

1981 Hungary
Clemence
Neal
Mills
Thompson
Watson
Robson
Coppell
McDermott
Mariner
Brooking
(Wilkins)
Keegan
Budapest 6 June: 3–1
Brooking 2, Keegan pen

1981 Norway
Clemence
Neal
Mills
Thompson
Osman
Robson
Keegan
Francis
Mariner
(Withe)
Hoddle
(Barnes)
McDermott
Oslo 9 Sept: 1–2
Robson

1981 Hungary
Shilton
Neal
Mills
Thompson
Martin
Robson
Keegan
Coppell
(Morley)
Mariner
Brooking
McDermott
Wembley 18 Nov: 1–0
Mariner

1982 N Ireland
Clemence
Anderson
Sansom
Wilkins
Watson
Foster
Keegan
Robson
Francis
(Regis)
Hoddle
Morley
(Woodcock)
Wembley 23 Feb: 4–0
Wilkins, Keegan,
Robson, Hoddle

1982 Wales
Corrigan
Neal
Sansom
Thompson
Butcher
Robson
Wilkins
Francis
(McDermott)
Withe
Hoddle
(Regis)
Morley
Cardiff 27 April: 1–0
Francis

1982 Holland
Shilton
Neal
Sansom
Thompson
Foster
Robson
Wilkins
Devonshire
(Rix)
Mariner
(Barnes)
McDermott
Woodcock

75

Wembley 25 May: 2–0
Mariner, Woodcock

1982 Scotland
Shilton
Mills
Sansom
Thompson
Butcher
Robson
Keegan
(McDermott)
Coppell
Mariner
(Francis)
Brooking
Wilkins
Glasgow 29 May: 1–0
Mariner

1982 Iceland
Corrigan
Anderson
Neal
Watson
Osman
McDermott
Hoddle
Devonshire
(Perryman)
Withe
Regis
(Goddard)
Morley
Reykjavik 2 June: 1–1
Goddard

1982 Finland
Clemence
Mills
Sansom
Thompson
Martin
Robson
(Rix)
Keegan
Coppell
(Francis)
Mariner
Brooking
(Woodcock)
Wilkins
Helsinki 3 June: 4–1
Robson 2, Mariner 2

1982 France†
Shilton
Mills
Sansom
(Neal)
Thompson
Butcher
Robson
Coppell
Francis
Mariner

Rix
Wilkins
Bilbao 16 June: 3–1
Robson 2, Mariner

1982 Czechoslovakia†
Shilton
Mills
Sansom
Thompson
Butcher
Robson
(Hoddle)
Coppell
Francis
Mariner
Rix
Wilkins
Bilbao 20 June: 2–0
Francis, 1 o.g.

1982 Kuwait†
Shilton
Neal
Mills
Thompson
Foster
Hoddle
Coppell
Francis
Mariner
Rix
Wilkins
Bilbao 25 June: 1–0
Francis

1982 W Germany
Shilton
Mills
Sansom
Thompson
Butcher
Robson
Coppell
Francis
(Woodcock)
Mariner
Rix
Wilkins
Madrid 29 June: 0–0

1982 Spain
Shilton
Mills
Sansom
Thompson
Butcher
Robson
Rix
(Brooking)
Francis
Mariner
Woodcock
(Keegan)
Wilkins
Madrid 5 July: 0–0

1982 Denmark
Shilton
Neal
Sansom
Wilkins
Osman
Butcher
Morley
(Hill)
Robson
Mariner
Francis
Rix
Copenhagen 22 Sept:
2–2 Francis 2

1982 W Germany
Shilton
Mabbutt
Sansom
Thompson
Butcher
Wilkins
Hill
Regis
(Woodcock)
Mariner
(Blissett)
Armstrong
(Rix)
Devonshire
Wembley 13 Oct: 1–2
Woodcock

1982 Greece
Shilton
Neal
Sansom
Thompson
Martin
Robson
Lee
Mabbutt
Mariner
Woodcock
Morley
Salonika 17 Nov: 3–0
Lee, Woodcock 2

1982 Luxembourg
Clemence
Neal
Sansom
Robson
Martin
Butcher
Coppell
(Chamberlain)
Lee
Woodcock
Blissett
Mabbutt
(Hoddle)
Luxembourg 12 Oct: 9–0
Neal, Coppell,
Woodcock,

Chamberlain, Hoddle,
Blissett 3, 1 o.g.

1983 Wales
Shilton
Neal
Statham
Lee
Martin
Butcher
Mabbutt
Blissett
Mariner
Cowans
Devonshire
Wembley 23 Feb: 2–1
Neal, Butcher

1983 Greece
Shilton
Neal
Sansom
Lee
Martin
Butcher
Coppell
Mabbutt
Francis
Woodcock
(Blissett)
Devonshire
(Rix)
Wembley 30 March:
0–0

1983 Hungary
Shilton
Neal
Sansom
Lee
Martin
Butcher
Mabbutt
Francis
Withe
Blissett
Cowans
Wembley 27 April: 2–0
Francis, Withe

1983 N Ireland
Shilton
Neal
Sansom
Hoddle
Roberts
Butcher
Mabbutt
Francis
Withe
Blissett
(Barnes J)
Cowans
Belfast 28 May: 0–0

1983 Scotland
Shilton

Neal
Sansom
Lee
Roberts
Butcher
Robson
(Mabbutt)
Francis
Withe
(Blissett)
Hoddle
Cowans
Wembley 1 June: 2–0
Robson, Cowans

1983 Australia
Shilton
Thomas
Statham
(Barnes)
Williams
Osman
Butcher
Barham
Gregory
Blissett
(Walsh)
Francis
Cowans *Sydney*
12 June: 0–0

1983 Australia
Shilton
Neal
Statham
(Williams)
Barham
Osman
Butcher
Gregory
Francis
Walsh
Cowans
Barnes
Brisbane 15 June: 1–0
Walsh

1983 Australia
Shilton
(Spink)
Neal
(Thomas)
Pickering
Lee
Osman
Butcher
Gregory
Francis
Walsh
(Blissett)
Cowans
Barnes
Melbourne 19 June: 1–1
Francis

1983 Denmark
Shilton

Neal
Sansom
Lee
(Blissett)
Osman
Butcher
Wilkins
Gregory
Mariner
Francis
Barnes
(Chamberlain)
Wembley 21 Sept: 0–1

1983 Hungary
Shilton
Gregory
Sansom
Lee
Martin
Butcher
Robson
Hoddle
Mariner
Blissett
(Withe)
Mabbutt
*Budapest 12 Oct: 3–0
Lee, Hoddle, Mariner*

1983 Luxembourg
Clemence
Duxbury
Sansom
Lee
Martin
Butcher
Robson
Hoddle
Mariner
Woodcock
(Barnes)
Devonshire
Luxembourg 16 Nov: 4–0 Butcher, Mariner, Robson 2

1984 France
Shilton
Duxbury
Sansom
Lee
(Barnes)
Roberts
Butcher
Robson
Stein
(Woodcock)
Walsh
Hoddle
Willams
Paris 29 Feb: 0–2

1984 N Ireland
Shilton
Anderson

Kennedy A
Lee
Roberts
Butcher
Robson
Wilkins
Woodcock
Francis
Rix
*Wembley 4 April: 1–0
Woodcock*

1984 Wales
Shilton
Duxbury
Kennedy A
Lee
Martin
(Fenwick)
Wright
Wilkins
Gregory
Walsh
Woodcock
Armstrong
(Blissett)
Wrexham 2 May: 0–1

1984 Scotland
Shilton
Duxbury
Sansom
Wilkins
Roberts
Fenwick
Chamberlain
(Hunt)
Robson
Woodcock
(Lineker)
Blissett
Barnes
*Glasgow 26 May: 1–1
Woodcock*

1984 USSR
Shilton
Duxbury
Sansom
Wilkins
Roberts
Fenwick
Chamberlain
Robson
Francis
(Hateley)
Blissett
Barnes
(Hunt)
Wembley 2 June: 0–2

1984 Brazil
Shilton
Duxbury
Sansom
Wilkins

Watson
Fenwick
Robson
Chamberlain
Hateley
Woodcock
(Allen)
Barnes
Rio de Janeiro 10 June: 2–0 Hateley, Barnes

1984 Uruguay
Shilton
Duxbury
Sansom
Wilkins
Watson
Fenwick
Robson
Chamberlain
Hateley
Allen
(Woodcock)
Barnes
Montevideo 13 June: 0–2

1984 Chile
Shilton
Duxbury
Sansom
Wilkins
Watson
Fenwick
Robson
Chamberlain
(Lee)
Hateley
Allen
Barnes
Santiago 17 June: 0–0

1984 East Germany
Shilton
Duxbury
Sansom
Williams
Wright
Butcher
Robson
Wilkins
Mariner
(Hateley)
Woodcock
(Francis)
Barnes
*Wembley 12 Sept: 1–0
Robson*

1984 Finland
Shilton
Duxbury
(Stevens)
Sansom
Williams
Wright
Butcher

Robson
(Chamberlain)
Wilkins
Hateley
Woodcock
Barnes
*Wembley 17 Oct: 5–0
Sansom, Robson, Hateley 2, Woodcock*

1984 Turkey
Shilton
Anderson
Sansom
Williams
(Stevens)
Wright
Butcher
Robson
Wilkins
Withe
Woodcock
(Francis)
Barnes
*Istanbul 14 Nov: 8–0
Anderson, Woodcock 2, Barnes 2, Robson 3*

1985 N Ireland
Shilton
Anderson
Sansom
Steven
Martin
Butcher
Stevens
Wilkins
Hateley
Woodcock
(Francis)
Barnes
*Belfast 27 Feb: 1–0
Hateley*

1985 Rep of Ireland
Bailey
Anderson
Sansom
Steven
Wright
Butcher
Robson
(Hoddle)
Wilkins
Hateley
(Davenport)
Lineker
Waddle
Wembley 26 March: 2–1 Steven, Lineker

1985 Romania
Shilton
Anderson
Sansom
Steven

Wright
Butcher
Robson
Wilkins
Mariner
(Lineker)
Francis
Barnes
(Waddle)
Bucharest 1 May: 0–0

1985 Finland
Shilton
Anderson
Sansom
Steven
(Waddle)
Fenwick
Butcher
Robson
Wilkins
Hateley
Francis
Barnes
*Helsinki 25 May: 1–1
Hateley*

1985 Scotland
Shilton
Anderson
Sansom
Hoddle
(Lineker)
Fenwick
Butcher
Robson
Wilkins
Hateley
Francis
Barnes
(Waddle)
Glasgow 25 May: 0–1

1985 Italy
Shilton
Stevens
Sansom
Steven
(Hoddle)
Wright
Butcher
Robson
Wilkins
Hateley
Francis
(Lineker)
Waddle
(Barnes)
Mexico City 6 June: 1–2 Hateley

1985 Mexico
Bailey
Anderson
Sansom
Hoddle

(Dixon)
Fenwick
Watson
Robson
Wilkins
(Reid)
Hateley
Francis
Barnes
(Waddle)
Mexico City 9 June:
0–1

1985 W Germany
Shilton
Stevens
Sansom
Hoddle
Wright
Butcher
Robson
(Bracewell)
Reid
Dixon
Lineker
(Barnes)
Waddle
Mexico City 12 June:
3–0 Robson, Dixon 2

1985 USA
Woods
Anderson
Sansom
(Watson)
Hoddle
(Steven)
Fenwick
Butcher
Robson
(Reid)
Bracewell
Dixon
Lineker
Waddle
(Barnes)
Los Angeles 16 June:
5–0 Steven, Dixon 2
Lineker 2

1985 Romania
Shilton
Stevens
Sansom
Reid
Wright
Fenwick
Robson
Hoddle
Hateley
Lineker
(Woodcock)
Waddle
(Barnes)
Wembley 11 Sept: 1–1
Hoddle

1985 Turkey
Shilton
Stevens
Sansom
Hoddle
Wright
Fenwick
Robson
(Steven)
Wilkins
Hateley
(Woodcock)
Lineker
Waddle
Wembley 16 Oct: 5–0
Robson, Waddle,
Lineker 3

1985 N Ireland
Shilton
Stevens
Sansom
Hoddle
Wright
Fenwick
Bracewell
Wilkins
Dixon
Lineker
Waddle
Wembley 13 Nov: 0–0

1986 Egypt
Shilton
(Woods)
Stevens
Sansom
Cowans
Wright
Fenwick
Steven
(Hill)
Wilkins
Hateley
Lineker
(Beardsley)
Wallace
Cairo 29 Jan: 4–0
Cowans, Steven,
Wallace, 1 o.g.

1986 Israel
Shilton
(Woods)
Stevens
Sansom
Hoddle
Martin
Butcher
Robson
Wilkins
Dixon
(Woodcock)
Beardsley
(Barnes)
Waddle

Tel Aviv 26 Feb: 2–1
Robson 2

1986 USSR
Shilton
Anderson
Sansom
Hoddle
Wright
Butcher
Cowans
(Hodge)
Wilkins
Beardsley
Lineker
Waddle
(Steven)
Tbilisi 26 March: 1–0
Waddle

1986 Scotland
Shilton
Stevens
Sansom
Hoddle
Watson
Butcher
Wilkins
(Reid)
Francis
Hateley
Hodge
(Stevens)
Waddle
Wembley 23 April: 2–1
Hoddle, Butcher

1986 Mexico
Shilton
Anderson
Sansom
Hoddle
Fenwick
Butcher
Robson
(Stevens)
Wilkins
(Steven)
Hateley
(Dixon)
Beardsley
Waddle
Los Angeles 17 May:
3–0 Hateley 2,
Beardsley

1986 Canada
Shilton
(Woods)
Stevens
Sansom
Hoddle
Martin
Butcher
Robson
Wilkins
Dixon
Hodge
Wilkins

(Reid)
Hateley
Lineker
(Beardsley)
Waddle
(Barnes)
Vancouver 24 May:
1–0 Hateley

1986 Portugal†
Shilton
Stevens
Sansom
Hoddle
Fenwick
Butcher
Robson
(Hodge)
Wilkins
Hateley
Lineker
Waddle
(Beardsley)
Monterrey 3 June: 0–1

1986 Morocco†
Shilton
Stevens
Sansom
Hoddle
Fenwick
Butcher
Robson
(Hodge)
Wilkins
Hateley
(Stevens)
Lineker
Waddle
Monterrey 6 June: 0–0

1986 Poland†
Shilton
Stevens
Sansom
Hoddle
Fenwick
Butcher
Hodge
Reid
Beardsley
(Waddle)
Lineker
Steven
Monterrey 11 June: 3–0
Lineker 3

1986 Paraguay†
Shilton
Stevens
Sansom
Hoddle
Martin
Butcher
Hodge
Reid

(Stevens)
Beardsley
(Hateley)
Lineker
Steven
Mexico City 18 June:
3–0 Beardsley,
Lineker 2

1986 Argentina†
Shilton
Stevens
Sansom
Hoddle
Fenwick
Butcher
Hodge
Reid
(Waddle)
Beardsley
Lineker
Steven
(Barnes)
Mexico City 22 June:
1–2 Lineker

1986 Sweden
Shilton
Anderson
Sansom
Hoddle
Martin
Butcher
Steven
(Cottee)
Wilkins
Dixon
Hodge
Barnes
(Waddle)
Stockholm 10 Sept:
0–1

1986 N Ireland
Shilton
Anderson
Samson
Hoddle
Watson
Butcher
Robson
Hodge
Beardsley
(Cottee)
Lineker
Waddle
Wembley 16 Oct: 3–0
Waddle, Lineker 2

1986 Yugoslavia
Woods
Anderson
Sansom
Hoddle
Wright
Butcher

78

Mabbutt
Hodge
(Wilkins)
Beardsley
Lineker
Waddle
(Steven)
Wembley 12 Nov: 2–0
Anderson, Mabbutt

1987 Spain
Shilton
(Woods)
Anderson
Sansom
Hoddle
Adams
Butcher
Robson
Hodge
Beardsley
Lineker
Waddle
(Steven)
Madrid 18 Feb: 4–2
Lineker 4

1987 N Ireland
Shilton
(Woods)
Anderson
Sansom
Mabbutt
Wright
Butcher
Robson
Hodge
Beardsley
Lineker
Waddle
Belfast 1 April: 2–0
Robson, Waddle

1987 Turkey
Woods
Anderson
Sansom
Hoddle
Adams
Mabbutt
Robson
Hodge
(Barnes)
Allen
(Hateley)
Lineker
Waddle
Izmir 29 April 0–0

1987 Brazil
Shilton
Stevens
Pearce
Reid
Adams
Butcher

Robson
Barnes
Beardsley
Lineker
(Hateley)
Waddle
Wembley 19 May: 1–1
Lineker

1987 Scotland
Woods
Stevens
Pearce
Hoddle
Wright
Butcher
Robson
Hodge
Beardsley
Hateley
Waddle
Glasgow 23 May: 0–0

1987 W Germany
Shilton
Anderson
Sansom
(Pearce)
Hoddle
(Webb)
Adams
Mabbutt
Reid
Barnes
Beardsley
Lineker
Waddle
(Hateley)
Düsseldorf 9 Sept: 1–3
Lineker

1987 Turkey
Shilton
Stevens
Sansom
Steven
(Hoddle)
Adams
Butcher
Robson
Webb
Beardsley
(Regis)
Lineker
Barnes
Wembley 14 Oct: 8–0
Robson, Webb,
Beardsley, Barnes 2,
Lineker 3

1987 Yugoslavia
Shilton
Stevens
Sansom
Steven
Adams

Butcher
Robson
(Reid)
Webb
(Hoddle)
Beardsley
Lineker
Barnes
Belgrade 11 Nov: 4–1
Adams, Robson,
Beardsley, Barnes

1988 Israel
Woods
Stevens
Pearce
Webb
Watson
Wright
(Fenwick)
Allen
(Harford)
McMahon
Beardsley
Barnes
Waddle
Tel Aviv 17 Feb: 0–0

1988 Holland
Shilton
Stevens
Sansom
Steven
Adams
Watson
(Wright)
Robson
Webb
(Hoddle)
Beardsley
(Hateley)
Lineker
Barnes
Wembley 23 March:
2–2 Adams, Lineker

1988 Hungary
Woods
Anderson
Pearce
(Stevens)
Steven
Adams
Pallister
Robson
McMahon
Beardsley
(Hateley)
Lineker
(Cottee)
Waddle
(Hoddle)
Budapest 27 April: 0–0

1988 Scotland
Shilton

Stevens
Sansom
Webb
Watson
Adams
Robson
Steven
(Waddle)
Beardsley
Lineker
Barnes
Wembley 21 May: 1–0
Beardsley

1988 Colombia
Shilton
Anderson
Sansom
McMahon
Wright
Adams
Robson
Waddle
(Hoddle)
Beardsley
(Hateley)
Lineker
Barnes
Wembley 24 May: 1–1
Lineker

1988 Switzerland
Shilton
(Woods)
Stevens
Sansom
Webb
Wright
Adams
(Watson)
Robson
(Reid)
Steven
(Waddle)
Beardsley
Lineker
Barnes
Lausanne 28 May: 1–0
Lineker

1988 Rep of Ireland
Shilton
Stevens
Sansom
Webb
(Hoddle)
Wright
Adams
Robson
Waddle
Beardsley
(Hateley)
Lineker
Barnes
Stuttgart 12 June: 0–1

1988 Holland
Shilton
Stevens
Sansom
Hoddle
Wright
Adams
Robson
Steven
(Waddle)
Beardsley
(Hateley)
Lineker
Barnes
Düsseldorf 15 June:
1–3 Robson

1988 USSR
Woods
Stevens
Sansom
Hoddle
Watson
Adams
Robson
Steven
McMahon
(Webb)
Lineker
(Hateley)
Barnes
Frankfurt 18 June: 1–3
Adams

1988 Denmark
Shilton
(Woods)
Stevens
Pearce
Rocastle
Adams
(Walker)
Butcher
Robson
Webb
Harford
(Cottee)
Beardsley
(Gascoigne)
Hodge
Wembley 14 Sept: 1–0
Webb

1988 Sweden
Shilton
Stevens
Pearce
Webb
Adams
(Walker)
Butcher
Robson
Beardsley
Waddle
Lineker
Barnes

(Cottee)
Wembley 19 Oct: 0–0

1988 Saudi Arabia
Seaman
Sterland
Pearce
Thomas
(Gascoigne)
Adams
Pallister
Robson
Rocastle
Beardsley
(Smith)
Lineker
Waddle
(Marwood)
Riyadh 16 Nov: 1–1
Adams

1989 Greece
Shilton
Stevens
Pearce
Webb
Walker
Butcher
Robson
Rocastle
Smith
(Beardsley)
Lineker
Barnes
Athens 8 Feb: 2–1
Robson, Barnes

1989 Albania
Shilton
Stevens
Pearce
Webb
Walker
Butcher
Robson
Rocastle
Waddle
(Beardsley)
Lineker
(Smith)
Barnes
Tirana 8 March: 2–0
Robson, Barnes

1989 Albania
Shilton
Stevens
(Parker)
Pearce
Webb
Walker
Butcher
Robson
Rocastle
(Gascoigne)
Beardsley

Lineker
Waddle
Wembley 26 April: 5–0
Lineker, Beardsley 2,
Waddle, Gascoigne

1989 Chile
Shilton
Parker
Pearce
Webb
Walker
Butcher
Robson
Gascoigne
Clough
Fashanu
(Cottee)
Waddle
Wembley 23 May: 0–0

1989 Scotland
Shilton
Stevens
Pearce
Webb
Walker
Butcher
Robson
Steven
Fashanu
(Bull)
Cottee
(Gascoigne)
Waddle
Glasgow 27 May: 2–0
Waddle, Bull

1989 Poland
Shilton
Stevens
Pearce
Webb
Walker
Butcher
Robson
Waddle
(Rocastle)
Beardsley
(Smith)
Lineker
Barnes
Wembley 3 June: 3–0
Webb, Lineker, Barnes

1989 Denmark
Shilton
(Seaman)
Parker
Pearce
Webb
(McMahon)
Walker
Butcher
Robson
Rocastle

Beardsley
(Bull)
Lineker
Barnes
(Waddle)
Copenhagen 7 June:
1–1 Lineker

1989 Sweden
Shilton
Stevens
Pearce
Webb
(Gascoigne)
Walker
Butcher
Beardsley
McMahon
Waddle
Lineker
Barnes
(Rocastle)
Stockholm 6 Sept: 0–0

1989 Poland
Shilton
Stevens
Pearce
McMahon
Walker
Butcher
Robson
Rocastle
Beardsley
Lineker
Waddle
Katowice 11 Oct: 0–0

1989 Italy
Shilton
(Beasant)
Stevens
Pearce
(Winterburn)
McMahon
(Hodge)
Walker
Butcher
Robson
(Phelan)
Waddle
Beardsley
(Platt)
Lineker
Barnes
Wembley 15 Nov: 0–0

1989 Yugoslavia
Shilton
(Beasant)
Parker
Pearce
(Dorigo)
Thomas
(Platt)
Walker

Butcher
Robson
(McMahon)
Rocastle)
(Hodge)
Bull
Lineker
Waddle
Wembley 13 Dec: 2–1
Robson 2

1990 Brazil
Shilton
(Woods)
Stevens
Pearce
McMahon
Walker
Butcher
Platt
Waddle
Beardsley
(Gascoigne)
Lineker
Barnes
Wembley 28 March:
1–0 Lineker

1990 Czechoslovakia
Shilton
(Seaman)
Dixon
Pearce
(Dorigo)
Steven
Walker
(Wright)
Butcher
Robson
(McMahon)
Gascoigne
Bull
Lineker
Hodge
Wembley 25 April: 4–2
Pearce, Gascoigne,
Bull 2

1990 Denmark
Shilton
(Woods)
Stevens
Pearce
(Dorigo)
McMahon
(Platt)
Walker
Butcher
Hodge
Gascoigne
Waddle
(Rocastle)
Lineker
(Bull)
Barnes
Wembley 15 May: 1–0
Lineker

1990 Uruguay
Shilton
Parker
Pearce
Hodge
(Beardsley)
Walker
Butcher
Robson
Gascoigne
Waddle
Lineker
(Bull)
Barnes
Wembley 22 May: 1–2
Barnes

1990 Tunisia
Shilton
Stevens
Pearce
Hodge
(Beardsley)
Walker
Butcher
(Wright)
Robson
Waddle
(Platt)
Gascoigne
Lineker
(Bull)
Barnes
Tunis 2 June: 1–1
Bull

1990 Rep of Ireland†
Shilton
Stevens
Pearce
Gascoigne
Walker
Butcher
Waddle
Robson
Beardsley
(McMahon)
Lineker
(Bull)
Barnes
Cagliari 11 June: 1–1
Lineker

1990 Holland†
Shilton
Parker
Pearce
Wright
Walker
Butcher
Robson
(Platt)
Waddle
(Bull)
Gascoigne
Lineker

Barnes
Cagliari 16 June: 0–0

1990 Egypt†
Shilton
Parker
Pearce
Gascoigne
Walker
Wright
McMahon
Waddle
(Platt)
Bull
(Beardsley)
Lineker
Barnes
Cagliari 21 June: 1–0
Wright

1990 Belgium†
Shilton
Parker
Pearce
Wright
Walker
Butcher
McMahon
(Platt)
Waddle
Gascoigne
Lineker
Barnes
(Bull)
Bologna 26 June: 1–0*
Platt

1990 Cameroon†
Shilton
Parker
Pearce
Wright
Walker
Butcher
(Steven)
Platt
Waddle
Gascoigne
Lineker
Barnes
(Beardsley)
Naples 1 July: 3–2*
Platt, Lineker 2 pens

1990 W Germany†
Shilton
Parker
Pearce
Wright
Walker
Butcher
(Steven)
Platt
Waddle
Gascoigne
Lineker
Beardsley

Turin 4 July: 1–1* (West Germany won 4–3 on pens) Lineker

1990 Italy†
Shilton
Stevens
Dorigo
Parker
Walker
Wright
(Waddle)
Platt
Steven
McMahon
(Webb)
Lineker
Beardsley
Bari 7 July: 1–2 Platt

1990 Hungary
Woods
Dixon
Pearce
(Dorigo)
Parker
Walker
Wright
Platt
Gascoigne
Bull
(Waddle)
Lineker
Barnes
Wembley 12 Sept: 1–0
Lineker

1990 Poland
Woods
Dixon
Pearce
Parker
Walker
Wright
Platt
Gascoigne
Bull
(Beardsley)
Lineker
(Waddle)
Barnes
Wembley 17 Oct:
2–0 Lineker pen,
Beardsley

1990 Rep of Ireland
Woods
Dixon
Pearce
Adams
Walker
Wright
Platt
Cowans
Beardsley
Lineker

McMahon
Dublin 14 Nov: 1–1
Platt

1991 Cameroon
Seaman
Dixon
Pearce
Steven
Walker
Wright
Robson
(Pallister)
Gascoigne
(Hodge)
Wright I
Lineker
Barnes
Wembley 6 Feb: 2–0
Lineker 2

1991 Rep of Ireland
Seaman
Dixon
Pearce
Adams
(Sharpe)
Walker
Wright
Robson
Platt
Beardsley
Lineker
(Wright I)
Barnes
Wembley 27 March:
1–1 Dixon

1991 Turkey
Seaman
Dixon
Pearce
Wise
Walker
Pallister
Platt
Thomas
(Hodge)
Smith
Lineker
Barnes
Izmir 1 May: 1–0 Wise

1991 USSR
Woods
Stevens
Dorigo
Wise
(Batty)
Parker
Wright
Platt
Thomas
Smith
Wright I
(Beardsley)

Barnes
Wembley 21 May: 3–1
Smith, Platt 2 (1 pen)

1991 Argentina
Seaman
Dixon
Pearce
Batty
Walker
Wright
Platt
Thomas
Smith
Lineker
Barnes
(Clough)
Wembley 25 May: 2–2
Platt, Lineker

1991 Australia
Woods
Parker
Pearce
Batty
Walker
Wright
Platt
Thomas
Clough
Lineker
(Wise)
Hirst
(Salako)
Sydney 1 June: 1–0
Gray o.g.

1991 New Zealand
Woods
Parker
Pearce
Batty
(Deane)
Walker
Barrett
Platt
Thomas
Wise
Lineker
Walters
(Salako)
Auckland 3 June: 1–0
Lineker

1991 New Zealand
Woods
Charles
Pearce
Wise
Walker
Wright
Platt
Thomas
Deane
(Hirst)
Wright I

Salako
Wellington 8 June: 2–0
Pearce, Hirst

1991 Malaysia
Woods
Charles
Pearce
Batty
Walker
Wright
Platt
Thomas
Clough
Lineker
Salako
Kuala Lumpur 12 June:
4–2 Lineker 4

1991 Germany
Woods
Dixon
Dorigo
Batty
Pallister
Parker
Platt
Steven
(Stewart)
Smith
Lineker
Salako
(Merson)
Wembley 11 Sept: 0–1

1991 Turkey
Woods
Dixon
Pearce
Batty
Walker
Mabbutt
Robson
Platt
Smith
Lineker
Waddle
Wembley 16 Oct: 1–0
Smith

1991 Poland
Woods
Dixon
Pearce
Gray
(Smith)
Walker
Mabbutt
Platt
Thomas
Rocastle
Lineker
Sinton
(Daley)
Poznan 13 Nov: 1–1
Lineker

81

1992 France
Woods
Jones
Pearce
Keown
Walker
Wright
Webb
Thomas
Clough
Shearer
Hirst
(Lineker)
Wembley 19 Feb: 2–0
Lineker, Shearer

1992 Czechoslovakia
Seaman
Keown
Pearce
Rocastle
(Dixon)
Walker
Mabbutt
(Lineker)
Platt
Merson
Clough
(Stewart)
Hateley
Barnes
(Dorigo)
Prague 25 March: 2–2
Merson, Keown

1992 CIS
Woods
(Martyn)
Steven
Sinton
(Curle)
Palmer
Walker
Keown
Platt
Steven
(Stewart)
Shearer
(Cough)
Lineker
Daley
Moscow 29 April: 2–2
Lineker, Steven

1992 Hungary
Martyn
(Seaman)
Stevens
Dorigo
Curle
(Sinton)
Walker
Keown
Webb
(Batty)
Palmer
Merson
(Smith)
Lineker
(Wright I)
Daley
Budapest 12 May: 1–0
Webb

1992 Brazil
Woods
Stevens
Dorigo
(Pearce)
Palmer
Walker
Keown
Daley
(Merson)
Steven
(Webb)
Platt
Lineker
Sinton
(Rocastle)
Wembley 17 May: 1–1
Platt

1992 Finland
Woods
Stevens
(Palmer)
Pearce
Keown
Walker
Wright
Platt
Steven
(Daley)
Webb
Lineker
Barnes
(Merson)
Helsinki 3 June: 2–1
Platt 2

1992 Denmark
Woods
Curle
(Daley)
Pearce
Keown
Walker
Platt
Steven
Lineker
Palmer
Merson
(Webb)
Smith
Malmö 11 June: 0–0

1992 France
Woods
Pearce
Keown
Walker
Platt
Steven
Lineker
Sinton
Palmer
Batty
Shearer
Malmö 14 June: 0–0

1992 Sweden
Woods
Pearce
Keown
Walker
Platt
Lineker
(Smith)
Sinton
(Merson)
Palmer
Webb
Daley
Batty
Stockholm 17 June: 1–2
Platt

Stuart Pearce of Nottingham Forest, a fiercely patriotic and loyal defender, has taken over from the retiring Lineker as the new England skipper

Caps 1872-1992

Abbott W (Everton)	1
A'Court A (Liverpool)	5
Adams T (Arsenal)	19
Adcock H (Leicester City)	5
Alcock C (Wanderers)	1
Alderson J (C Palace)	1
Aldridge A (WBA, Walsall Town Swifts)	2
Allen A (Stoke)	3
Allen A (Aston Villa)	1
Allen C (QPR, Spurs)	5
Allen H (Wolves)	5
Allen J (Portsmouth)	2
Allen R (WBA)	5
Alsford W (Spurs)	1
Amos A (Old Carthusians)	2
Anderson R (Old Etonians)	1
Anderson S (Sunderland)	2
Anderson V (Nottm Forest, Arsenal, Man Utd)	30
Angus J (Burnley)	1
Armfield J (Blackpool)	43
Armitage G (Charlton)	1
Armstrong D (Middlesbrough, Southampton)	3
Armstrong K (Chelsea)	1
Arnold J (Fulham)	1
Arthur J (Blackburn)	7
Ashcroft J (Woolwich Arsenal)	3
Ashmore G (WBA)	1
Ashton C (Corinthians)	1
Ashurst W (Notts County)	5
Astall G (Birmingham)	2
Astle J (WBA)	5
Aston J (Man Utd)	17
Athersmith W (Aston Villa)	12
Atyeo J (Bristol City)	6
Austin S (Man City)	1
Bach P (Sunderland)	1
Bache J (Aston Villa)	7
Baddeley T (Wolves)	5
Bagshaw J (Derby County)	1
Bailey G (Man Utd)	2
Bailey H (Leicester Fosse)	5
Bailey M (Charlton)	2
Bailey N (Clapham Rovers)	19
Baily E (Spurs)	9
Bain J (Oxford Univ)	1
Baker A (Arsenal)	1
Baker B (Everton, Chelsea)	2
Baker J (Hibernian, Arsenal)	8
Ball A (Blackpool, Everton, Arsenal)	72
Ball J (Bury)	1
Balmer W (Everton)	1
Bamber J (Liverpool)	1
Bambridge A (Swifts)	3
Bambridge E C (Swifts)	18
Bambridge E H (Swifts)	1
Banks G (Leicester City, Stoke)	73
Banks H (Millwall)	1
Banks T (Bolton)	6
Bannister W (Burnley, Bolton)	2
Barclay R (Sheff Wed)	3
Barham M (Norwich)	2
Barkas S (Man City)	5
Barker J (Derby County)	11
Barker R (Herts Rangers)	1
Barker R R (Casuals)	1
Barlow R (WBA)	1
Barnes J (Watford, Liverpool)	67
Barnes P (Man City, WBA, Leeds Utd)	22
Barnet H (Royal Engineers)	1
Barrass M (Bolton)	3
Barrett A (Fulham)	1
Barrett E (Oldham)	1
Barrett J (W Ham)	1
Barry L (Leicester City)	5
Barson F (Aston Villa)	1
Barton J (Blackburn)	1
Barton P (Birmingham)	7
Bassett W (WBA)	16
Bastard S (Upton Park)	1
Bastin C (Arsenal)	21
Batty D (Leeds Utd)	10
Baugh R (Stafford Road, Wolves)	2
Bayliss A (WBA)	1
Baynham R (Luton)	3
Beardsley P (Newcastle, Liverpool)	49
Beasant D (Chelsea)	2
Beasley A (Huddersfield)	1
Beats W (Wolves)	2
Beattie K (Ipswich)	9
Becton F (Preston, Liverpool)	2
Bedford H (Blackpool)	2
Bell C (Man City)	48
Bennett W (Sheff Utd)	2
Benson R (Sheff Utd)	1
Bentley R (Chelsea)	12
Beresford J (Aston Villa)	1
Berry A (Oxford Univ)	1
Berry J (Man Utd)	4
Bestall J (Grimsby)	1
Betmead H (Grimsby)	1
Betts M (Old Harrovians)	1
Betts W (Sheff Wed)	1
Beverley J (Blackburn)	3
Birkett R H (Clapham Rovers)	1
Birkett R (Middlesbrough)	1
Birley F (Oxford Univ, Wanderers)	2
Birtles G (Nottm Forest)	3
Bishop S (Leicester City)	4
Blackburn F (Blackburn)	3
Blackburn G (Aston Villa)	1
Blenkinsop E (Sheff Wed)	26
Bliss H (Spurs)	1
Blissett L (Watford)	14
Blockley J (Arsenal)	1
Bloomer S (Derby County, Middlesbrough)	23
Blunstone F (Chelsea)	5
Bond R (Preston, Bradford City)	8
Bonetti P (Chelsea)	7
Bonsor A (Wanderers)	2
Booth F (Man City)	1
Booth T (Blackburn, Everton)	2
Bowden E (Arsenal)	6
Bower A (Corinthians)	5
Bowers J (Derby County)	3
Bowles S (QPR)	5
Bowser S (WBA)	1
Boyer P (Norwich)	1
Boyes W (WBA, Everton)	3
Boyle T (Burnley)	1
Brabrook P (Chelsea)	3
Bracewell P (Everton)	3
Bradford G (Bristol Rovers)	1
Bradford J (Birmingham)	12
Bradley W (Man Utd)	3
Bradshaw F (Sheff Wed)	1
Bradshaw T (Liverpool)	1
Bradshaw W (Blackburn)	4
Brann G (Swifts)	3
Brawn W (Aston Villa)	2
Bray J (Man City)	6
Brayshaw E (Sheff Wed)	1
Bridges B (Chelsea)	4
Bridgett A (Sunderland)	11
Brindle T (Darwen)	2
Brittleton J (Sheff Wed)	5
Britton C (Everton)	9
Broadbent P (Wolves)	7
Broadis I A (Man City, Newcastle)	14
Brockbank J (Cambridge Univ)	1
Brodie J B (Wolves)	3
Bromilow T G (Liverpool)	5
Bromley-Davenport W E (Oxford Univ)	2
Brook E (Man City)	18
Brooking T (West Ham)	47
Brooks J (Spurs)	3
Broome F H (Aston Villa)	7
Brown A (Aston Villa)	1
Brown A S (Sheff Utd)	2
Brown G (Huddersfield, Aston Villa)	9
Brown J (Blackburn)	5
Brown J H (Sheff Wed)	6
Brown K (West Ham)	1
Brown T (WBA)	3
Brown W (West Ham)	1
Bruton J (Burnley)	3
Bryant W (Clapton)	1
Buchan C (Sunderland)	6
Buchanan W (Clapham Rovers)	1
Buckley F C (Derby County)	1
Bull S (Wolves)	13
Bullock F E (Huddersfield)	1
Bullock N (Bury)	3
Burgess H (Man City)	4
Burgess H (Sheff Wed)	4
Burnup C (Cambridge Univ)	1
Burrows H (Sheff Wed)	3
Burton F E (Nottm Forest)	1
Bury L (Cambridge Univ, Old Etonians)	2
Butcher T (Ipswich)	77
Butler J (Arsenal)	1
Butler W (Bolton)	1

83

Name	Caps
Byrne G (Liverpool)	2
Byrne J J (C Palace, West Ham)	11
Byrne R (Man Utd)	33
Callaghan I (Liverpool)	4
Calvey J (Nottm Forest)	1
Campbell A (Blackburn, Huddersfield)	8
Camsell G (Middlesbrough)	9
Capes A (Stoke)	1
Carr J (Middlesbrough)	2
Carr J (Newcastle)	2
Carr W H (Owlerton)	1
Carter H S (Sunderland, Derby County)	13
Carter J H (WBA)	3
Catlin A E (Sheff Wed)	5
Chadwick A (Southampton)	2
Chadwick E (Everton)	7
Chamberlain M (Stoke)	8
Chambers H (Liverpool)	8
Channon M (Southampton, Man City)	46
Charles G (Nottm Forest)	2
Charlton J (Leeds Utd)	35
Charlton R (Man Utd)	106
Charnley R (Blackpool)	1
Charnsley C (Small Heath)	1
Chedgzoy S (Everton)	8
Chenery C (C Palace)	3
Cherry T (Leeds Utd)	27
Chilton A (Man Utd)	2
Chippendale H (Blackburn)	1
Chivers M (Spurs)	24
Christian E (Old Etonians)	1
Clamp E (Wolves)	4
Clapton D (Arsenal)	1
Clare T (Stoke)	4
Clarke A (Leeds Utd)	19
Clarke H (Spurs)	1
Clay T (Spurs)	4
Clayton R (Blackburn)	35
Clegg J (Sheff Wed)	1
Clegg W (Sheff Wed, Sheff Albion)	2
Clemence R (Liverpool, Spurs)	61
Clement D (QPR)	5
Clough B (Middlesbrough)	2
Clough N (Nottm Forest)	7
Coates R (Burnley, Spurs)	4
Cobbold W (Cambridge Univ, Old Carthusians)	9
Cock J (Huddersfield, Chelsea)	2
Cockburn H (Man Utd)	13
Cohen G (Fulham)	37
Colclough H (C Palace)	1
Coleman E (Dulwich Hamlet)	1
Coleman J (Woolwich Arsenal)	1
Common A (Sheff Utd, Middlesbrough)	3
Compton L H (Arsenal)	2
Conlin J (Bradford City)	1
Connelly J (Burnley, Man Utd)	20
Cook T E (Brighton)	1
Cooper N C (Cambridge Univ)	1
Cooper T (Derby County)	15
Cooper T (Leeds Utd)	20
Coppell S (Man Utd)	42
Copping W (Leeds Utd, Arsenal)	20
Corbett B (Corinthians)	1
Corbett R (Old Malvernians)	1
Corbett W (Birmingham)	3
Corrigan J (Man City)	9
Cottee A (West Ham, Everton)	7
Cotterill G (Cambridge Univ, Old Brightonians)	4
Cottle J (Bristol City)	1
Cowan S (Man City)	3
Cowan S G (Aston Villa, Bari)	10
Cowell A (Blackburn)	1
Cox J (Liverpool)	3
Cox J D (Derby County)	1
Crabtree J (Burnley, Aston Villa)	14
Crawford J F (Chelsea)	1
Crawford R (Ipswich)	2
Crawshaw T (Sheff Wed)	10
Crayston W (Arsenal)	8
Creek N (Corinthians)	1
Cresswell W (South Shields, Sunderland, Everton)	7
Crompton R (Blackburn)	41
Crooks S (Derby County)	26
Crowe C (Wolves)	1
Cuggy F (Sunderland)	2
Cullis S (Wolves)	12
Cunliffe A (Blackburn)	2
Cunliffe D (Portsmouth)	1
Cunliffe J (Everton)	1
Cunningham L (WBA, Real Madrid)	6
Curle K (Man City)	6
Currey E (Oxford Univ)	2
Currie A (Sheff Utd, Leeds Utd)	17
Cursham A (Notts County)	6
Cursham H (Notts County)	8
Daft H (Notts County)	5
Daley A (Aston Villa)	7
Danks T (Nottm Forest)	1
Davenport J (Bolton)	2
Davenport P (Nottm Forest)	1
Davis G (Derby County)	2
Davis H (Sheff Wed)	3
Davison J (Sheff Wed)	1
Dawson J (Burnley)	2
Day S (Old Malvernians)	3
Dean W (Everton)	16
Deane B (Sheff Utd)	2
Deeley N (Wolves)	2
Devey J (Aston Villa)	2
Devonshire A (West Ham)	8
Dewhurst F (Preston)	9
Dewhurst G (Liverpool Ramblers)	1
Dickinson J (Portsmouth)	48
Dimmock J (Spurs)	3
Ditchburn E (Spurs)	6
Dix R (Derby County)	1
Dixon J (Notts County)	1
Dixon K (Chelsea)	8
Dixon L (Arsenal)	12
Dobson A (Notts County)	4
Dobson C (Notts County)	1
Dobson M (Burnley, Everton)	5
Doggart A (Corinthians)	1
Dorigo A (Chelsea, Leeds Utd)	10
Dorrell A (Aston Villa)	4
Douglas B (Blackburn)	36
Downs R (Everton)	1
Doyle M (Man City)	5
Drake E (Arsenal)	5
Ducat A (Woolwich Arsenal, Aston Villa)	6
Dunn A T (Cambridge Univ, Old Etonians)	4
Duxbury M (Man Utd)	10
Earle S (Clapton, West Ham)	2
Eastham G (Arsenal)	19
Eastham G R (Bolton)	1
Eckersley W (Blackburn)	17
Edwards D (Man Utd)	18
Edwards J (Shropshire Wanderers)	1
Edwards W (Leeds Utd)	16
Ellerington W (Southampton)	2
Elliott G (Middlesbrough)	3
Elliott W (Burnley)	5
*Evans R (Sheff Utd)	4
Ewer F (Casuals)	2
Fairclough P (Old Foresters)	1
Fairhurst D (Newcastle)	1
Fantham J (Sheff Wed)	1
Fashanu J (Wimbledon)	2
Felton W (Sheff Wed)	1
Fenton M (Middlesbrough)	1
Fenwick T (QPR, Spurs)	20
Field E (Clapham Rovers)	2
Finney T (Preston NE)	76
Fleming H (Swindon)	11
Fletcher A (Wolves)	2
Flowers R (Wolves)	49
Forman F (Nottm Forest)	9
Forman F R (Nottm Forest)	3
Forrest J (Blackburn)	11
Fort J (Millwall)	1
Foster R (Oxford Univ, Corinthians)	5
Foster S (Brighton and Hove Albion)	3
Foulke W (Sheff Utd)	1
Foulkes W (Man Utd)	1
Fox F (Gillingham)	1
Francis G (QPR)	12
Francis T (Birmingham, Nottm Forest, Man City, Sampdoria)	52
Franklin C (Stoke)	27
Freeman B (Everton, Burnley)	5
Froggatt J (Portsmouth)	13
Froggatt R (Sheff Wed)	4
Fry C (Corinthians)	1
Furness W (Leeds Utd)	1
Galley T (Wolves)	2
Gardner T (Aston Villa)	2
Garfield B (WBA)	1
Garratty W (Aston Villa)	1
Garrett T (Blackpool)	3
Gascoigne P (Spurs)	20
Gates E (Ipswich)	2
Gay L (Cambridge Univ, Old Brightonians)	3

Name	Count
Geary F (Everton)	2
Geaves R (Clapham Rovers)	1
Gee C (Everton)	3
Geldard A (Everton)	4
George C (Derby County)	1
George W (Aston Villa)	3
Gibbins W (Clapton)	2
Gidman J (Aston Villa)	1
Gillard I (QPR)	3
Gilliat W (Old Carthusians)	1
Goddard P (West Ham)	1
Goodall F (Huddersfield)	25
Goodall J (Preston, Derby County)	14
Goodhart H (Old Etonians)	3
Goodwyn A (Royal Engineers)	1
Goodyer A (Nottm Forest)	1
Gosling R (Old Etonians)	5
Gosnell A (Newcastle)	1
Gough H (Sheff Utd)	1
Goulden L (West Ham)	14
Graham L (Millwall)	2
Graham T (Nottm Forest)	2
Grainger C (Sheff Utd, Sunderland)	7
Gray A (Crystal Palace)	1
Greaves J (Chelsea, Spurs)	57
Green G (Sheff Utd)	8
Green T (Wanderers)	1
Greenhalgh E (Notts County)	2
Greenhoff B (Man Utd, Leeds Utd)	18
Greenwood D (Blackburn)	2
Gregory J (QPR)	6
Grimsdell A (Spurs)	6
Grosvenor A (Birmingham)	3
Gunn W (Notts County)	2
Gurney R (Sunderland)	1
Hacking J (Oldham)	3
Hadley H (WBA)	1
Hagan J (Sheff Utd)	1
Haines J (WBA)	1
Hall A (Aston Villa)	1
Hall G (Spurs)	10
Hall J (Birmingham)	17
Halse H (Man Utd)	1
Hammond H (Oxford Univ)	1
Hampson J (Blackpool)	3
Hampton H (Aston Villa)	4
Hancocks J (Wolves)	3
Hapgood E (Arsenal)	30
Hardinge H (Sheff Utd)	1
Hardman E (Everton)	4
Hardwick G (Middlesbrough)	13
Hardy H (Stockport County)	1
Hardy S (Liverpool, Aston Villa)	21
Harford M (Luton)	2
Hargreaves F (Blackburn)	3
Hargreaves J (Blackburn)	2
Harper E (Blackburn)	1
Harris G (Burnley)	1
Harris P (Portsmouth)	2
Harris S (Cambridge Univ, Old Westminsters)	6
Harrison A (Old Westminsters)	2
Harrison G (Everton)	2
Harrow J (Chelsea)	2
Hart E (Leeds Utd)	8
Hartley F (Oxford City)	1
Harvey A (Wednesbury Strollers)	1
Harvey J (Everton)	1
Hassall H (Huddersfield, Bolton)	5
Hateley M (Portsmouth, AC Milan, Monaco, Rangers)	32
Hawkes R (Luton)	5
Haworth G (Accrington)	5
Hawtrey J (Old Etonians)	2
Haygarth E (Swifts)	1
Haynes J (Fulham)	56
Healless H (Blackburn)	2
Hector K (Derby County)	2
Hedley G (Sheff Utd)	1
Hegan K (Corinthians)	4
Hellawell M (Birmingham)	2
Henfrey A (Cambridge Univ, Corinthians)	5
Henry R (Spurs)	1
Heron F (Wanderers)	1
Heron G (Uxbridge, Wanderers)	5
Hibbert W (Bury)	1
Hibbs H (Birmingham)	25
Hill F (Bolton)	2
Hill G (Man Utd)	6
Hill J (Burnley)	11
Hill R (Luton)	3
Hill R H (Millwall)	1
Hillman J (Burnley)	1
Hills A (Old Harrovians)	1
Hilsdon G (Chelsea)	8
Hine E (Leicester City)	6
Hinton A (Wolves, Nottm Forest)	3
Hirst D (Sheff Wed)	3
Hitchens G (Aston Villa, Inter-Milan)	7
Hobbis H (Charlton)	2
Hoddle G (Spurs, Monaco)	53
Hodge S (Aston Villa, Spurs, Nottm Forest)	24
Hodgetts D (Aston Villa)	6
Hodgkinson A (Sheff Utd)	5
Hodgson G (Liverpool)	3
Hodkinson J (Blackburn)	3
Hogg W (Sunderland)	3
Holdcroft G (Preston)	2
Holden A (Bolton)	5
Holden G (Wednesbury OA)	4
Holden-White C (Corinthians)	2
Holford T (Stoke)	1
Holley G (Sunderland)	10
Holliday E (Middlesbrough)	3
Hollins J (Chelsea)	1
Holmes R (Preston)	7
Holt J (Everton, Reading)	10
Hopkinson E (Bolton)	14
Hossack A (Corinthians)	2
Houghton W (Aston Villa)	7
Houlker A (Blackburn, Portsmouth, Southampton)	5
Howarth R (Preston, Everton)	5
Howe D (WBA)	23
Howe J (Derby County)	3
Howell L (Wanderers)	1
Howell R (Sheff Utd, Liverpool)	2
Hudson A (Stoke)	2
Hudson J (Sheffield)	1
Hudspeth F (Newcastle)	1
Hufton A (West Ham)	6
Hughes E (Liverpool, Wolves)	62
Hughes L (Liverpool)	3
Hulme J (Arsenal)	9
Humphreys P (Notts County)	1
Hunt G (Spurs)	3
Hunt Rev. K (Leyton)	2
Hunt R (Liverpool)	34
Hunt S (WBA)	2
Hunter J (Sheff Heeley)	7
Hunter N (Leeds Utd)	28
Hurst G (West Ham)	49
Iremonger J (Nottm Forest)	2
Jack D (Bolton, Arsenal)	9
Jackson E (Oxford Univ)	1
Jarrett B (Cambridge Univ)	3
Jefferis F (Everton)	2
Jezzard B (Fulham)	2
Johnson D (Ipswich, Liverpool)	8
Johnson E (Saltley Coll, Stoke)	2
Johnson J (Stoke)	5
Johnson T (Man City, Everton)	5
Johnson W (Sheff Utd)	6
Johnston H (Blackpool)	10
Jones A (Walsall Swifts, Great Lever)	3
Jones H (Blackburn)	6
Jones H (Nottm Forest)	1
Jones M (Sheff Utd, Leeds Utd)	3
Jones R (Liverpool)	1
Jones W (Bristol City)	1
Jones W (Liverpool)	2
Joy B (Casuals)	1
Kail E (Dulwich Hamlet)	3
Kay T (Everton)	1
Kean F (Sheff Wed, Bolton)	9
Keegan K (Liverpool, SV Hamburg, Southampton)	63
Keen E (Derby County)	4
Kelly R (Burnley, Sunderland, Huddersfield)	14
Kennedy A (Liverpool)	2
Kennedy R (Liverpool)	17
Kenyon-Slaney (Wanderers)	1
Keown M (Everton)	9
Kevan D (WBA)	14
Kidd B (Man Utd)	2
King R (Oxford Univ)	1
Kingsford R (Wanderers)	1
Kingsley M (Newcastle)	1
Kinsey G (Wolves, Derby County)	4
Kirchen A (Arsenal)	3
Kirton W (Aston Villa)	1
Knight A (Portsmouth)	1
Knowles C (Spurs)	4
Labone B (Everton)	26

Name	Count
Lampard F (West Ham)	2
Langley E (Fulham)	3
Langton R (Blackburn, Preston, Bolton)	11
Latchford R (Everton)	12
Latheron E (Blackburn)	2
Lawler C (Liverpool)	4
Lawton T (Everton, Chelsea, Notts County)	23
Leach T (Sheff Wed)	2
Leake A (Aston Villa)	5
Lee E (Southampton)	1
Lee F (Man City)	27
Lee J (Derby County)	1
Lee S (Liverpool)	14
Leighton J (Nottm Forest)	1
Lilley H (Sheff Utd)	1
Linacre H (Nottm Forest)	2
Lindley T (Cambridge Univ, Nottm Forest)	13
Lindsay A (Liverpool)	4
Lindsay W (Wanderers)	1
Lineker G (Leicester City, Everton, Barcelona, Spurs)	80
Lintott E (QPR, Bradford City)	7
Lipsham H (Sheff Utd)	1
Little B (Aston Villa)	1
Lloyd L (Liverpool, Nottm Forest)	4
Lockett A (Stoke)	1
Lodge L (Cambridge Univ, Corinthians)	5
Lofthouse J (Blackburn, Accrington)	7
Lofthouse N (Bolton)	33
Longworth E (Liverpool)	5
Lowder A (Wolves)	1
Lowe E (Aston Villa)	3
Lucas T (Liverpool)	3
Luntley E (Nottm Forest)	2
Lyttelton Hon A (Cambridge Univ)	1
Lyttelton Hon E (Cambridge Univ)	1
McCall J (Preston)	5
McDermott T (Liverpool)	25
McDonald C (Burnley)	8
McFarland R (Derby County)	28
McGarry W (Huddersfield)	4
McGuinness W (Man Utd)	2
McInroy A (Sunderland)	1
McMahon S (Liverpool)	17
McNab R (Arsenal)	4
McNeal R (WBA)	2
McNeil M (Middlesbrough)	9
Mabbutt G (Spurs)	16
Macauley R (Cambridge Univ)	1
Macdonald M (Newcastle)	14
Macrae S (Notts County)	6
Maddison F (Oxford Univ)	1
Madeley P (Leeds Utd)	24
Magee J (WBA)	5
Makepeace H (Everton)	4
Male C (Arsenal)	19
Mannion W (Middlesbrough)	26
Mariner P (Ipswich, Arsenal)	35
Marsden J (Darwen)	1
Marsden W (Sheff Wed)	3
Marsh R (QPR, Man City)	9
Marshall T (Darwen)	2
Martin A (West Ham)	17
Martin H (Sunderland)	1
Martyn N (Crystal Palace)	2
Marwood B (Arsenal)	1
Maskrey H (Derby County)	1
Mason C (Wolves)	3
Matthews R (Coventry)	5
Matthews S (Stoke, Blackpool)	54
Matthews V (Sheff Utd)	2
Maynard W (1st Surrey Rifles)	2
Meadows J (Man City)	1
Medley L (Spurs)	6
Meehan T (Chelsea)	1
Melia J (Liverpool)	2
Mercer D (Sheff Utd)	2
Mercer J (Everton)	5
Merrick G (Birmingham)	23
Merson P (Arsenal)	7
Metcalfe V (Huddersfield)	2
Mew J (Man Utd)	1
Middleditch B (Corinthians)	1
Milburn J (Newcastle)	13
Miller B (Burnley)	1
Miller H (Charlton)	1
Mills G (Chelsea)	3
Mills M (Ipswich)	42
Milne G (Liverpool)	14
Milton A (Arsenal)	1
Milward A (Everton)	4
Mitchell C (Upton Park)	5
Mitchell J (Man City)	1
Moffat H (Oldham)	1
Molyneux G (Southampton)	4
Moon W (Old Westminsters)	7
Moore H (Notts County)	2
Moore J (Derby County)	1
Moore R (West Ham)	108
Moore W (West Ham)	1
Mordue J (Sunderland)	2
Morice C (Barnes)	1
Morley A (Aston Villa)	6
Morley H (Notts County)	1
Morren T (Sheff Utd)	1
Morris F (WBA)	2
Morris J (Derby County)	3
Morris W (Wolves)	3
Morse H (Notts County)	1
Mort T (Aston Villa)	3
Morten A (C Palace)	1
Mortensen S (Blackpool)	25
Morton J (West Ham)	1
Mosforth W (Sheff Wed, Sheff Albion)	9
Moss F (Arsenal)	4
Moss F (Aston Villa)	5
Mosscrop E (Burnley)	2
Mozley B (Derby County)	3
Mullen J (Wolves)	12
Mullery A (Spurs)	35
Neal P (Liverpool)	50
Needham E (Sheff Utd)	16
Newton K (Blackburn, Everton)	27
Nicholls J (WBA)	2
Nicholson W (Spurs)	1
Nish D (Derby County)	5
Norman M (Spurs)	23
Nuttall H (Bolton)	3
Oakley W (Oxford Univ, Corinthians)	16
O'Dowd J (Chelsea)	3
O'Grady M (Huddersfield, Leeds Utd)	2
Ogilvie R (Clapham Rovers)	1
Oliver L (Fulham)	1
Olney B (Aston Villa)	2
Osborne F (Fulham, Spurs)	4
Osborne R (Leicester City)	1
Osgood P (Chelsea)	4
Osman R (Ipswich)	11
Ottaway C (Oxford Univ)	2
Owen J (Sheffield)	1
Owen S (Luton)	3
Page L (Burnley)	7
Paine T (Southampton)	19
Pallister G (Middlesbrough, Man Utd)	5
Palmer C (Sheff Wed)	7
Pantling H (Sheff Utd)	1
Paravacini P J de (Cambridge Univ)	3
Parker P (QPR, Man Utd)	17
Parker T (Southampton)	1
Parkes P (QPR)	1
Parkinson J (Liverpool)	2
Parr P (Oxford Univ)	1
Parry E (Old Carthusians)	3
Parry R (Bolton)	2
Patchitt B (Corinthians)	2
Pawson F (Cambridge Univ, Swifts)	2
Payne J (Luton)	1
Peacock A (Middlesbrough, Leeds Utd)	6
Peacock J (Middlesbrough)	3
Pearce S (Nottm Forest)	50
Pearson H (WBA)	1
Pearson J H (Crewe)	1
Pearson J S (Stuart) (Man Utd)	15
Pearson S C (Stan) (Man Utd)	8
Pease W (Middlesbrough)	1
Pegg D (Man Utd)	1
Pejic M (Stoke)	4
Pelly F (Old Foresters)	3
Pennington J (WBA)	25
Pentland F (Middlesbrough)	5
Perry C (WBA)	3
Perry T (WBA)	1
Perry W (Blackpool)	3
Perryman S (Spurs)	1
Peters M (West Ham, Spurs)	67
Phelan M (Man Utd)	1
Phillips L (Portsmouth)	3
Pickering F (Everton)	3
Pickering J (Sheff Utd)	1
Pickering N (Sunderland)	1
Pike T (Cambridge Univ)	1
Pilkington B (Burnley)	1
Plant J (Bury)	1
Platt D (Aston Villa, Bari)	32
Plum S (Charlton)	1
Pointer R (Burnley)	3
Porteous T (Sunderland)	1

Jimmy Greaves, the impish Tottenham forward who had a magnificent goalscoring record for England of 44 goals in just 57 international appearances, the highest ratio of any modern international

Priest A (Sheff Utd)	1
Prinsep J (Clapham Rovers)	1
Puddefoot S (Blackburn)	2
Pye J (Wolves)	1
Pym R (Bolton)	3
Quantrill A (Derby County)	4
Quixall A (Sheff Wed)	5
Radford J (Arsenal)	2
Raikes G (Oxford Univ)	4
Ramsey A (Southampton, Spurs)	32
Rawlings A (Preston)	1
Rawlings W (Southampton)	2
Rawlinson J (Cambridge Univ)	1
Rawson H (Royal Engineers)	1
Rawson W (Oxford Univ)	2
Read A (Tufnell Park)	1
Reader J (WBA)	1
Reaney P (Leeds Utd)	3
Reeves K (Norwich, Man City)	2
Regis C (WBA, Coventry)	5
Reid P (Everton)	13
Revie D (Man City)	6
†Reynolds J (WBA, Aston Villa)	8
Richards C (Nottm Forest)	1
Richards G (Derby County)	1
Richards J (Wolves)	1
Richardson J (Newcastle)	2
Richardson W (WBA)	1
Rickaby S (WBA)	1
Rigby A (Blackburn)	5
Rimmer E (Sheff Wed)	4
Rimmer J (Arsenal)	1
Rix G (Arsenal)	17
Robb G (Spurs)	1
Roberts C (Man Utd)	3
Roberts F (Man City)	4
Roberts G (Spurs)	6
Roberts H (Arsenal)	1
Roberts H (Millwall)	1
Roberts R (WBA)	3
Roberts W (Preston)	2
Robinson J (Sheff Wed)	4
Robinson J W (Derby County, New Brighton Tower, Southampton)	11
Robson B (WBA, Man Utd)	90
Robson R (WBA)	20
Rocastle D (Arsenal)	14
Rose W (Wolves, Preston)	5
Rostron T (Darwen)	2
Rowe A (Spurs)	1
Rowley J (Man Utd)	6
Rowley W (Stoke)	2
Royle J (Everton, Man City)	6
Ruddlesdin H (Sheff Wed)	3
Ruffell J (West Ham)	6
Russell B (Royal Engineers)	1
Rutherford J (Newcastle)	11
Sadler D (Man Utd)	4
Sagar C (Bury)	2
Sagar E (Everton)	4
Salako J (C Palace)	5
Sandford E (WBA)	1
Sandilands R (Old Westminsters)	5
Sands J (Nottm Forest)	1
Sansom K (C Palace, Arsenal)	86
Saunders F (Swifts)	1
Savage A (C Palace)	1
Sayer J (Stoke)	1
Scattergood E (Derby County)	1
Schofield J (Stoke)	3
Scott L (Arsenal)	17
Scott W (Brentford)	1
Seaman D (QPR, Arsenal)	9
Seddon J (Bolton)	6
Seed J (Spurs)	5
Settle J (Bury, Everton)	6
Sewell J (Sheff Wed)	6
Sewell W (Blackburn)	1
Shackleton L (Sunderland)	5
Sharp J (Everton)	2
Sharpe L (Man Utd)	1
Shaw G E (WBA)	1
Shaw G L (Sheff Utd)	5
Shea D (Blackburn)	2
Shearer A (Southampton)	3
Shellito K (Chelsea)	1
Shelton A (Notts County)	6
Shelton C (Notts Rangers)	1
Shepherd A (Bolton, Newcastle)	2
Shilton P (Leicester City, Stoke, Nottm Forest, Southampton, Derby County)	125
Shimwell E (Blackpool)	1
Shutt G (Stoke)	1
Silcock J (Man Utd)	3
Sillett P (Chelsea)	3
Simms E (Luton)	1
Simpson J (Blackburn)	8
Sinton A (QPR)	5
Slater W (Wolves)	12
Smalley T (Wolves)	1
Smart T (Aston Villa)	5
Smith A (Nottm Forest)	3
Smith A K (Oxford Univ)	1
Smith A M (Arsenal)	13
Smith B (Spurs)	2
Smith C E (C Palace)	1
Smith G O (Oxford Univ, Old Carthusians, Corinthians)	20
Smith H (Reading)	4
Smith J (WBA)	2
Smith Joe (Bolton)	5
Smith J C R (Millwall)	2
Smith J W (Portsmouth)	3
Smith Leslie (Brentford)	1
Smith Lionel (Arsenal)	6
Smith R A (Spurs)	15
Smith S (Aston Villa)	1
Smith S C (Leicester City)	1
Smith T (Birmingham)	2
Smith T (Liverpool)	1
Smith W H (Huddersfield)	3
Sorby T (Thursday Wanderers)	1
Southworth J (Blackburn)	3
Sparks F (Herts Rangers, Clapham Rovers)	3
Spence J (Man Utd)	2
Spence R (Chelsea)	2
Spencer C (Newcastle)	2
Spencer H (Aston Villa)	6
Spiksley F (Sheff Wed)	7
Spilsbury B (Cambridge Univ)	3
Spink N (Aston Villa)	1
Spouncer W (Nottm Forest)	1
Springett R (Sheff Wed)	33
Sproston B (Leeds Utd, Spurs, Man City)	11
Squire R (Cambridge Univ)	3
Stanbrough M (Old Carthusians)	1
Staniforth R (Huddersfield)	8
Starling R (Sheff Wed, Aston Villa)	2
Statham D (WBA)	3
Steele F (Stoke)	6
Stein B (Luton)	1
Stephenson C (Huddersfield)	1
Stephenson G (Derby County, Sheff Wed)	3

87

Stephenson J (Leeds Utd)	2	Ufton D (Charlton)	1	Whitham M (Sheff Utd)	1
Stepney A (Man Utd)	1	Underwood A (Stoke)	2	Whitworth S (Leicester)	7
Sterland M (Sheff Wed)	1	Urwin T (Middlesbrough, Newcastle)	4	Whymark T (Ipswich)	1
Steven T (Everton, Glasgow R, Marseille)	36	Utley G (Barnsley)	1	Widdowson S (Nottm Forest)	1
				Wignall F (Nottm Forest)	2
Stevens G A (Spurs)	7	Vaughton O (Aston Villa)	5	Wilkes A (Aston Villa)	5
Stevens G (Everton, Rangers)	46	Veitch C (Newcastle)	6	Wilkins R (Chelsea, Man Utd, A C Milan)	84
Stewart J (Sheff Wed, Newcastle)	3	Veitch J (Old Westminsters)	1		
Stewart P (Spurs)	3	Venables T (Chelsea)	2	Wilkinson B (Sheff Utd)	1
Stiles N (Man Utd)	28	Vidal R (Oxford Univ)	1	Wilkinson L (Oxford Univ)	1
Stoker J (Birmingham)	3	Viljoen C (Ipswich)	2	Williams B (Wolves)	24
Storer H (Derby County)	2	Viollet D (Man Utd)	2	Williams O (Clapton Orient)	2
Storey P (Arsenal)	19	Von Donop (Royal Engineers)	2	Williams S (Southampton)	6
Storey-Moore I (Nottm Forest)	1			Williams W (WBA)	6
Strange A (Sheff Wed)	20	Wace H (Wanderers)	3	Williamson E (Arsenal)	2
Stratford A (Wanderers)	1	Waddle C (Newcastle, Spurs, Marseille)	62	Williamson R (Middlesbrough)	7
Streten B (Luton)	1			Willingham C (Huddersfield)	12
Sturgess A (Sheff Utd)	2	Wadsworth S (Huddersfield)	9	Willis A (Spurs)	1
Summerbee M (Man City)	8	Wainscoat W (Leeds Utd)	1	Wilshaw D (Wolves)	12
Sunderland A (Arsenal)	1	Waiters A (Blackpool)	5	Wilson C P (Hendon)	2
Sutcliffe J (Bolton, Millwall)	5	Walker D (Nottm Forest)	47	Wilson C W (Oxford Univ)	2
Swan P (Sheff Wed)	19	Walden F (Spurs)	2	Wilson G (Sheff Wed)	12
Swepstone H (Pilgrims)	6	Walker W (Aston Villa)	18	Wilson G P (Corinthians)	2
Swift F (Man City)	19	Wall G (Man Utd)	7	Wilson R (Huddersfield, Everton)	63
		Wallace C (Aston Villa)	3	Wilson T (Huddersfield)	1
Tait G (Birmingham Excelsior)	1	Wallace D (Southampton)	1	Winckworth W (Old Westminsters)	2
Talbot B (Ipswich, Arsenal)	6	Walsh P (Luton)	5	Windridge J (Chelsea)	8
Tambling R (Chelsea)	3	Walters A (Cambridge Univ, Old Carthusians)	9	Wingfield-Stratford C (Royal Engineers)	1
Tate J (Aston Villa)	3				
Taylor E (Blackpool)	1	Walters M (Rangers)	1	Winterburn N (Arsenal)	1
Taylor E H (Huddersfield)	8	Walters P (Oxford Univ, Old Carthusians)	13	Wise D (Chelsea)	5
Taylor J (Fulham)	2			Withe P (Aston Villa)	11
Taylor P H (Liverpool)	3	Walton N (Blackburn)	1	Wollaston C (Wanderers)	4
Taylor P J (C Palace)	4	Ward J (Blackburn Olympic)	1	Wolstenholme S (Everton, Blackburn)	3
Taylor T (Man Utd)	19	Ward P (Brighton and Hove Albion)	1	Wood H (Wolves)	3
Temple D (Everton)	1	Ward T (Derby County)	2	Wood R (Man Utd)	3
Thickett H (Sheff Utd)	2	Waring T (Aston Villa)	5	Woodcock A (Nottm Forest, Cologne, Arsenal)	42
Thomas D (Coventry)	2	Warner C (Upton Park)	1		
Thomas D (QPR)	8	Warren B (Derby County, Chelsea)	22	Woodger G (Oldham)	1
Thomas G (C Palace)	9	Waterfield G (Burnley)	1	Woodhall G (WBA)	2
Thomas M (Arsenal)	2	Watson D (Norwich, Everton)	12	Woodley V (Chelsea)	19
Thompson P (Peter) (Liverpool)	16	Watson D V (Sunderland, Man City, Werder Bremen, Southampton, Stoke)	65	Woods C (Norwich, Glasgow R, Sheff Wed)	34
Thompson P B (Phil) (Liverpool)	42				
Thompson T (Aston Villa, Preston)	2			Woodward V (Spurs, Chelsea)	23
Thomson R (Wolves)	8	Watson V (West Ham)	5	Woosnam M (Man City)	1
Thornewell G (Derby County)	4	Watson W (Burnley)	3	Worrall F (Portsmouth)	2
Thornley I (Man City)	1	Watson W (Sunderland)	4	Worthington F (Leicester City)	8
Tilson S (Man City)	4	Weaver S (Newcastle)	3	Wreford-Brown C (Oxford Univ, Old Carthusians)	4
Titmuss F (Southampton)	2	Webb G (West Ham)	2		
Todd C (Derby County)	27	Webb N (Nottm Forest, Man Utd)	26	Wright E (Cambridge Univ)	1
Toone G (Notts County)	2	Webster M (Middlesbrough)	3	Wright I (C Palace, Arsenal)	5
Topham A (Casuals)	1	Wedlock W (Bristol City)	26	Wright J (Newcastle)	1
Topham R (Wolves, Casuals)	2	Weir D (Bolton)	2	Wright M (Southampton, Derby County, Liverpool)	42
Towers A (Sunderland)	3	Welch R de C (Wanderers, Harrow Chequers)	2		
Townley W (Blackburn)	2			Wright T (Everton)	11
Townrow J (Clapton Orient)	2	Weller K (Leicester City)	4	Wright W (Wolves)	105
Tremelling D (Birmingham)	1	Welsh D (Charlton)	3	Wylie J (Wanderers)	1
Tresadern J (West Ham)	2	West G (Everton)	3		
Tueart D (Man City)	6	Westwood R (Bolton)	6	Yates J (Burnley)	1
Tunstall F (Sheff Utd)	7	Whateley O (Aston Villa)	2	York R (Aston Villa)	2
Turnbull R (Bradford City)	1	Wheeler J (Bolton)	1	Young A (Huddersfield)	9
Turner A (Southampton)	2	Wheldon G (Aston Villa)	4	Young G (Sheff Wed)	1
Turner H (Huddersfield)	2	White T (Everton)	1		
Turner J (Bolton, Stoke, Derby County)	3	Whitehead J (Accrington, Blackburn)	2	*Evans R also played for Wales	
Tweedy G (Grimsby)	1	Whitfield H (Old Etonians)	1	†Reynolds J also played for Ireland	

International Goalscorers 1946–1992

(Up to and including 17 June, 1992)

Charlton R	49	Hateley	9	Bull	4	Eastham	2	Keown	1
Lineker	48	Ball	8	Dixon K	4	Froggatt J	2	Kidd	1
Greaves	44	Beardsley	8	Hassall	4	Froggatt R	2	Langton	1
Finney	30	Broadis	8	Revie	4	Gascoigne	2	Lawler	1
Lofthouse	30	Byrne J	8	Robson R	4	Haines	2	Lee J	1
Robson B	26	Hoddle	8	Steven	4	Hancocks	2	Mabbutt	1
Hurst	24	Kevan	8	Watson D	4	Hunter	2	Marsh	1
Mortensen	23	Connelly	7	Webb	4	Lee S	2	Medley	1
Channon	21	Coppell	7	Baker	3	Moore	2	Melia	1
Keegan	21	Paine	7	Blissett	3	Pearce	2	Merson	1
Peters	20	Charlton J	6	Butcher	3	Perry	2	Mullery	1
Haynes	18	Johnson	6	Currie	3	Pointer	2	Nicholls	1
Hunt R	18	Macdonald	6	Elliott	3	Royle	2	Nicholson	1
Lawton	16	Mullen	6	Francis G	3	Smith A	2	Parry	1
Taylor T	16	Rowley	6	Grainger	3	Taylor P	2	Sansom	1
Woodcock	16	Waddle	6	Kennedy R	3	Tueart	2	Shackleton	1
Chivers	13	Atyeo	5	McDermott	3	Wignall	2	Shearer	1
Mariner	13	Baily	5	Matthews S	3	Worthington	2	Stiles	1
Smith R	13	Brooking	5	Morris	3	A'Court	1	Summerbee	1
Francis T	12	Carter	5	O'Grady	3	Astall	1	Tambling	1
Douglas	11	Edwards	5	Peacock	3	Beattie	1	Thompson P B	
Mannion	11	Hitchens	5	Ramsey	3	Bowles	1	(Phil)	1
Platt	11	Latchford	5	Sewell	3	Bradford	1	Viollet	1
Barnes J	10	Neal	5	Wilkins	3	Bridges	1	Wallace	1
Clarke A	10	Pearson S C		Wright W	3	Chamberlain	1	Walsh	1
Flowers	10	(Stan)	5	Allen R	2	Crawford	1	Weller	1
Lee F	10	Pearson J S		Anderson	2	Dixon L	1	Wise	1
Milburn	10	(Stuart)	5	Bradley	2	Goddard	1	Withe	1
Wilshaw	10	Pickering F	5	Broadbent	2	Hirst	1	Wright M	1
Bell	9	Adams	4	Brooks	2	Hughes E	1		
Bentley	9	Barnes P	4	Cowans	2	Kay	1		

England International Appearances 1991–92

Barnes	2	1992 v Cz, Fin
Batty	5	1991 v G, T; 1992 v H (sub), F, Se
Clough	3	1992 v F, Cz, CIS (sub)
Curle	3	1992 v CIS (sub), H, D
Daley	7	1991 v Pol (sub); 1992 v CIS, H, Br, Fin (sub), D (sub), Se
Dixon	4	1991 v G, T, Pol; 1992 v Cz (sub)
Dorigo	4	1991 v G; 1992 v Cz (sub), H, Br
Gray	1	1991 v Pol
Hateley	1	1992 v Cz
Hirst	1	1992 v F
Jones	1	1992 v F
Keown	9	1992 v F, Cz, CIS, H, Br, Fin, D, F, Se
Lineker	12	1991 v G, T, Pol; 1992 v F (sub), Cz (sub), CIS, H, Br, Fin, D, F, Se
Mabbutt	3	1991 v T, Pol; 1992 v Cz
Martyn	2	1992 v CIS (sub), H
Merson	7	1991 v G (sub); 1992 v Cz, H, Br (sub), Fin (sub), D, Se (sub)
Pallister	1	1991 v G
Palmer	7	1992 v CIS, H, Br, Fin (sub), D, F, Se
Parker	1	1991 v G
Pearce	9	1991 v T, Pol; 1992 v F, Cz, Br (sub), Fin, D, F, Se
Platt	10	1991 v G, T, Pol; 1992 v Cz, CIS, Br, Fin, D, F, Se
Robson	1	1991 v T
Rocastle	3	1991 v Pol; 1992 v Cz, Br (sub)
Salako	1	1991 v G
Seaman	2	1992 v Cz, H (sub)
Shearer	3	1992 v F, CIS, F

Sinton	6	1991 v Pol; 1992 v CIS, H (sub), Br, F, Se
Smith	6	1991 v G, T, Pol (sub); 1992 v H (sub), D, Se (sub)
Steven	6	1991 v G; 1992 v CIS, Br, Fin, D, F
Stevens	4	1992 v CIS, H, Br, Fin
Stewart	3	1991 v G (sub); 1992 v Cz (sub), CIS (sub)
Thomas	2	1991 v Pol; 1992 v F
Waddle	1	1991 v T
Walker	11	1991 v T, Pol; 1992 v F, Cz, CIS, H, Br, Fin, D, F, Se
Webb	6	1992 v F, H, Br (sub), Fin, D (sub), Se
Woods	10	1991 v G, T, Pol; 1992 v F, CIS, Br, Fin, D, F, Se
Wright I	1	1992 v H (sub)
Wright M	2	1992 v F, Fin

Br – Brazil; CIS – Commonwealth of Independent States;
Cz – Czechoslovakia: D – Denmark; Fin – Finland; F – France;
G – Germany; H – Hungary; Pol – Poland; Se – Sweden; T – Turkey.

International Goalscorers 1991–92

Platt	4	v Brazil, Finland 2, Sweden
Lineker	3	v Poland, France, CIS
Keown	1	v Czechoslovakia
Merson	1	v Czechoslovakia
Shearer	1	v France
Smith A	1	v Turkey
Steven	1	v CIS
Webb	1	v Hungary

Above: Chris Woods shows the tourists in Moscow's Red Square that not only can he hold a football but he can do tricks with it as well

Below: Gary Mabbutt, the most reliable of defenders, has been an excellent B captain and, when needed, played solidly for Graham Taylor's senior side

International Matches 1991–92

ECQ European Championship Qualifier   ECF Eurpoean Championship Finals

Year	Date	Venue	Goals	Scorers
England v Germany				
1991	11 Sept	Wembley	0–1	
England v Turkey				
1991	16 Oct	Wembley	1–0 (ECQ)	Smith
England v Poland				
1991	13 Nov	Poznan	1–1 (ECQ)	Lineker
England v France				
1992	19 Feb	Wembley	2–0	Shearer, Lineker
England v Czechoslovakia				
1992	25 March	Prague	2–2	Merson, Keown
England v CIS				
1992	29 April	Moscow	2–2	Lineker, Steven
England v Hungary				
1992	12 May	Budapest	1–0	Webb
England v Brazil				
1992	17 May	Wembley	1–1	Platt
England v Finland				
1992	3 June	Helsinki	2–1	Platt (2)
England v Denmark				
1992	11 June	Malmö	0–0 (ECF)	
England v France				
1992	14 June	Malmö	0–0 (ECF)	
England v Sweden				
1992	17 June	Stockholm	1–2 (ECF)	Platt

Country-by-Country Results 1872–1992

WCQ World Cup Qualifier   WCF World Cup Final   ECQ European Championship Qualifier   ECF European Championship Final
RC Rous Cup   BJT Brazilian Jubilee Tournament   ENC European Nations' Cup   USBT US Bicentennial Tournament

v Albania
| 1989 | 8 March | Tirana | W | 2–0 (WCQ) |
| 1989 | 26 April | Wembley | W | 5–0 (WCQ) |

P 2, W 2, D 0, L 0, F 7, A 0

v Argentina
1951	9 May	Wembley	W	2–1
1953	17 May	Buenos Aires	D	0–0*
1962	2 June	Rancagua	W	3–1 (WCF)
1964	6 June	Rio de Janeiro	L	0–1 (BJT)
1966	23 July	Wembley	W	1–0 (WCF)
1974	22 May	Wembley	D	2–2
1977	12 June	Buenos Aires	D	1–1
1980	13 May	Wembley	W	3–1
1986	22 June	Mexico City	L	1–2 (WCF)
1991	25 May	Wembley	D	2–2

P 10, W 4, D 4, L 2, F 15, A 11

*abandoned after 21 mins

v Australia
1980	31 May	Sydney	W	2–1
1983	12 June	Sydney	D	0–0
1983	15 June	Brisbane	W	1–0
1983	19 June	Melbourne	D	1–1
1991	1 June	Sydney	W	1–0

P 5, W 3, D 2, L 0, F 5, A 2

v Austria
1908	6 June	Vienna	W	6–1
1908	8 June	Vienna	W	11–1
1909	1 June	Vienna	W	8–1
1930	14 May	Vienna	D	0–0
1932	7 Dec	Chelsea	W	4–3
1936	6 May	Vienna	L	1–2
1951	28 Nov	Wembley	D	2–2
1952	25 May	Vienna	W	3–2
1958	15 June	Boras	D	2–2 (WCF)
1961	27 May	Vienna	L	1–3
1962	4 April	Wembley	W	3–1
1965	20 Oct	Wembley	L	2–3
1967	27 May	Vienna	W	1–0
1973	26 Sept	Wembley	W	7–0
1979	13 June	Vienna	L	3–4

P 15, W 8, D 3, L 4, F 54 A 25

v Belgium
1921	21 May	Brussels	W	2–0
1923	19 March	Arsenal	W	6–1
1923	1 Nov	Antwerp	D	2–2
1924	8 Dec	West Bromwich	W	4–0
1926	24 May	Antwerp	W	5–3
1927	11 May	Brussels	W	9–1
1928	19 May	Antwerp	W	3–1
1929	11 May	Brussels	W	5–1
1931	16 May	Brussels	W	4–1
1936	9 May	Brussels	L	2–3
1947	21 Sept	Brussels	W	5–2
1950	18 May	Brussels	W	4–1
1952	26 Nov	Wembley	W	5–0
1954	17 June	Basle	D	4–4 (WCF)
1964	21 Oct	Wembley	D	2–2
1970	20 Feb	Brussels	W	3–1
1980	12 June	Turin	D	1–1 (ECF)
1990	26 June	Bologna	W	1–0 (WCF)

P 18, W 13, D 4, L 1, F 67, A 24

v Bohemia
| 1908 | 13 June | Prague | W | 4–0 |

P 1, W 1, D 0, L 0, F 4, A 0

v Brazil
1956	9 May	Wembley	W	4–2
1958	11 June	Gothenburg	D	0–0 (WCF)
1959	13 May	Rio de Janeiro	L	0–2
1962	10 June	Vina del Mar	L	1–3 (WCF)
1963	8 May	Wembley	D	1–1
1964	30 May	Rio de Janeiro	L	1–5 (BJT)
1969	12 June	Rio de Janeiro	L	1–2
1970	7 June	Guadalajara	L	0–1 (WCF)
1976	23 May	Los Angeles	L	0–1 (USBT)
1977	8 June	Rio de Janeiro	D	0–0
1978	19 April	Wembley	D	1–1
1981	12 May	Wembley	L	0–1
1984	10 June	Rio de Janeiro	W	2–0
1987	19 May	Wembley	D	1–1 (RC)
1990	28 March	Wembley	W	1–0
1992	17 May	Wembley	D	1–1

P 16, W 3, D 6, L 7, F 14, A 21

v Bulgaria
1962	7 June	Rancagua	D	0–0 (WCF)
1968	11 Dec	Wembley	D	1–1
1974	1 June	Sofia	W	1–0
1979	6 June	Sofia	W	3–0 (ECQ)
1979	22 Nov	Wembley	W	2–0 (ECQ)

P 5, W 3, D 2, L 0, F 7, A 1

v Cameroon
| 1990 | 1 July | Naples | W | 3–2* (WCF) |
| 1991 | 6 Feb | Wembley | W | 2–0 |

P 2, W 2, D 0, L 0, F 5, A 2

* after extra time

v Canada
| 1986 | 24 May | Vancouver | W | 1–0 |

P 1, W 1, D 0, L 0, F 1, A 0

v Chile
1950	25 June	Rio de Janeiro	W	2–0 (WCF)
1953	24 May	Santiago	W	2–1
1984	17 June	Santiago	D	0–0
1989	23 May	Wembley	D	0–0 (RC)

P 4, W 2, D 2, L 0, F 4, A 1

v Colombia
1970	20 May	Bogota	W	4–0
1988	24 May	Wembley	D	1–1 (RC)

P 2, W 1, D 1, L 0, F 5, A 1

v CIS
1992	29 April	Moscow	D	2–2

P 1, W 0, D 1, L 0, F 2, A 2

v Cyprus
1975	16 April	Wembley	W	5–0 (ECQ)
1975	11 May	Limassol	W	1–0 (ECQ)

P 2, W 2, D 0, L 0, F 6, A 0

v Czechoslovakia
1934	16 May	Prague	L	1–2
1937	1 Dec	Tottenham	W	5–4
1963	29 May	Bratislava	W	4–2
1966	2 Nov	Wembley	D	0–0
1970	11 June	Guadalajara	W	1–0 (WCF)
1973	27 May	Prague	D	1–1
1974	30 Oct	Wembley	W	3–0 (ECF)
1975	30 Oct	Bratislava	L	1–2 (ECF)
1978	29 Nov	Wembley	W	1–0
1982	20 June	Bilbao	W	2–0 (WCF)
1990	25 April	Wembley	W	4–2
1992	25 March	Prague	D	2–2

P 12, W 7, D 3, L 2, F 25, A 15

v Denmark
1948	26 Sept	Copenhagen	D	0–0
1955	2 Oct	Copenhagen	W	5–1
1956	5 Dec	Wolverhampton	W	5–2 (WCQ)
1957	15 May	Copenhagen	W	4–1 (WCQ)
1966	3 July	Copenhagen	W	2–0
1978	20 Sept	Copenhagen	W	4–3 (ECQ)
1979	12 Sept	Wembley	W	1–0 (ECQ)
1982	22 Sept	Copenhagen	D	2–2 (ECQ)
1983	21 Sept	Wembley	L	0–1 (ECQ)
1988	14 Sept	Wembley	W	1–0
1989	7 June	Copenhagen	D	1–1
1990	15 May	Wembley	W	1–0
1992	11 June	Malmö	D	0–0 (ECF)

P 13, W 8, D 4, L 1, F 26, A 11

v Ecuador
1970	24 May	Quito	W	2–0

P 1, W 1, D 0, L 0, F 2, A 0

v Egypt
1986	29 Jan	Cairo	W	4–0
1990	21 June	Cagliari	W	1–0 (WCF)

P 2, W 2, D 0, L 0, F 5, A 0

v FIFA
1953	21 Oct	Wembley	D	4–4

P 1, W 0, D 1, L 0, F 4, A 4

v Finland
1937	20 May	Helsinki	W	8–0
1956	20 May	Helsinki	W	5–1
1966	26 June	Helsinki	W	3–0
1976	13 June	Helsinki	W	4–1 (WCQ)
1976	13 Oct	Wembley	W	2–1 (WCQ)
1982	3 June	Helsinki	W	4–1
1984	17 Oct	Wembley	W	5–0 (WCQ)
1985	22 May	Helsinki	D	1–1 (WCQ)
1992	3 June	Helsinki	W	2–1

P 9, W 8, D 1, L 0, F 34, A 6

v France
1923	10 May	Paris	W	4–1
1924	17 May	Paris	W	3–1
1925	21 May	Paris	W	3–2
1927	26 May	Paris	W	6–0
1928	17 May	Paris	W	5–1
1929	9 May	Paris	W	4–1
1931	14 May	Paris	L	2–5
1933	6 Dec	Tottenham	W	4–1
1938	26 May	Paris	W	4–2
1947	3 May	Arsenal	W	3–0
1949	22 May	Paris	W	3–1
1951	3 Oct	Arsenal	D	2–2
1955	15 May	Paris	L	0–1
1957	27 Nov	Wembley	W	4–0
1962	3 Oct	Sheffield	D	1–1 (ENC)
1963	27 Feb	Paris	L	2–5 (ENC)
1966	20 July	Wembley	W	2–0 (WCF)
1969	12 March	Wembley	W	5–0
1982	16 June	Bilbao	W	3–1 (WCF)
1984	29 Feb	Paris	L	0–2
1992	19 Feb	Wembley	W	2–0
1992	14 June	Malmo	D	0–0 (ECF)

P 22, W 15, D 3, L 4, F 62, A 27

v East Germany
1963	2 June	Leipzig	W	2–1
1970	25 Nov	Wembley	W	3–1
1974	29 May	Leipzig	D	1–1
1984	12 Sept	Wembley	W	1–0

P 4, W 3, D 1, L 0, F 7, A 3

v West Germany
†1930	10 May	Berlin	D	3–3
†1935	4 Dec	Tottenham	W	3–0
†1938	14 May	Berlin	W	6–3
1954	1 Dec	Wembley	W	3–1
1956	26 May	Berlin	W	3–1
1965	12 May	Nuremberg	W	1–0
1966	23 Feb	Wembley	W	1–0
1966	30 July	Wembley	W	4–2 (WCF)
1968	1 June	Hanover	L	0–1
1970	14 June	Leon	L	2–3 (WCF)
1972	29 April	Wembley	L	1–3 (ECQ)
1972	13 May	Berlin	D	0–0 (ECQ)
1975	12 March	Wembley	W	2–0
1978	22 Feb	Munich	L	1–2
1982	29 June	Madrid	D	0–0 (WCF)
1982	13 Oct	Wembley	L	1–2
1985	12 June	Mexico City	W	3–0
1987	9 Sept	Düsseldorf	L	1–3
1990	4 July	Turin	L	1–1* (WCF)

P 19, W 9, D 3, L 7, F 36, A 25

* after extra time (England lost 3–4 on pens)
† as Germany

v Germany

| 1991 | 11 Sept | Wembley | L | 0–1 |

P 1, W 0, D 0, L 1, F 0, A 1

v Greece

1971	21 April	Wembley	W	3–0 (ECQ)
1971	1 Dec	Athens	W	2–0 (ECQ)
1982	17 Nov	Salonika	W	3–0 (ECQ)
1983	30 March	Wembley	D	0–0 (ECQ)
1989	8 Feb	Athens	W	2–1

P 5, W 4, D 1, L 0, F 10, A 1

v Holland

1935	18 May	Amsterdam	W	1–0
1946	27 Nov	Huddersfield	W	8–2
1964	9 Dec	Amsterdam	D	1–1
1969	5 Nov	Amsterdam	W	1–0
1970	14 Jan	Wembley	D	0–0
1977	9 Feb	Wembley	L	0–2
1982	25 May	Wembley	W	2–0
1988	23 March	Wembley	D	2–2
1988	15 June	Düsseldorf	L	1–3 (ECF)
1990	16 June	Cagliari	D	0–0 (WCF)

P 10, W 4, D 4, L 2, F 16, A 10

v Hungary

1908	10 June	Budapest	W	7–0
1909	29 May	Budapest	W	4–2
1909	31 May	Budapest	W	8–2
1934	10 May	Budapest	L	1–2
1936	2 Dec	Arsenal	W	6–2
1953	25 Nov	Wembley	L	3–6
1954	23 May	Budapest	L	1–7
1960	22 May	Budapest	L	0–2
1962	31 May	Rancagua	L	1–2 (WCF)
1965	5 May	Wembley	W	1–0
1978	24 May	Wembley	W	4–1
1981	6 June	Budapest	W	3–1 (WCQ)
1981	18 Nov	Wembley	W	1–0 (WCQ)
1983	27 April	Wembley	W	2–0 (ECQ)
1983	12 Oct	Budapest	W	3–0 (ECQ)
1988	27 April	Budapest	D	0–0
1990	12 Sept	Wembley	W	1–0
1992	12 May	Budapest	W	1–0

P 18, W 12, D 1, L 5, F 47, A 27

v Iceland

| 1982 | 2 June | Reykjavik | D | 1–1 |

P 1, W 0, D 1, L 0, F 1, A 1

v Ireland

1882	18 Feb	Belfast	W	13–0
1883	24 Feb	Liverpool	W	7–0
1884	23 Feb	Belfast	W	8–1
1885	28 Feb	Manchester	W	4–0
1886	13 March	Belfast	W	6–1
1887	5 Feb	Sheffield	W	7–0
1888	31 March	Belfast	W	5–1
1889	2 March	Everton	W	6–1
1890	15 March	Belfast	W	9–1
1891	7 March	Wolverhampton	W	6–1
1892	5 March	Belfast	W	2–0
1893	25 Feb	Birmingham	W	6–1
1894	3 March	Belfast	D	2–2
1895	9 March	Derby	W	9–0
1896	7 March	Belfast	W	2–0
1897	20 Feb	Nottingham	W	6–0
1898	5 March	Belfast	W	3–2
1899	18 Feb	Sunderland	W	13–2
1900	17 March	Dublin	W	2–0
1901	9 March	Southampton	W	3–0
1902	22 March	Belfast	W	1–0
1903	14 Feb	Wolverhampton	W	4–0
1904	12 March	Belfast	W	3–1
1905	25 Feb	Middlesbrough	D	1–1
1906	17 Feb	Belfast	W	5–0
1907	16 Feb	Everton	W	1–0
1908	15 Feb	Belfast	W	3–1
1909	13 Feb	Bradford	W	4–0
1910	12 Feb	Belfast	D	1–1
1911	11 Feb	Derby	W	2–1
1912	10 Feb	Dublin	W	6–1
1913	15 Feb	Belfast	L	1–2
1914	14 Feb	Middlesbrough	L	0–3
1919	25 Oct	Belfast	D	1–1
1920	23 Oct	Sunderland	W	2–0
1921	22 Oct	Belfast	D	1–1
1922	21 Oct	West Bromwich	W	2–0
1923	20 Oct	Belfast	L	1–2
1924	22 Oct	Everton	W	3–1
1925	24 Oct	Belfast	D	0–0
1926	20 Oct	Liverpool	D	3–3
1927	22 Oct	Belfast	L	0–2
1928	22 Oct	Everton	W	2–1
1929	19 Oct	Belfast	W	3–0
1930	20 Oct	Sheffield	W	5–1
1931	17 Oct	Belfast	W	6–2
1932	17 Oct	Blackpool	W	1–0
1933	14 Oct	Belfast	W	3–0
1935	6 Feb	Everton	W	2–1
1935	19 Oct	Belfast	W	3–1
1936	18 Nov	Stoke	W	3–1
1937	23 Oct	Belfast	W	5–1
1938	16 Nov	Manchester	W	7–0
1946	28 Sept	Belfast	W	7–2
1947	5 Nov	Everton	D	2–2
1948	9 Oct	Belfast	W	6–2
1949	16 Nov	Manchester	W	9–2 (WCQ)
1950	7 Oct	Belfast	W	4–1
1951	14 Nov	Aston Villa	W	2–0
1952	4 Oct	Belfast	D	2–2
1953	11 Nov	Everton	W	3–1 (WCQ)
1954	2 Oct	Belfast	W	2–0
1955	2 Nov	Wembley	W	3–0
1956	6 Oct	Belfast	D	1–1
1957	6 Nov	Wembley	L	2–3
1958	4 Oct	Belfast	D	3–3
1959	18 Nov	Wembley	W	2–1
1960	8 Oct	Belfast	W	5–2
1961	22 Nov	Wembley	D	1–1
1962	20 Oct	Belfast	W	3–1
1963	20 Nov	Wembley	W	8–3
1964	3 Oct	Belfast	W	4–3
1965	10 Nov	Wembley	W	2–1
1966	20 Oct	Belfast	W	2–0 (ECQ)
1967	22 Nov	Wembley	W	2–0 (ECQ)
1969	3 May	Belfast	W	3–1
1970	21 April	Wembley	W	3–1
1971	15 May	Belfast	W	1–0

93

1972	23 May	Wembley	L	0–1
1973	12 May	Everton	W	2–1
1974	15 May	Wembley	W	1–0
1975	17 May	Belfast	D	0–0
1976	11 May	Wembley	W	4–0
1977	28 May	Belfast	W	2–1
1978	16 May	Wembley	W	1–0
1979	7 Feb	Wembley	W	4–0 (ECQ)
1979	19 May	Belfast	W	2–0
1979	17 Oct	Belfast	W	5–1 (ECQ)
1980	20 May	Wembley	D	1–1
1982	23 Feb	Wembley	W	4–0
1983	28 May	Belfast	D	0–0
1984	4 April	Wembley	W	1–0
1985	27 Feb	Belfast	W	1–0 (WCQ)
1985	13 Nov	Wembley	D	0–0 (WCQ)
1986	15 Oct	Wembley	W	3–0 (ECQ)
1987	1 April	Belfast	W	2–0 (ECQ)

P 96, W 74, D 16, L 6, F 319, A 80

v Israel

| 1986 | 26 Feb | Tel Aviv | W | 2–1 |
| 1988 | 17 Feb | Tel Aviv | D | 0–0 |

P 2, W 1, D 1, L 0, F 2, A 1

v Italy

1933	13 May	Rome	D	1–1
1934	14 Nov	Arsenal	W	3–2
1939	13 May	Milan	D	2–2
1948	16 May	Turin	W	4–0
1949	30 Nov	Tottenham	W	2–0
1952	18 May	Florence	D	1–1
1959	6 May	Wembley	D	2–2
1961	24 May	Rome	W	3–2
1973	14 June	Turin	L	0–2
1973	14 Nov	Wembley	L	0–1
1976	28 May	New York	W	3–2 (USBT)
1976	17 Nov	Rome	L	0–2 (WCQ)
1977	16 Nov	Wembley	W	2–0 (WCQ)
1980	15 June	Turin	L	0–1 (ECF)
1985	6 June	Mexico City	L	1–2
1989	15 Nov	Wembley	D	0–0
1990	7 July	Bari	L	1–2 (WCF)

P 17, W 6, D 5, L 6, F 25, A 22

v Kuwait

| 1982 | 25 June | Bilbao | W | 1–0 (WCF) |

P 1, W 1, D 0, L 0, F 1, A 0

v Luxembourg

1927	21 May	Luxembourg	W	5–2
1960	19 Oct	Luxembourg	W	9–0 (WCQ)
1961	28 Sept	Arsenal	W	4–1 (WCQ)
1977	30 March	Wembley	W	5–0 (WCQ)
1977	12 Oct	Luxembourg	W	2–0 (WCQ)
1982	15 Dec	Wembley	W	9–0 (ECQ)
1983	16 Nov	Luxembourg	W	4–0 (ECQ)

P 7, W 7, D 0, L 0, F 38, A 3

v Malaysia

| 1991 | 12 June | Kuala Lumpur | W | 4–2 |

P 1, W 1, D 0, L 0, F 4, A 2

v Malta

| 1971 | 3 Feb | Valletta | W | 1–0 (ECQ) |
| 1971 | 12 May | Wembley | W | 5–0 (ECQ) |

P 2, W 2, D 0, L 0, F 6, A 0

v Mexico

1959	24 May	Mexico City	L	1–2
1961	10 May	Wembley	W	8–0
1966	16 July	Wembley	W	2–0 (WCF)
1969	1 June	Mexico City	D	0–0
1985	9 June	Mexico City	L	0–1
1986	17 May	Los Angeles	W	3–0

P 6, W 3, D 1, L 2, F 14, A 3

v Morocco

| 1986 | 6 June | Monterrey | D | 0–0 (WCF) |

P 1, W 0, D 1, L 0, F 0, A 0

v New Zealand

| 1991 | 3 June | Auckland | W | 1–0 |
| 1991 | 8 June | Wellington | W | 2–0 |

P 2, W 2, D 0, L 0, F 3, A 0

v Northern Ireland **see** *Ireland*

v Norway

1937	14 May	Oslo	W	6–0
1938	9 Nov	Newcastle	W	4–0
1949	18 May	Oslo	W	4–1
1966	29 June	Oslo	W	6–1
1980	10 Sept	Wembley	W	4–0 (WCQ)
1981	9 Sept	Oslo	L	1–2 (WCQ)

P 6, W 5, D 0, L 1, F 25, A 4

v Paraguay

| 1986 | 18 June | Mexico City | W | 3–0 (WCF) |

P 1, W 1, D 0, L 0, F 3, A 0

v Peru

| 1959 | 17 May | Lima | L | 1–4 |
| 1962 | 20 May | Lima | W | 4–0 |

P 2, W 1, D 0, L 1, F 5, A 4

v Poland

1966	5 Jan	Everton	D	1–1
1966	5 July	Chorzow	W	1–0
1973	6 June	Chorzow	L	0–2 (WCQ)
1973	17 Oct	Wembley	D	1–1 (WCQ)
1986	11 June	Monterrey	W	3–0 (WCF)
1989	3 June	Wembley	W	3–0 (WCQ)
1989	11 Oct	Katowice	D	0–0 (WCQ)
1990	17 Oct	Wembley	W	2–0 (ECQ)
1991	13 Nov	Poznan	D	1–1 (ECQ)

P 9, W 4, D 4, L 1, F 12, A 5

v Portugal

1947	25 May	Lisbon	W	10–0
1950	14 May	Lisbon	W	5–3
1951	19 May	Everton	W	5–2
1955	22 May	Oporto	L	1–3
1958	7 May	Wembley	W	2–1
1961	21 May	Lisbon	D	1–1 (WCQ)
1961	25 Oct	Wembley	W	2–0 (WCQ)

1964	17 May	Lisbon	W	4–3	
1964	4 June	Sao Paolo	D	1–1	(BJT)
1966	26 July	Wembley	W	2–1	(WCF)
1969	10 Dec	Wembley	W	1–0	
1974	3 April	Lisbon	D	0–0	
1974	20 Nov	Wembley	D	0–0	(ECQ)
1975	19 Nov	Lisbon	D	1–1	(ECQ)
1986	3 June	Monterrey	L	0–1	(WCF)

P 15, W 8, D 5, L 2, F 35, A 17

v Republic of Ireland

1946	30 Sept	Dublin	W	1–0	
1949	21 Sept	Everton	L	0–2	
1957	8 May	Wembley	W	5–1	(WCQ)
1957	19 May	Dublin	D	1–1	(WCQ)
1964	24 May	Dublin	W	3–1	
1976	8 Sept	Wembley	D	1–1	
1978	25 Oct	Dublin	D	1–1	(ECQ)
1980	6 Feb	Wembley	W	2–0	(ECQ)
1985	26 March	Wembley	W	2–1	
1988	12 June	Stuttgart	L	0–1	(ECF)
1990	11 June	Cagliari	D	1–1	(WCF)
1990	14 Nov	Dublin	D	1–1	(ECQ)
1991	27 March	Wembley	D	1–1	(ECQ)

P 13, W 5, D 6, L 2, F 19, A 12

v Rest of Europe

1938	26 Oct	Arsenal	W	3–0	

P 1, W 1, D 0, L 0, F 3, A 0

v Rest of the World

1963	23 Oct	Wembley	W	2–1	

P 1, W 1, D 0, L 0, F 2, A 1

v Romania

1939	24 May	Bucharest	W	2–0	
1968	6 Nov	Bucharest	D	0–0	
1969	15 Jan	Wembley	D	1–1	
1970	2 June	Guadalajara	W	1–0	(WCF)
1980	15 Oct	Bucharest	L	1–2	(WCQ)
1981	29 April	Wembley	D	0–0	(WCQ)
1985	1 May	Bucharest	D	0–0	(WCQ)
1985	11 Sept	Wembley	D	1–1	(WCQ)

P 8, W 2, D 5, L 1, F 6, A 4

v Saudi Arabia

1988	16 Nov	Riyadh	D	1–1	

P 1, W 0, D 1, L 0, F 1, A 1

v Scotland

1872	30 Nov	Glasgow	D	0–0	
1873	8 March	Kennington	W	4–2	
1874	7 March	Glasgow	L	1–2	
1875	6 March	Kennington	D	2–2	
1876	4 March	Glasgow	L	0–3	
1877	3 March	Kennington	L	1–3	
1878	2 March	Glasgow	L	2–7	
1879	5 April	Kennington	W	5–4	
1880	13 March	Glasgow	L	4–5	
1881	12 March	Kennington	L	1–6	
1882	11 March	Glasgow	L	1–5	
1883	10 March	Sheffield	L	2–3	
1884	15 March	Glasgow	L	0–1	
1885	21 March	Kennington	D	1–1	
1886	31 March	Glasgow	D	1–1	
1887	19 March	Blackburn	L	2–3	
1888	17 March	Glasgow	W	5–0	
1889	13 April	Kennington	L	2–3	
1890	5 April	Glasgow	D	1–1	
1891	6 April	Blackburn	W	2–1	
1892	2 April	Glasgow	W	4–1	
1893	1 April	Richmond	W	5–2	
1894	7 April	Glasgow	D	2–2	
1895	6 April	Everton	W	3–0	
1896	4 April	Glasgow	L	1–2	
1897	3 April	Crystal Palace	L	1–2	
1898	2 April	Glasgow	W	3–1	
1899	8 April	Birmingham	W	2–1	
1900	7 April	Glasgow	L	1–4	
1901	30 March	Crystal Palace	D	2–2	
1902	3 March	Birmingham	D	2–2	
1903	4 April	Sheffield	L	1–2	
1904	9 April	Glasgow	W	1–0	
1905	1 April	Crystal Palace	W	1–0	
1906	7 April	Glasgow	L	1–2	
1907	6 April	Newcastle	D	1–1	
1908	4 April	Glasgow	D	1–1	
1909	3 April	Crystal Palace	W	2–0	
1910	2 April	Glasgow	L	0–2	
1911	1 April	Everton	D	1–1	
1912	23 March	Glasgow	D	1–1	
1913	5 April	Chelsea	W	1–0	
1914	14 April	Glasgow	L	1–3	
1920	10 April	Sheffield	W	5–4	
1921	9 April	Glasgow	L	0–3	
1922	8 April	Aston Villa	L	0–1	
1923	14 April	Glasgow	D	2–2	
1924	12 April	Wembley	D	1–1	
1925	4 April	Glasgow	L	0–2	
1926	17 April	Manchester	L	0–1	
1927	2 April	Glasgow	W	2–1	
1928	31 March	Wembley	L	1–5	
1929	13 April	Glasgow	L	0–1	
1930	5 April	Wembley	W	5–2	
1931	28 March	Glasgow	L	0–2	
1932	9 April	Wembley	W	3–0	
1933	1 April	Glasgow	L	1–2	
1934	14 April	Wembley	W	3–0	
1935	6 April	Glasgow	L	0–2	
1936	4 April	Wembley	D	1–1	
1937	17 April	Glasgow	L	1–3	
1938	9 April	Wembley	L	0–1	
1939	15 April	Glasgow	W	2–1	
1947	12 April	Wembley	D	1–1	
1948	10 April	Glasgow	W	2–0	
1949	9 April	Wembley	L	1–3	
1950	15 April	Glasgow	W	1–0	(WCQ)
1951	14 April	Wembley	L	2–3	
1952	5 April	Glasgow	W	2–1	
1953	18 April	Wembley	D	2–2	
1954	3 April	Glasgow	W	4–2	(WCQ)
1955	2 April	Wembley	W	7–2	
1956	14 April	Glasgow	D	1–1	
1957	6 April	Wembley	W	2–1	
1958	19 April	Glasgow	W	4–0	
1959	11 April	Wembley	W	1–0	
1960	9 April	Glasgow	D	1–1	
1961	15 April	Wembley	W	9–3	
1962	14 April	Glasgow	L	0–2	

1963	6 April	Wembley	L	1–2
1964	11 April	Glasgow	L	0–1
1965	10 April	Wembley	D	2–2
1966	2 April	Glasgow	W	4–3
1967	15 April	Wembley	L	2–3 (ECQ)
1968	24 Feb	Glasgow	D	1–1 (ECQ)
1969	10 May	Wembley	W	4–1
1970	25 April	Glasgow	D	0–0
1971	22 May	Wembley	W	3–1
1972	27 May	Glasgow	W	1–0
1973	14 Feb	Glasgow	W	5–0
1973	19 May	Wembley	W	1–0
1974	18 May	Glasgow	L	0–2
1975	24 May	Wembley	W	5–1
1976	15 May	Glasgow	L	1–2
1977	4 June	Wembley	L	1–2
1978	20 May	Glasgow	W	1–0
1979	26 May	Wembley	W	3–1
1980	24 May	Glasgow	W	2–0
1981	23 May	Wembley	L	0–1
1982	29 May	Glasgow	W	1–0
1983	1 June	Wembley	W	2–0
1984	26 May	Glasgow	D	1–1
1985	25 May	Glasgow	L	0–1 (RC)
1986	23 April	Wembley	W	2–1 (RC)
1987	23 May	Glasgow	D	0–0 (RC)
1988	21 May	Wembley	W	1–0 (RC)
1989	27 May	Glasgow	W	2–0 (RC)

P 107, W 43, D 24, L 40, F 188, A 168

v Spain

1929	15 May	Madrid	L	3–4
1931	9 Dec	Arsenal	W	7–1
1950	2 July	Rio de Janeiro	L	0–1 (WCF)
1955	18 May	Madrid	D	1–1
1955	30 Nov	Wembley	W	4–1
1960	15 May	Madrid	L	0–3
1960	26 Oct	Wembley	W	4–2
1965	8 Dec	Madrid	W	2–0
1967	24 May	Wembley	W	2–0
1968	3 April	Wembley	W	1–0 (ECQ)
1968	8 May	Madrid	W	2–1 (ECQ)
1980	26 March	Barcelona	W	2–0
1980	18 June	Naples	W	2–1 (ECF)
1981	25 March	Wembley	L	1–2
1982	5 July	Madrid	D	0–0 (WCF)
1987	18 Feb	Madrid	W	4–2

P 16, W 10, D 2, L 4, F 35, A 19

v Sweden

1923	21 May	Stockholm	W	4–2
1923	24 May	Stockholm	W	3–1
1937	17 May	Stockholm	W	4–0
1947	19 Nov	Arsenal	W	4–2
1949	13 May	Stockholm	L	1–3
1956	16 May	Stockholm	D	0–0
1959	28 Oct	Wembley	L	2–3
1965	16 May	Gothenburg	W	2–1
1968	22 May	Wembley	W	3–1
1979	10 June	Stockholm	D	0–0
1986	10 Sept	Stockholm	L	0–1
1988	19 Oct	Wembley	D	0–0 (WCQ)
1989	6 Sept	Stockholm	D	0–0 (WCQ)
1992	17 June	Stockholm	L	1–2 (ECF)

P 14, W 6, D 4, L 4, F 24, A 16

v Switzerland

1933	29 May	Berne	W	4–0
1938	21 May	Zurich	L	1–2
1947	18 May	Zurich	L	0–1
1948	2 Dec	Arsenal	W	6–0
1952	28 May	Zurich	W	3–0
1954	20 June	Berne	W	2–0 (WCF)
1962	9 May	Wembley	W	3–1
1963	5 June	Basle	W	8–1
1971	13 Oct	Basle	W	3–2 (ECQ)
1971	10 Nov	Wembley	D	1–1 (ECQ)
1975	3 Sept	Basle	W	2–1
1977	7 Sept	Wembley	D	0–0
1980	19 Nov	Wembley	W	2–1 (WCQ)
1981	30 May	Basle	L	1–2 (WCQ)
1988	28 May	Lausanne	W	1–0

P 15, W 10, D 2, L 3, F 37, A 12

v Tunisia

| 1990 | 2 June | Tunis | D | 1–1 |

P 1, W 0, D 1, L 0, F 1, A 1

v Turkey

1984	14 Nov	Istanbul	W	8–0 (WCQ)
1985	16 Oct	Wembley	W	5–0 (WCQ)
1987	29 April	Izmir	D	0–0 (ECQ)
1987	14 Oct	Wembley	W	8–0 (ECQ)
1991	1 May	Izmir	W	1–0 (ECQ)
1991	16 Oct	Wembley	W	1–0 (ECQ)

P 6, W 5, D 1, L 0, F 23, A 0

v USA

1950	29 June	Belo Horizonte	L	0–1 (WCF)
1953	8 June	New York	W	6–3
1959	28 May	Los Angeles	W	8–1
1964	27 May	New York	W	10–0
1985	16 June	Los Angeles	W	5–0

P 5, W 4, D 0, L 1, F 29, A 5

v USSR (see also CIS)

1958	18 May	Moscow	D	1–1
1958	8 June	Gothenburg	D	2–2 (WCF)
1958	17 June	Gothenburg	L	0–1 (WCF)
1958	22 Oct	Wembley	W	5–0
1967	6 Dec	Wembley	D	2–2
1968	8 June	Rome	W	2–0 (ECF)
1973	10 June	Moscow	W	2–1
1984	2 June	Wembley	L	0–2
1986	26 March	Tbilisi	W	1–0
1988	18 June	Frankfurt	L	1–3 (ECF)
1991	21 May	Wembley	W	3–1

P 11, W 5, D 3, L 3, F 19, A 13

v Uruguay

1953	31 May	Montevideo	L	1–2
1954	26 June	Basle	L	2–4 (WCF)
1964	6 May	Wembley	W	2–1
1966	11 July	Wembley	D	0–0 (WCF)
1969	8 June	Montevideo	W	2–1
1977	15 June	Montevideo	D	0–0
1984	13 June	Montevideo	L	0–2
1990	22 May	Wembley	L	1–2

P 8, W 2, D 2, L 4, F 8, A 12

v Wales

1879	18 Jan	Kennington	W	2–1
1880	15 March	Wrexham	W	3–2
1881	26 Feb	Blackburn	L	0–1
1882	13 March	Wrexham	L	3–5
1883	3 Feb	Kennington	W	5–0
1884	17 March	Wrexham	W	4–0
1885	14 March	Blackburn	D	1–1
1886	29 March	Wrexham	W	3–1
1887	26 Feb	Kennington	W	4–0
1888	4 Feb	Crewe	W	5–1
1889	23 Feb	Stoke	W	4–1
1890	15 March	Wrexham	W	3–1
1891	7 May	Sunderland	W	4–1
1892	5 March	Wrexham	W	2–0
1893	13 March	Stoke	W	6–0
1894	12 March	Wrexham	W	5–1
1895	18 March	Kensington	D	1–1
1896	16 March	Cardiff	W	9–1
1897	29 March	Sheffield	W	4–0
1898	28 March	Wrexham	W	3–0
1899	20 March	Bristol	W	4–0
1900	26 March	Cardiff	D	1–1
1901	18 March	Newcastle	W	6–0
1902	3 March	Wrexham	D	0–0
1903	2 March	Portsmouth	W	2–1
1904	29 Feb	Wrexham	D	2–2
1905	27 March	Liverpool	W	3–1
1906	19 March	Cardiff	W	1–0
1907	18 March	Fulham	D	1–1
1908	16 March	Wrexham	W	7–1
1909	15 March	Nottingham	W	2–0
1910	14 March	Cardiff	W	1–0
1911	13 March	Millwall	W	3–0
1912	11 March	Wrexham	W	2–0
1913	17 March	Bristol	W	4–3
1914	16 March	Cardiff	W	2–0
1920	15 March	Arsenal	L	1–2
1921	14 March	Cardiff	D	0–0
1922	13 March	Liverpool	W	1–0
1923	5 March	Cardiff	D	2–2
1924	3 March	Blackburn	L	1–2
1925	28 Feb	Swansea	W	2–1
1926	1 March	Crystal Palace	L	1–3
1927	12 Feb	Wrexham	D	3–3
1927	28 Nov	Burnley	L	1–2
1928	17 Nov	Swansea	W	3–2
1929	20 Nov	Chelsea	W	6–0
1930	22 Nov	Wrexham	W	4–0
1931	18 Nov	Liverpool	W	3–1
1932	16 Nov	Wrexham	D	0–0
1933	15 Nov	Newcastle	L	1–2
1934	29 Sept	Cardiff	W	4–0
1936	5 Feb	Wolverhampton	L	1–2
1936	17 Oct	Cardiff	L	1–2
1937	17 Nov	Middlesbrough	W	2–1
1938	22 Oct	Cardiff	L	2–4
1946	13 Nov	Manchester	W	3–0
1947	18 Oct	Cardiff	W	3–0
1948	10 Nov	Aston Villa	W	1–0
1949	15 Oct	Cardiff	W	4–1 (WCQ)
1950	15 Nov	Sunderland	W	4–2
1951	20 Oct	Cardiff	D	1–1
1952	12 Nov	Wembley	W	5–2
1953	10 Oct	Cardiff	W	4–1 (WCQ)
1954	10 Nov	Wembley	W	3–2
1955	22 Oct	Cardiff	L	1–2
1956	14 Nov	Wembley	W	3–1
1957	19 Oct	Cardiff	W	4–0
1958	26 Nov	Aston Villa	D	2–2
1959	17 Oct	Cardiff	D	1–1
1960	23 Nov	Wembley	W	5–1
1961	14 Oct	Cardiff	D	1–1
1962	21 Nov	Wembley	W	4–0
1963	12 Oct	Cardiff	W	4–0
1964	18 Nov	Wembley	W	2–1
1965	2 Oct	Cardiff	D	0–0
1966	16 Nov	Wembley	W	5–1 (ECQ)
1967	21 Oct	Cardiff	W	3–0 (ECQ)
1969	7 May	Wembley	W	2–1
1970	18 April	Cardiff	D	1–1
1971	19 May	Wembley	D	0–0
1972	20 May	Cardiff	W	3–0
1972	15 Nov	Cardiff	W	1–0 (WCQ)
1973	24 Jan	Wembley	D	1–1 (WCQ)
1973	15 May	Wembley	W	3–0
1974	11 May	Cardiff	W	2–0
1975	21 May	Wembley	D	2–2
1976	24 March	Wrexham	W	2–1
1976	8 May	Cardiff	W	1–0
1977	31 May	Wembley	L	0–1
1978	3 May	Cardiff	W	3–1
1979	23 May	Wembley	D	0–0
1980	17 May	Wrexham	L	1–4
1981	20 May	Wembley	D	0–0
1982	27 April	Cardiff	W	1–0
1983	23 Feb	Wembley	W	2–1
1984	2 May	Wrexham	L	0–1

P 97, W 62, D 21, L 14, F 239, A 90

v Yugoslavia

1939	18 May	Belgrade	L	1–2
1950	22 Nov	Highbury	D	2–2
1954	16 May	Belgrade	L	0–1
1956	28 Nov	Wembley	W	3–0
1958	11 May	Belgrade	L	0–5
1960	11 May	Wembley	D	3–3
1965	9 May	Belgrade	D	1–1
1966	4 May	Wembley	W	2–0
1968	5 June	Florence	L	0–1 (ECF)
1972	11 Oct	Wembley	D	1–1
1974	5 June	Belgrade	D	2–2
1986	12 Nov	Wembley	W	2–0 (ECQ)
1987	11 Nov	Belgrade	W	4–1 (ECQ)
1989	13 Dec	Wembley	W	2–1

P 14, W 5, D 5, L 4, F 23, A 2

England's Managers Since Walter Winterbottom

SIR ALF RAMSEY
Record: P110, W67, D26, L17, F224, A98
First game: 27 Feb, 1963 v France at Paris (European Championship qualifier)
England lost 5–2
Last game: 3 April, 1974 v Portugal at Lisbon (friendly)
England drew 0–0
Reason for leaving: Sacked (May 1974)

JOE MERCER (CARETAKER MANAGER)
Record: P7, W3, D3, L1, F9, A7
First game: 11 May, 1974 v Wales at Cardiff (Home International Championship)
England won 2–0
Last game: 5 June, 1974 v Yugoslavia at Belgrade (friendly)
England drew 2–2

DON REVIE
Record: P29, W14, D8, L7 F49, A25
First game: 30 Oct, 1974 v Czechoslovakia at Wembley (European Championship qualifier)
England won 3–0
Last game: 15 June, 1977 v Uruguay at Montevideo (South American tour)
England drew 0–0
Reason for leaving: Resigned to take up position as manager of the United Arab Emirates national team

RON GREENWOOD
Record: P55, W33, D12, L10, F93, A40
First game: 7 Sept, 1977 v Switzerland at Wembley (friendly)
England drew 0–0
Last game: 5 July, 1982 v Spain at Madrid (World Cup Finals, second stage)
England drew 0–0
Reason for leaving: Retired

BOBBY ROBSON
Record: P95, W47, D30, L18, F154, A60
First game: 22 Sept, 1982 v Denmark at Copenhagen (European Championship qualifier)
England drew 2–2
Last game: 7 July, 1990 v Italy at Bari (World Cup third place play-off)
England lost 1–2
Reason for leaving: To join Dutch club PSV Eindhoven as manager, his contract as England manager having expired after the World Cup.

GRAHAM TAYLOR
Record*: P25, W13, D9, L3, F34, A18
First game: 12 Sept, 1990 v Hungary at Wembley (friendly)
England won 1–0

* to 9 Sept, 1992

B Internationals

Caps 1949–1992

(up to and including 30 May, 1992) Clubs named are those they were playing with at time of selection

Player	Caps
Ablett G (Liverpool)	1
Adams T (Arsenal)	4
Anderson V (Nottm Forest)	7
Armstrong D (Middlesbrough)	2
Atkinson D (Sheff Wed)	1
Bailey G (Man Utd)	2
Bailey J (Everton)	1
Barnes P (WBA)	1
Barrett E (Oldham)	4
Barton W (Wimbledon)	1
Batson B (WBA)	3
Batty D (Leeds Utd)	5
Beagrie P (Everton)	2
Beardsley P (Liverpool)	2
Beasant D (Wimbledon)	7
Birtles G (Nottm Forest)	1
Bishop I (West Ham)	1
Blissett L (Watford)	1
Bond K (Norwich, Man City)	2
Borrows B (Coventry City)	1
Brock K (QPR)	1
Bruce S (Norwich)	1
Bull S (Wolves)	5
Burrows D (Liverpool)	3
Butcher T (Ipswich)	1
Callaghan N (Watford)	1
Campbell K (Arsenal)	1
Chapman L (Leeds Utd)	1
Clough N (Nottm Forest)	3
Corrigan J (Man City)	10
Coton T (Man City)	1
Cowans G (Aston Villa)	2
Crook I (Norwich)	1
Cunningham L (WBA)	1
Curle K (Wimbledon, Man City)	4
Daley S (Wolves)	6
Daley T (Aston Villa)	1
Davenport P (Nottm Forest)	1
Davis P (Arsenal)	1
Deane B (Sheff Utd)	3
Devonshire A (West Ham)	1
Dicks J (West Ham)	2
Dixon L (Arsenal)	4
Dorigo T (Chelsea, Leeds Utd)	7
Ebbrell J (Everton)	1
Elliott P (Celtic)	1
Elliott S (Sunderland)	3
Eves M (Wolves)	3
Fairclough C (Spurs)	1
Fairclough D (Liverpool)	1
Fashanu J (Nottm Forest)	1
Flanagan M (Charlton, C Palace)	3
Ford T (WBA)	3
Forsyth M (Derby County)	1
Gabbiadini M (Sunderland)	1
Gallagher J (Birmingham)	1
Gascoigne P (Spurs)	4
Geddis D (Ipswich)	1
Gibson C (Aston Villa)	1
Gidman J (Aston Villa)	2
Goddard P (West Ham)	1
Gordon D (Norwich)	2
Greenhoff B (Man Utd)	1
Harford M (Luton)	1
Hazell R (Wolves)	1
Heath A (Everton)	1
Hilaire V (C Palace)	1
Hill G (Man Utd, Derby County)	6
Hirst D (Sheff Wed)	3
Hoddle G (Spurs)	2
Hodge S (Nottm Forest)	2
Hollins J (QPR)	5
Hurlock T (Millwall)	3
Ince P (Man Utd)	1
Jobson R (Oldham)	2
Johnston C (Liverpool)	1
Joseph R (Wimbledon)	2
Kennedy A (Liverpool)	7
Keown M (Everton)	1
King P (Sheff Wed)	1
Lake P (Man City)	1
Langley T (Chelsea)	3

Laws B (Nottm Forest)	1	Mountfield D (Everton)	1	Richards J (Wolves)	3	Sunderland A (Arsenal)	7
Le Saux G (Chelsea)	2	Mowbray T (Middlesbrough)	3	Rix G (Arsenal)	3		
Le Tissier M (Southampton)	5	Mutch A (Wolves)	3	Roberts G (Spurs)	1	Talbot B (Ipswich, Arsenal)	8
Lineker G (Leicester City)	1			Robson B (WBA, Man United)	3	Thomas G (C Palace)	3
Linighan A (Norwich)	4	Naylor S (WBA)	3			Thomas M (Liverpool)	5
Lukic J (Leeds Utd)	1	Needham D (Nottm Forest)	6	Rocastle D (Arsenal)	2	Thomas M (Spurs)	1
Lyons M (Everton)	1	Newell M (Everton)	2	Roeder G (Orient, QPR)	5	Thompson P (Liverpool)	1
McCall S (Ipswich)	1	Osman R (Ipswich)	2	Sansom K (C Palace)	2	Waldron M (Southampton)	1
McDermott T (Liverpool)	1	Owen G (Man City)	7	Seaman D (QPR)	6	Wallace D (Man Utd)	1
McLeary A (Millwall)	3			Sharpe L (Man United)	1	Wallace R (Southampton)	1
McMahon S (Aston Villa, Liverpool)	2	Pallister G (Middlesbrough, Man Utd)	9	Shearer A (Southampton)	1	Walters M (Rangers)	1
				Sims S (Leicester City)	1	Ward P (Nottm Forest)	2
Mabbutt G (Spurs)	9	Palmer C (Sheff Wed)	5	Sinton A (QPR)	3	Webb N (Man Utd)	4
Mackenzie S (Man City, Charlton)	3	Parker G (Nottm Forest)	1	Slater S (West Ham)	2	White D (Man City)	1
		Parker P (QPR)	3	Smith A (Arsenal)	4	Williams P (Charlton)	3
Mariner P (Ipswich)	7	Parkes P (West Ham)	2	Snodin I (Everton)	2	Williams S (Southampton)	4
Martin A (West Ham)	2	Peach D (Southampton)	1	Speight M (Sheff Utd)	4	Winterburn N (Arsenal)	3
Martyn N (Bristol Rovers, C Palace)	5	Platt D (Aston Villa)	3	Spink N (Aston Villa)	2	Wise D (Wimbledon)	3
		Power P (Man City)	2	Statham D (WBA)	2	Woodcock T (Cologne)	1
Merson P (Arsenal)	2	Preece D (Luton)	3	Sterland M (Sheff Wed, Leeds)	3	Woods C (Norwich, Rangers)	2
Money R (Liverpool)	1						
Morley T (Aston Villa)	2	Reeves K (Man City)	3	Stevens G (Everton)	1	Wright B (Everton)	2
Mortimer D (Aston Villa)	3	Regis C (WBA)	3	Stewart P (Spurs)	5	Wright I (C Palace, Arsenal)	3

Country-by-Country Results 1949–1992

v Algeria
1990　11 Dec　Algiers　D　0–0

v Australia
1980　17 Nov　Birmingham　W　1–0

v CIS
1992　28 April　Moscow　D　1–1

v Czechoslovakia
1978　28 Nov　Prague　W　1–0
1990　24 April　Sunderland　W　2–0
1992　24 March　Ceske Budejovice　W　1–0

v Finland
1949　15 May　Helsinki　W　4–0

v France
1952　22 May　Le Havre　L　1–7
1992　18 Feb　Q P R　W　3–0

v West Germany
1954　24 March　Gelsenkirchen　W　4–0
1955　23 March　Sheffield　D　1–1
1978　21 Feb　Augsburg　W　2–1

v Holland
1949　18 May　Amsterdam　W　4–0
1950　22 Feb　Newcastle　W　1–0
1950　17 May　Amsterdam　L　0–3
1952　26 March　Amsterdam　W　1–0

v Iceland
1989　19 May　Reykjavik　W　2–0
1991　27 April　Watford　W　1–0

v Italy
1950　11 May　Milan　L　0–5
1989　14 Nov　Brighton　D　1–1

v Luxembourg
1950　21 May　Luxembourg　W　2–1

v Malaysia
1978　30 May　Kuala Lumpur　D　1–1

v Malta
1987　14 Oct　Ta'Qali　W　2–0

v New Zealand
1978　7 June　Christchurch　W　4–0
1978　11 June　Wellington　W　3–1
1978　14 June　Auckland　W　4–0
1979　15 Oct　Leyton Orient　W　4–1
1984　13 Nov　Nottingham Forest　W　2–0

v Norway
1989　22 May　Stavanger　W　1–0

v Republic of Ireland
1990　27 March　Cork　L　1–4

v Scotland
1953　11 March　Edinburgh　D　2–2
1954　3 March　Sunderland　D　1–1
1956　29 Feb　Dundee　D　2–2
1957　6 Feb　Birmingham　W　4–1

v Singapore
1978　18 June　Singapore　W　8–0

v Spain
1980　26 March　Sunderland　W　1–0
1981　25 March　Granada　L　2–3
1991　18 Dec　Castellon　W　1–0

v Switzerland
1950　18 Jan　Sheffield　W　5–0

1954	22 May	Basle	L	0–2	
1956	21 March	Southampton	W	4–1	
1989	16 May	Winterthur	W	2–0	
1991	20 May	Walsall	W	2–1	

v USA

1980	14 Oct	Manchester	W	1–0	

v Wales

1991	5 Feb	Swansea	W	1–0	

v Yugoslavia

1954	16 May	Ljubljana	L	1–2
1955	19 Oct	Manchester	W	5–1
1989	12 Dec	Millwall	W	2–1

Under-21 Internationals

Caps 1976–1992

Player	Caps
Ablett G (Liverpool)	1
Adams N (Everton)	1
Adams T (Arsenal)	5
Allen C (QPR, C Palace)	3
Allen M (QPR)	2
Allen P (West Ham, Spurs)	3
Anderson V (Nottm Forest)	1
Andrews I (Leicester City)	1
Atkinson B (Sunderland)	5
Bailey G (Man Utd)	14
Baker G (Southampton)	2
Bannister G (Sheff Wed)	1
Barker S (Blackburn)	4
Barnes J (Watford)	2
Barnes P (Man City)	9
Barrett E (Oldham)	4
Batty D (Leeds Utd)	7
Beagrie P (Sheff Utd)	2
Beardsmore R (Man Utd)	5
Beeston C (Stoke)	1
Bertschin K (Birmingham)	3
Birtles G (Nottm Forest)	2
Blackwell D (Wimbledon)	6
Blake M (Aston Villa)	7
Blissett L (Watford)	4
Bracewell P (Stoke, Sunderland, Everton)	13
Bradshaw P (Wolves)	4
Breacker T (Luton)	2
Brennan M (Ipswich)	5
Brightwell I (Man City)	4
Brock K (Oxford Utd)	4
Bull S (Wolves)	5
Burrows D (WBA, Liverpool)	7
Butcher T (Ipswich)	7
Butters G (Spurs)	3
Butterworth I (Coventry City, Nottm Forest)	8
Caesar G (Arsenal)	3
Callaghan N (Watford)	9
Campbell K (Arsenal)	2
Carr C (Fulham)	1
Carr F (Nottm Forest)	9
Caton T (Man City, Arsenal)	14
Chamberlain M (Stoke)	4
Chapman L (Stoke)	1
Charles G (Nottm Forest)	4
Chettle S (Nottm Forest)	12
Clough N (Nottm Forest)	15
Coney D (Fulham)	4
Connor T (Brighton and Hove Albion)	1
Cooke R (Spurs)	1
Cooper C (Middlesbrough)	8
Corrigan J (Man City)	3
Cottee T (West Ham)	8
Cowans G (Aston Villa)	5
Cranson I (Ipswich)	5
Crooks G (Stoke)	4
Crossley M (Nottm Forest)	3
Cundy J (Chelsea)	2
Cunningham L (WBA)	6
Curbishley A (Birmingham)	1
Daniel P (Hull)	7
Davis P (Arsenal)	11
D'Avray M (Ipswich)	2
Deehan J (Aston Villa)	7
Dennis M (Birmingham)	3
Dickens A (West Ham)	1
Dicks J (West Ham)	4
Digby F (Swindon)	5
Dillon K (Birmingham)	1
Dixon K (Chelsea)	1
Dobson T (Coventry City)	4
Dodd J (Southampton)	6
Donowa L (Norwich)	3
Dorigo T (Aston Villa)	11
Dozzell J (Ipswich)	9
Draper M (Notts County)	1
Duxbury M (Man Utd)	7
Dyson P (Coventry City)	4
Ebbrell J (Everton)	12
Elliott P (Luton, Aston Villa)	3
Fairclough C (Nottm Forest, Spurs)	7
Fairclough D (Liverpool)	1
Fashanu Justin (Norwich, Nottm Forest)	11
Fenwick T (QPR)	11
Fereday W (QPR)	5
Flowers T (Southampton)	3
Forsyth M (Derby County)	1
Foster S (Brighton and Hove Albion)	1
Futcher P (Luton, Man City)	11
Gabbiadini M (Sunderland)	2
Gale T (Fulham)	1
Gascoigne P (Newcastle)	13
Gayle H (Birmingham)	3
Gernon I (Ipswich)	1
Gibbs N (Watford)	5
Gibson C (Aston Villa)	1
Gilbert W (C Palace)	11
Goddard P (West Ham)	8
Gordon D (Norwich)	4
Gray A (Aston Villa)	2
Haigh P (Hull)	1
Hardyman P (Portsmouth)	2
Hateley M (Coventry City, Portsmouth)	10
Hayes M (Arsenal)	3
Hazell R (Wolves)	1
Heath A (Stoke, Everton)	8
Hesford I (Blackpool)	7
Hilaire V (C Palace)	9
Hillier D (Arsenal)	1
Hinchcliffe A (Man City)	1
Hinshelwood P (C Palace)	2
Hirst D (Sheff Wed)	7
Hoddle G (Spurs)	12
Hodge S (Nottm Forest, Aston Villa)	8
Hodgson D (Middlesbrough, Liverpool)	7
Holdsworth D (Watford)	1
Horne B (Millwall)	5
Hucker P (QPR)	2
Ince P (West Ham)	2
James D (Watford)	7
James J (Luton)	2
Jemson N (Nottm Forest)	1
Johnson T (Notts County)	2
Johnson C (Middlesbrough)	2
Jones C (Spurs)	1
Jones D (Everton)	1
Keegan G (Oldham)	1
Keown M (Aston Villa)	8
Kerslake D (QPR)	1
Kilcline B (Notts County)	2
King A (Everton)	2
Kitson P (Leicester City)	3
Knight A (Portsmouth)	2
Knight I (Sheff Wed)	2
Lake P (Man City)	5
Langley T (Chelsea)	1
Lee D (Chelsea)	9
Lee R (Charlton)	2
Lee S (Liverpool)	6
Le Saux G (Chelsea)	4
Lowe D (Ipswich)	2
Lukic J (Leeds Utd)	7
Lund G (Grimsby)	1
Mabbutt G (Bristol Rovers, Spurs)	6
McCall S (Ipswich)	6
McDonald N (Newcastle)	5
McGrath L (Coventry City)	1
MacKenzie S (WBA)	3
McLeary A (Millwall)	1
McMahon S (Everton, Aston Villa)	6
McManaman S (Liverpool)	2
Martin L (Man Utd)	2
Martyn N (Bristol Rovers)	11
Matthew D (Chelsea)	7
May A (Man City)	1
Merson P (Arsenal)	4
Middleton J (Nottm Forest, Derby County)	3
Miller A (Arsenal)	4
Mills G (Nottm Forest)	2
Mimms R (Rotherham, Everton)	3
Minto S (Charlton)	1
Moran S (Southampton)	2
Morgan S (Leicester City)	2
Mortimer P (Charlton)	2
Moses R (WBA, Man Utd)	8
Mountfield D (Everton)	1
Muggleton C (Leicester City)	1
Mutch A (Wolves)	1
Newell M (Luton)	4
Oldfield D (Luton)	1
Olney I (Aston Villa)	9
Ord R (Sunderland)	3
Osman R (Ipswich)	7
Owen G (Man City, WBA)	22

100

Painter I (Stoke)	1	Rix G (Arsenal)	7	Statham D (WBA)	6	Wallace D (Southampton)	14
Palmer C (Sheff Wed)	4	Robins M (Man Utd)	6	Stein B (Luton)	3	Wallace Ray (Southampton)	4
Parker G (Hull, Nottm Forest)	6	Robson B (WBA)	7	Sterland M (Sheff Wed)	7	Wallace Rod (Southampton)	11
Parker P (Fulham)	8	Robson S (Arsenal, West Ham)	8	Steven T (Everton)	2	Walsh G (Man Utd)	2
Parkes P (QPR)	1	Rocastle D (Arsenal)	14	Stevens G (Everton)	1	Walsh P (Luton)	4
Parkin S (Stoke)	5	Rodger G (Coventry City)	4	Stevens G (Brighton and Hove Albion, Spurs)	7	Walters M (Aston Villa)	9
Peach D (Southampton)	6	Rosario R (Norwich)	4	Stewart P (Man City)	1	Ward P (Brighton and Hove Albion)	2
Peake A (Leicester City)	1	Rowell G (Sunderland)	1	Stuart G (Chelsea)	5	Warhurst P (Oldham)	7
Pearce S (Nottm Forest)	1	Ruddock N (Southampton)	4	Suckling P (Coventry City, Man City, C Palace)	10	Watson D (Norwich)	7
Pickering N (Sunderland, Coventry City)	15	Ryan J (Oldham)	1	Sunderland A (Wolves)	1	Watson G (Sheff Wed)	2
Platt D (Aston Villa)	3	Samways V (Spurs)	5	Swindlehurst D (C Palace)	1	Webb N (Portsmouth, Nottm Forest)	3
Porter G (Watford)	12	Sansom K (C Palace)	8			White D (Man City)	6
Pressman K (Sheff Wed)	1	Seaman D (Birmingham)	10	Talbot B (Ipswich)	1	Whyte C (Arsenal)	4
Proctor M (Middlesbrough, Nottm Forest)	5	Sedgley S (Coventry City, Spurs)	11	Thomas D (Coventry City, Spurs)	7	Wicks S (QPR)	1
		Sellars S (Blackburn)	3	Thomas M (Arsenal)	12	Wilkins R (Chelsea)	1
Ramage C (Derby County)	3	Sharpe L (Man Utd)	8	Thomas M (Luton)	3	Wilkinson P (Grimsby, Everton)	4
Ranson R (Man City)	10	Shaw G (Aston Villa)	7	Thomas R (Watford)	1	Williams P (Charlton)	4
Redmond S (Man City)	14	Shearer A (Southampton)	9	Thompson G (Coventry City)	6	Williams P (Derby County)	3
Reeves K (Norwich, Man City)	10	Shelton G (Sheff Wed)	1	Thorn A (Wimbledon)	5	Williams S (Southampton)	14
Regis C (WBA)	6	Sheringham T (Millwall)	1	Tiler C (Barnsley, Nottm Forest)	11	Winterburn N (Wimbledon)	1
Reid N (Man City)	6	Sherwood T (Norwich)	4			Wise D (Wimbledon)	1
Reid P (Bolton)	6	Simpson P (Man City)	5	Venison B (Sunderland)	10	Woodcock A (Nottm Forest)	2
Richards J (Wolves)	2	Sims S (Leicester City)	10	Vinnicombe C (Rangers)	9	Woods C (Nottm Forest, QPR, Norwich)	6
Rideout P (Aston Villa, Bari)	5	Sinnott L (Watford)	1			Wright M (Southampton)	4
Ripley S (Middlesbrough)	8	Slater S (West Ham)	3	Waddle C (Newcastle)	1	Wright W (Everton)	6
Ritchie A (Brighton and Hove Albion)	1	Smith D (Coventry City)	10	Walker D (Nottm Forest)	7		
		Smith M (Sheff Wed)	5	Walker I (Spurs)	1	Yates D (Notts County)	5
		Snodin I (Doncaster)	4				
		Statham B (Spurs)	3				

Goalscorers 1976–1992

Adams	1	Cole	1	Duxbury	1	Hirst	1	Parker P	1	Sedgley	1	Wallace R	3
Allen	1	Coney	1	Dyson	1	Hoddle	2	Peach	1	Shaw	2	Walsh	4
Barnes P	2	Connor	1	Ebbrell	1	Hodge	3	Pickering N	1	Shearer	13	Walters	1
Batty	1	Cottee	1	Elliott	1	Hodgson	2	Porter	1	Simpson	1	Ward	3
Birtles	1	Cranson	1	Fashanu	5	Johnson T	2	Reeves	2	Sims	2	Watson D	1
Blake	1	Crooks	3	Fairclough C	1	King A	1	Regis	3	Stein B	3	Watson G	1
Brightwell	2	Cundy	1	Gascoigne	6	Kitson	3	Rideout	1	Sterland	3	White D	2
Bull	3	Cunningham	2	Gayle H	1	Mabbutt	2	Ripley	1	Stewart P	1	Wilkinson P	1
Butterworth	1	Daniel	1	Goddard	5	Matthew	1	Robins	7	Stuart	2	Williams P	3
Campbell	1	Davis	2	Hateley	8	Mortimer P	2	Robson B	2	Thomas M	3	Woodcock	5
Carr	1	D'Avray	1	Hazell	1	Olney	3	Robson S	2	Thompson G	3		
Chamberlain	1	Deehan	6	Heath	3	Owen G	4	Rocastle	2	Waddle	1		
Clough	3	Dixon K	1	Hilaire	1	Parker G	1	Samways	1	Wallace D	1		

Country-by-Country Results 1976–1992

UQ UEFA Competition Qualifier   UF UEFA Competition Final

v Albania

1989	7 March	Shkoder	W	2–1 (UQ)
1989	25 April	Ipswich	W	2–0 (UQ)

v Bulgaria

1979	5 June	Pernik	W	3–1 (UQ)
1979	20 Nov	Leicester	W	5–0 (UQ)
1989	5 June	Toulon	L	2–3

v Czechoslovakia

1990	27 May	Toulon	W	2–1
1992	26 May	Toulon	L	1–2

v Denmark

1978	19 Sept	Hvidovre	W	2–1 (UQ)
1979	11 Sept	Watford	W	1–0 (UQ)
1982	21 Sept	Hvidovre	W	4–1 (UQ)
1983	20 Sept	Norwich	W	4–1 (UQ)

1986	12 March	Copenhagen	W	1–0 (UF)
1986	26 March	Manchester City	D	1–1 (UF)
1988	13 Sept	Watford	D	0–0

v Finland
1977	26 May	Helsinki	W	1–0 (UQ)
1977	12 Oct	Hull	W	8–1 (UQ)
1984	16 Oct	Southampton	W	2–0 (UQ)
1985	21 May	Mikkeli	L	1–3 (UQ)

v France
1984	28 Feb	Sheffield Wed	W	6–1 (UF)
1984	28 March	Rouen	W	1–0 (UF)
1987	11 June	Toulon	L	0–2
1988	13 April	Besançon	L	2–4 (UF)
1988	27 April	Arsenal	D	2–2 (UF)
1988	12 June	Toulon	L	2–4
1990	23 May	Aix en Provence	W	7–3
1991	3 June	Toulon	W	1–0
1992	28 May	Aubagne	D	0–0

v East Germany
1980	16 April	Sheffield United	L	1–2 (UF)
1980	23 April	Jena	L	0–1 (UF)

v West Germany
1982	21 Sept	Sheffield United	W	3–1 (UF)
1982	12 Oct	Bremen	L	2–3 (UF)
1987	8 Sept	Lüdenscheid	L	0–2

v Germany
1991	10 Sept	Scunthorpe	W	2–1

v Greece
1982	16 Nov	Piraeus	L	0–1 (UQ)
1983	29 March	Portsmouth	W	2–1 (UQ)
1989	7 Feb	Patras	L	0–1

v Hungary
1981	5 June	Keszthely	W	2–1 (UQ)
1981	17 Nov	Nottingham Forest	W	2–0 (UQ)
1983	26 April	Newcastle	W	1–0 (UQ)
1983	11 Oct	Nyiregyhaza	W	2–0 (UQ)
1990	11 Sept	Southampton	W	3–1
1992	12 May	Vac	D	2–2

v Israel
1985	27 Feb	Tel Aviv	W	2–1

v Italy
1978	8 March	Manchester City	W	2–1 (UF)
1978	5 April	Rome	D	0–0 (UF)
1984	18 April	Manchester City	W	3–1 (UF)
1984	2 May	Florence	L	0–1 (UF)
1986	9 April	Pisa	L	0–2 (UF)
1986	23 April	Swindon	D	1–1 (UF)

v Mexico
1988	5 June	Toulon	W	2–1
1991	29 May	Vitrolles	W	6–0
1992	24 May	Six-Fours	D	1–1

v Morocco
1987	7 June	Toulon	W	2–0
1988	9 June	Toulon	W	1–0

v Norway
1977	1 June	Bergen	W	2–1 (UQ)
1977	6 Sept	Brighton	W	6–0 (UQ)
1980	9 Sept	Southampton	W	3–0
1981	8 Sept	Drammen	D	0–0

v Poland
1982	17 March	Warsaw	W	2–1 (UF)
1982	7 April	West Ham	D	2–2 (UF)
1989	2 June	Plymouth	W	2–1 (UQ)
1989	10 Oct	Jastrzebie Zdroj	W	3–1 (UQ)
1990	16 Oct	Tottenham	L	0–1 (UQ)
1991	12 Nov	Pila	L	1–2 (UQ)

v Portugal
1987	13 June	Sollies-Pont	D	0–0
1990	21 May	Six-Fours	L	0–1

v Republic of Ireland
1981	25 Feb	Liverpool	W	1–0
1985	25 March	Portsmouth	W	3–2
1989	9 June	Six-Fours	D	0–0
1990	13 Nov	Cork	W	3–0 (UQ)
1991	26 March	Brentford	W	3–0 (UQ)

v Romania
1980	14 Oct	Ploesti	L	0–4 (UQ)
1981	28 April	Swindon	W	3–0 (UQ)
1985	30 April	Brasov	D	0–0 (UQ)
1985	9 Sept	Ipswich	W	3–0 (UQ)

v Scotland
1977	27 April	Sheffield United	W	1–0
1980	12 Feb	Coventry	W	2–1 (UF)
1980	4 March	Aberdeen	D	0–0 (UF)
1982	19 April	Glasgow	W	1–0 (UF)
1982	28 April	Manchester City	D	1–1 (UF)
1988	16 Feb	Aberdeen	W	1–0 (UF)
1988	22 March	Nottingham Forest	W	1–0 (UF)

v Senegal
1989	7 June	Sainte-Maxime	W	6–1
1991	27 May	Arles	W	2–1

v Spain
1984	17 May	Seville	W	1–0 (UF)
1984	24 May	Sheffield United	W	2–0 (UF)
1987	18 Feb	Burgos	W	2–1

v Sweden
1979	9 June	Vasteras	W	2–1
1986	9 Sept	Oestersund	D	1–1
1988	18 Oct	Coventry	D	1–1 (UQ)
1989	5 Sept	Uppsala	L	0–1 (UQ)

v Switzerland
1980	18 Nov	Ipswich	W	5–0 (UQ)
1981	31 May	Neuenburg	D	0–0 (UQ)
1988	28 May	Lausanne	D	1–1

v Turkey
1984	13 Nov	Bursa	D	0–0 (UQ)
1985	15 Oct	Bristol	W	3–0 (UQ)
1987	28 April	Izmir	D	0–0 (UQ)
1987	13 Oct	Sheffield	D	1–1 (UQ)

| 1991 | 30 April | Izmir | D | 2–2 (UQ) |
| 1991 | 15 Oct | Reading | W | 2–0 (UQ) |

v USA

| 1989 | 11 June | Toulon | L | 0–2 |

v USSR

1987	9 June	La Ciotat	D	0–0
1988	7 June	Six-Fours	W	1–0
1990	25 May	Toulon	W	2–1
1991	31 May	Aix-en-Provence	W	2–1

v Wales

1976	15 Dec	Wolverhampton	D	0–0
1979	6 Feb	Swansea	W	1–0
1990	5 Dec	Tranmere	D	0–0

v Yugoslavia

1978	19 April	Novi Sad	L	1–2 (UF)
1978	2 May	Manchester City	D	1–1 (UF)
1986	11 Nov	Peterborough	D	1–1 (UQ)
1987	10 Nov	Zemun	W	5–1 (UQ)

Under-23 Internationals

Caps 1954–1976

A'Court A (Liverpool)	7
Allen A (Stoke)	7
Allen L (Spurs)	1
Anderson S (Sunderland)	4
Angus J (Burnley)	7
Armfield J (Blackpool)	9
Armstrong D (Middlesbrough)	4
Armstrong G (Arsenal)	5
Ashurst L (Sunderland)	1
Aston J (Man Utd)	1
Atyeo J (Bristol City)	2
Ayre R (Charlton)	2
Badger L (Sheff Utd)	13
Bailey M (Charlton)	5
Baker J (Hibernian, Arsenal)	6
Baldwin T (Chelsea)	2
Ball A (Blackpool)	8
Banks G (Leicester City)	2
Barnwell J (Arsenal)	1
Barrett L (Fulham)	1
Barrowclough S (Newcastle)	5
Beattie K (Ipswich)	9
Bell C (Man City)	2
Bennett A (Rotherham)	1
Bernard M (Stoke)	3
Birchenall A (Sheff Utd, Chelsea)	4
Blockley J (Coventry City, Arsenal)	10
Bloomfield J (Arsenal)	2
Blunstone F (Chelsea)	5
Bonds W (West Ham)	2
Bonetti P (Chelsea)	12
Booth C (Wolves)	1
Booth T (Man City)	4
Boyer P (Norwich)	2
Brabrook P (Chelsea)	9
Broadbent P (Wolves)	1
Brooking T (West Ham)	1
Buckley M (Everton)	2
Burnside D (WBA)	1
Burrows H (Aston Villa)	1
Byrne G (Liverpool)	1
Byrne J (C Palace, West Ham)	7
Callaghan I (Liverpool)	4
Cantello L (WBA)	8
Case J (Liverpool)	1
Cattlin C (Coventry City)	2
Channon M (Southampton)	9
Charlton R (Man Utd)	6
Cheesebrough A (Burnley)	1
Chisnall P (Man Utd)	4
Chivers M (Southampton)	17
Clark C (WBA)	1
Clarke A (Fulham, Leicester City)	6
Clayton R (Blackburn)	6
Clemence R (Liverpool)	4
Clough B (Middlesbrough)	3
Coates R (Burnley)	8
Cohen G (Fulham)	8
Connelly J (Burnley)	1
Coppell S (Man Utd)	1
Corrigan J (Man City)	1
Crawford B (Blackpool)	1
Cross G (Leicester City)	11
Crowe C (Leeds Utd, Blackburn)	4
Crowther S (Aston Villa)	3
Currie A (Sheff Utd)	13
Curry W (Newcastle)	1
Davies R (Derby County)	1
Day M (West Ham)	5
Deakin A (Aston Villa)	6
Dobing P (Blackburn)	7
Dobson C (Sheff Wed)	2
Dobson M (Burnley)	1
Dodd A (Stoke)	6
Dodgin W (Arsenal)	1
Douglas B (Blackburn)	5
Doyle M (Man City)	8
Dyson J (Man City)	1
Dyson K (Newcastle)	1
Eastham G (Newcastle)	6
Edwards D (Man Utd)	6
Edwards P (Man Utd)	3
Ellis S (Sheff Wed)	3
Ellis S (Charlton)	1
Evans A (Liverpool)	4
Fantham J (Sheff Wed)	1
Farmer E (Wolves)	2
Farmer J (Stoke)	1
Finney A (Sheff Wed)	3
Fletcher P (Burnley)	4
Flowers R (Wolves)	2
Ford D (Sheff Wed)	2
Foulkes W (Man Utd)	2
Francis G (QPR)	6
Francis T (Birmingham)	5
Garland C (Bristol City)	1
George C (Arsenal)	5
Gidman J (Aston Villa)	4
Gillard I (QPR)	5
Glazier W (Coventry)	3
Gowling A (Man Utd)	1
Greaves J (Chelsea, Spurs)	12
Greenhoff B (Man Utd)	4
Greenhoff J (Birmingham)	5
Groves V (Arsenal)	1
Grummitt P (Nottm Forest)	3
Gunter P (Portsmouth)	1
Hankin R (Burnley)	3
Harris Gordon (Burnley)	2
Harris Gerry (Wolves)	4
Harris J (Everton)	1
Harris R (Chelsea)	4
Harrison M (Chelsea)	3
Harvey J (Everton)	5
Hayes J (Man City)	2
Haynes J (Fulham)	8
Hibbitt K (Wolves)	1
Hill F (Bolton)	10
Hill G (Man Utd)	1
Hill S (Blackpool)	4
Hindley P (Nottm Forest)	1
Hinton A (Wolves, Nottm Forest)	7
Hinton M (Charlton)	3
Hitchens G (Cardiff City)	1
Hodgkinson A (Sheff Utd)	7
Holliday E (Middlesbrough)	5
Hollins J (Chelsea)	12
Hooper H (West Ham)	2
Hopkinson E (Bolton)	6
Howe D (WBA)	6
Hudson A (Chelsea, Stoke)	10
Hughes E (Liverpool)	8
Hunt R P (Swindon, Wolves)	3
Hunter N (Leeds Utd)	3
Hurst G (West Ham)	4
Hurst J (Everton)	9
Husband J (Everton)	5
Hutchinson I (Chelsea)	2
Iley J (Spurs)	1
Jeffrey A (Doncaster)	2
Jeffries D (Man City)	1
Johnson D (Ipswich)	9
Jones G (Middlesbrough)	9
Jones M (Sheff Utd)	9
Jones R (Bournemouth)	1
Kay T (Sheff Wed)	7
Kaye A (Barnsley)	1
Keegan K (Liverpool)	5
Kember S (C Palace, Chelsea)	3
Kendall H (Everton)	6
Kennedy A (Newcastle)	6
Kennedy R (Arsenal)	6
Kevan D (WBA)	4
Kidd B (Man Utd)	10
Kirkham J (Wolves)	2
Kirkup J (West Ham)	3
Knowles C (Spurs)	6
Knowles P (Wolves)	4
Labone B (Everton)	7
Lampard F (West Ham)	4
Latchford P (WBA)	2
Latchford R (Birmingham, Everton)	6
Lawler C (Liverpool)	4

103

Leary S (Charlton)	1	Newton K (Blackburn)	4	Richards J (Wolves)	6	Sullivan C (Plymouth)	2
Le Flem R (Nottm Forest)	1	Nicholls J (WBA)	1	Riley H (Leicester City)	2	Summerbee M (Man City)	1
Lloyd L (Liverpool)	8	Nisbet G (WBA)	1	Robson B (Newcastle)	2	Sunderland A (Wolves)	1
Lock K (West Ham)	4	Nish D (Leicester City)	10	Robson J (Burnley)	1	Swan P (Sheff Wed)	3
Lyons M (Everton)	5	Norman M (Spurs)	3	Robson J (Derby County, Aston Villa)	7	Sydenham J (Southampton)	2
McDermott T (Newcastle)	1	O'Grady M (Huddersfield, Leeds Utd)	3	Robson R (Fulham)	1	Talbut J (Burnley)	7
Macdonald M (Newcastle)	4	O'Neil B (Burnley)	1	Rofe D (Leicester City)	1	Tambling R (Chelsea)	13
McDowell J (West Ham)	13	O'Rourke J (Middlesbrough)	1	Rogers D (Swindon)	2	Taylor P (C Palace)	4
McFarland R (Derby County)	5	Osgood P (Chelsea)	6	Royle J (Everton)	10	Taylor T (West Ham)	11
McGrath J (Newcastle)	1					Thomas D (Burnley, QPR)	11
McGuinness W (Man Utd)	4	Pacey D (Luton)	1	Sadler D (Man Utd)	3	Thompson P (Liverpool)	4
McNeil M (Middlesbrough)	9	Paddon G (West Ham)	1	Sammels J (Arsenal)	9	Thompson P B (Liverpool)	2
Macedo E (Fulham)	10	Paine T (Southampton)	4	Scanlon A (Man Utd)	5	Thompson R (Wolves)	15
Maddren W (Middlesbrough)	5	Palmer G (Wolves)	2	Scott M (Chelsea)	4	Todd C (Sunderland, Derby County)	14
Mannion G (Wolves)	2	Pardoe G (Man City)	4	Setters M (WBA, Man Utd)	16		
Marsh R (QPR)	2	Parkes P (QPR)	6	Shaw B (Sheff Utd)	2	Towers A (Man City, Sunderland)	7
Marshall G (Hearts)	1	Parkin D (Wolves)	5	Shaw G (Sheff Utd)	5		
Matthews R (Coventry City)	4	Parry R (Bolton)	4	Shawcross D (Man City)	1	Tueart D (Man City)	1
Miller B (Burnley)	3	Payne D (C Palace)	1	Shellito K (Chelsea)	1		
Mills D (Middlesbrough)	8	Pearson S (Man Utd)	1	Shilton P (Leicester City)	13	Usher B (Sunderland)	1
Mills M (Ipswich)	5	Pegg D (Man Utd)	3	Sillett P (Chelsea)	3		
Mills S J (Southampton)	1	Pejic M (Stoke)	8	Sissons J (West Ham)	10	Venables T (Chelsea)	4
Mobley V (Sheff Wed)	3	Perryman S (Spurs)	17	Sleeuwenhoek J (Aston Villa)	2	Wallington M (Leicester City)	2
Montgomery J (Sunderland)	6	Peters M (West Ham)	5	Smith J (West Ham)	1		
Moore I (Nottm Forest)	2	Pickering F (Blackburn)	3	Smith T (Liverpool)	10	West A (Burnley)	1
Moore R (West Ham)	8	Piper N (Plymouth, Portsmouth)	4	Smith T (Birmingham)	15	West G (Blackpool, Everton)	3
Moores I (Stoke Utd)	2	Pointer R (Burnley)	5	Smith W (Sheff Wed)	6	Whitefoot G (Man Utd)	1
Morgan R (Spurs)	1	Powell B (Wolves)	4	Springett P (Sheff Wed)	6	Whitham J (Sheff Wed)	1
Morley M (Preston)	1	Powell S (Derby County)	1	Stephenson A (C Palace, West Ham)	7	Whittle A (Everton)	1
Mortimer D (Coventry City)	6	Pugh J (Sheff Wed)	1	Stepney A (Millwall)	3	Whitworth S (Leicester City)	6
Mullery A (Fulham)	3			Stevens D (Bolton)	2	Whymark T (Ipswich)	7
Murray A (Chelsea)	6	Quixall A (Sheff Wed)	1	Stevenson A (Burnley)	11	Wilkins R (Chelsea)	2
Murray J (Wolves)	2			Stiles N (Man Utd)	3	Wilson D (Preston)	7
		Radford J (Arsenal)	4	Stokes A (Spurs)	1	Wood R (Man Utd)	1
Nattrass I (Newcastle)	1	Rankin A (Everton)	1	Stokes D (Huddersfield)	4	Wothington F (Huddersfield)	2
Neal R (Lincoln, Birmingham)	4	Reaney P (Leeds Utd)	5	Suddick A (Newcastle)	2	Wright T (Everton)	7
Newton H (Nottm Forest)	4						

Youth Internationals

Country-by-Country Results 1947–1992

WYC World Youth Championship   IYT International Youth Tournament   *Qualifying Competition   †Professionals   §Abandoned

v Algeria
†1984 22 April   Cannes   W   3–0

v Argentina
†1981 5 Oct   Sydney   D   1–1 (WYC)

v Australia
†1981 8 Oct   Sydney   D   1–1 (WYC)

v Austria
1949 19 April   Zeist   W   4–2 (IYT)
1952 17 April   Barcelona   D   5–5 (IYT)
1957 16 April   Barcelona   L   0–3 (IYT)
1958 4 March   Highbury   W   3–2
1958 1 June   Graz   W   4–3
1960 20 April   Vienna   L   0–1 (IYT)
†1964 1 April   Rotterdam   W   2–1 (IYT)
†1980 6 Sept   Pazin   L   0–1
†1981 29 May   Bonn   W   7–0 (IYT)
†1981 3 Sept   Umag   W   3–0 (IYT)
†1984 6 Sept   Izola   D   2–2 (IYT)

v Belgium
1948 16 April   West Ham   W   3–1 (IYT)
1951 22 March   Cannes   D   1–1 (IYT)
1953 31 March   Brussels   W   2–0 (IYT)
§1956 7 Nov   Brussels   A   3–2
1957 13 Nov   Sheffield   W   2–0
†1965 15 April   Ludwigshafen   W   3–0 (IYT)
1969 11 March   West Ham   W   1–0 (IYT*)
1972 13 May   Palma   D   0–0 (IYT*)
†1973 4 June   Viareggio   D   0–0 (IYT)
†1977 19 May   Lokeren   W   1–0 (IYT)
†1979 17 Jan   Brussels   W   4–0
†1980 8 Sept   Labin   W   6–1

†1983 13 April	Birmingham	D	1–1		
†1988 20 May	Chatel	D	0–0		
†1990 24 July	Nyiregyhaza	D	1–1 (IYT)		
†1990 16 Oct	Sunderland	D	0–0 (IYT*)		
†1991 16 Oct	Eernegem	L	0–1 (IYT)		

v Brazil

†1986 29 March	Cannes	D	0–0
†1986 13 May	Peking	L	1–2
†1987 2 June	Niteroi	L	0–2

v Bulgaria

1956 28 March	Salgotarjan	L	1–2 (IYT)
1960 16 April	Graz	L	0–1 (IYT)
1962 24 April	Ploesti	D	0–0 (IYT)
†1968 7 April	Nimes	D	0–0 (IYT)
†1969 26 March	Waregem	W	2–0 (IYT)
†1972 13 May	Palma	D	0–0 (IYT)
†1979 31 May	Vienna	L	0–1 (IYT)

v Cameroon

†1981 3 Oct	Sydney	W	2–0 (WYC)
†1985 1 June	Toulon	W	1–0

v China

†1983 31 March	Cannes	W	5–1
†1985 26 Aug	Baku	L	0–2 (WYC)
†1986 5 May	Peking	W	1–0

v Czechoslovakia

1955 7 April	Lucca	L	0–1 (IYT)
†1966 21 May	Rijeka	L	2–3 (IYT)
†1969 20 May	Leipzig	W	3–1 (IYT)
1979 24 May	Bischofshofen	W	3–0 (IYT)
†1979 8 Sept	Pula	L	1–2
†1982 11 April	Cannes	L	0–1
†1983 20 May	Highbury	D	1–1 (IYT)
†1989 26 Apr	Bystrica	L	0–1 (IYT*)
†1989 14 Nov	Portsmouth	W	1–0 (IYT*)
†1990 25 April	Wembley	D	1–1

v Denmark

†1955 1 Oct	Plymouth	W	9–2
1956 20 May	Esbjerg	W	2–1
†1979 31 Oct	Esbjerg	W	3–1 (IYT*)
1980 26 March	Coventry	W	4–0 (IYT*)
†1982 15 July	Stjordal	W	5–2
†1983 16 July	Holbeck	L	0–1
†1987 16 Feb	Manchester	W	2–1
†1990 28 March	Wembley	D	0–0
†1991 6 Feb	Oxford	L	1–5

v Egypt

†1981 11 Oct	Sydney	W	4–2 (WYC)

v Finland

†1975 19 May	Berne	D	1–1 (IYT)

v France

1957 24 March	Fontainebleau	W	1–0
1958 22 March	Eastbourne	L	0–1
†1966 23 May	Rijeka	L	1–2 (IYT)
†1987 11 May	Istanbul	W	2–0 (IYT)
†1968 25 Jan	Paris	L	0–1
1978 8 Feb	Crystal Palace	W	3–1 (IYT)*
1978 1 March	Paris	D	0–0 (IYT*)
†1979 2 June	Vienna	D	0–0 (IYT)
†1982 12 April	Cannes	L	0–1
†1983 2 April	Cannes	L	0–2
1984 1 March	Watford	W	4–0
†1984 23 April	Cannes	L	1–2
†1985 7 June	Toulon	L	1–3
†1986 31 March	Cannes	L	1–2
†1986 11 May	Peking	D	1–1
†1988 22 May	Monthey	L	1–2
†1988 15 Nov	Bradford	D	1–1 (IYT*)
†1989 11 Oct	Martigues	D	0–0 (IYT*)
†1990 22 May	Wembley	L	1–3

v East Germany

1958 7 April	Neunkirchen	W	1–0 (IYT)
1959 8 March	Zwickau	L	3–4
1960 2 April	Portsmouth	D	1–1
†1965 25 April	Essen	L	2–3 (IYT)
†1969 22 May	Magdeburg	L	0–4 (IYT)
†1973 10 June	Florence	W	3–2 (IYT)
†1984 25 May	Moscow	D	1–1 (IYT)
†1988 21 May	Monthey	W	1–0

West Germany

1953 4 April	Boom	W	3–1 (IYT)
1954 15 April	Gelsenkirchen	D	2–2 (IYT)
1956 1 April	Sztalinvaros	W	2–1 (IYT)
1957 31 March	Oberhausen	W	4–1
1958 12 March	Bolton	L	1–2
1961 12 March	Flensberg	L	0–2
†1962 31 March	Northampton	W	1–0
†1967 14 Feb	Möenchengladbach	W	1–0
†1972 22 May	Barcelona	W	2–0 (IYT)
†1975 25 Jan	Las Palmas	W	4–2
†1976 14 Nov	Monte Carlo	D	1–1
†1979 28 May	Salzburg	W	2–0 (IYT)
†1979 1 Sept	Pula	D	1–1
†1983 5 Sept	Pazin	W	2–0

v Greece

1957 18 April	Barcelona	L	2–3 (IYT)
1959 2 April	Dimitrovo	W	4–0 (IYT)
†1977 23 May	Beveren	D	1–1 (IYT)
†1983 28 June	Puspokladany	W	1–0
†1988 26 Oct	Birkenhead	W	5–0 (IYT*)
†1989 8 March	Xanthi	W	5–0 (IYT*)

v Holland

1948 17 April	Tottenham	W	3–2 (IYT)
1951 26 March	Cannes	W	2–1 (IYT)
†1954 21 Nov	Arnhem	L	2–3
†1955 5 Nov	Norwich	W	3–1
1957 2 March	Brentford	D	5–5
1957 14 April	Barcelona	L	1–2 (IYT)
1957 2 Oct	Amsterdam	W	3–2
1961 9 March	Utrecht	L	0–1
†1962 31 Jan	Brighton	W	4–3
†1962 22 April	Ploesti	L	0–3 (IYT)
†1963 13 April	Wimbledon	W	5–0 (IYT)
1968 9 April	Nimes	W	1–0 (IYT)
†1974 13 Feb	West Bromwich	D	1–1 (IYT*)
†1974 27 Feb	The Hague	W	1–0 (IYT*)
†1980 23 May	Halle	W	1–0 (IYT*)
†1982 9 April	Cannes	W	1–0

105

†1985	7 April	Cannes	L	1–3
†1987	1 Aug	Wembley	W	3–1

v Hungary

1954	11 April	Düsseldorf	L	1–3 (IYT)
1956	31 March	Tatabanya	L	2–4 (IYT)
†1956	23 Oct	Tottenham	W	2–1
†1956	25 Oct	Sunderland	W	2–1
†1965	21 April	Wuppertal	W	5–0 (IYT)
†1975	16 May	Olten	W	3–1 (IYT)
†1977	16 Oct	Las Palmas	W	3–0
†1979	5 Sept	Pula	W	2–0
†1980	11 Sept	Pula	L	1–2
†1981	7 Sept	Porec	W	4–0
†1983	29 July	Debrecen	L	1–2
†1983	3 Sept	Umag	W	3–2
†1986	30 March	Cannes	W	2–0

v Iceland

†1973	31 May	Viareggio	W	2–0 (IYT)
†1977	21 May	Turnhout	D	0–0 (IYT)
†1983	7 Sept	Reykjavik	W	3–0 (IYT*)
1983	19 Sept	Blackburn	W	4–0 (IYT*)
†1983	1 Nov	Crystal Palace	W	3–0 (IYT*)
†1984	16 Oct	Manchester	W	4–3 (IYT*)
†1985	11 Sept	Reykjavik	W	5–0 (IYT*)
†1990	12 Sept	Reykjavik	W	3–2 (IYT*)
†1991	12 Sept	Crystal Palace	W	2–1 (IYT*)

v Ireland

1948	15 May	Belfast	D	2–2
1949	18 April	Haarlem	D	3–3 (IYT)
1949	14 May	Hull	W	4–2
1950	6 May	Belfast	L	0–1
1951	5 May	Liverpool	W	5–2
1952	19 April	Belfast	L	0–2
1953	11 April	Wolverhampton	D	0–0
1954	10 April	Bruehl	W	5–0 (IYT)
1954	8 May	Newtonards	D	2–2
1955	14 May	Watford	W	3–0
1956	12 May	Belfast	D	0–1
1957	11 May	Leyton	W	6–2
1958	10 May	Bangor	L	2–4
1959	9 May	Liverpool	W	5–0
1960	14 May	Belfast	W	5–2
1961	13 May	Manchester	W	2–0
1962	12 May	Londonderry	L	1–2
†1963	23 April	Wembley	W	4–0 (IYT)
1963	11 May	Oldham	D	1–1
1964	25 Jan	Belfast	W	3–1
1965	22 Jan	Birkenhead	L	2–3
1966	26 Feb	Belfast	W	4–0
1967	25 Feb	Stockport	W	3–0
1968	23 Feb	Belfast	L	0–2
1969	28 Feb	Birkenhead	L	0–2
1970	28 Feb	Lurgan	L	1–3
1971	6 March	Blackpool	D	1–1 (IYT)
1972	11 March	Chester	D	1–1
1973	24 March	Wellington	W	3–0
1974	19 April	Birkenhead	L	1–2
†1975	13 May	Kriens	W	3–0 (IYT)
†1980	16 May	Amstadt	W	1–0 (IYT)
†1981	11 Feb	Walsall	W	1–0 (IYT*)
†1981	11 March	Belfast	W	3–0 (IYT*)

v Israel

†1962	20 May	Tel Aviv	W	3–1
†1962	22 May	Haifa	L	1–2

v Italy

1958	13 April	Luxembourg	L	0–1 (IYT)
1959	25 March	Sofia	L	1–3 (IYT)
1961	4 April	Braga	L	2–3 (IYT)
†1965	23 April	Marl-Huels	W	3–1 (IYT)
†1966	25 May	Rijeka	D	1–1 (IYT)
†1967	5 May	Izmir	W	1–0 (IYT)
†1973	14 Feb	Cava Dei Tirreni	L	0–1
†1973	14 March	Highbury	W	1–0
†1973	7 June	Viareggio	W	1–0 (IYT)
†1978	19 Nov	Monte Carlo	L	1–2
†1979	28 Feb	Rome	W	1–0 (IYT*)
†1979	4 April	Birmingham	W	2–0 (IYT*)
†1983	22 May	Watford	D	1–1 (IYT)
†1984	20 April	Cannes	W	1–0
†1985	5 April	Cannes	D	2–2

v Luxembourg

1950	25 May	Vienna	L	1–2 (IYT)
1954	17 April	Bad Neuenahr	L	0–2 (IYT)
1957	2 Feb	West Ham	W	7–1
1957	17 Nov	Luxembourg	W	3–0
1958	9 April	Esch Sur Alzette	W	5–0 (IYT)
†1984	29 May	Moscow	W	2–0 (IYT)

v Malta

†1969	18 May	Wolfen	W	6–0 (IYT)
†1979	26 May	Salzburg	W	3–0 (IYT)

v Mexico

†1984	18 April	Cannes	W	4–0
†1985	5 June	Toulon	W	2–0
†1985	29 Aug	Baku	L	0–1 (WYC)
†1991	27 March	Port of Spain	L	1–3

v Norway

†1982	13 July	Levanger	L	1–4
†1983	14 July	Korsor	W	1–0

v Paraguay

†1985	24 Aug	Baku	D	2–2 (WYC)

v Poland

1960	18 April	Graz	W	4–2 (IYT)
†1964	26 March	Breda	D	1–1 (IYT)
†1971	26 May	Presov	D	0–0 (IYT)
†1972	20 May	Valencia	W	1–0 (IYT)
†1975	21 Jan	Las Palmas	D	1–1
1978	9 May	Chorzow	L	0–2 (IYT)
†1979	3 Sept	Porec	L	0–1
†1980	25 May	Leipzig	W	2–1 (IYT)
†1982	17 July	Steinkver	W	3–2
†1983	12 July	Seagelse	W	1–0
†1990	15 May	Wembley	W	3–0
†1992	20 July	Regensburg	W	6–1 (IYT)

v Portugal

1954	18 April	Bonn	L	0–2 (IYT)
1961	2 April	Lisbon	L	0–4 (IYT)
1964	3 April	The Hague	W	4–0 (IYT)
†1971	30 May	Prague	W	3–0 (IYT)

Rod Wallace, being dragged here by an unfriendly hand, has been involved with England at Under-21, B and senior level

†1978 13 Nov	Monte Carlo		W	2–0
†1980 18 May	Rosslau		D	1–1 (IYT)
†1982 7 April	Cannes		W	3–0
†1992 22 July	Schweinfurt		L	1–1 (IYF)
(*aet*; Portugal won on pens)				

v Qatar

†1981 14 Oct	Sydney		L	1–2 (WYC)
†1983 4 April	Cannes		D	1–1

v Rep of Ireland

1953 5 April	Leuven		W	2–0 (IYT)
†1964 30 March	Middleburg		W	6–0 (IYT)
†1968 7 Feb	Dublin		D	0–0 (IYT*)
†1968 28 Feb	Portsmouth		W	4–1 (IYT*)
†1970 14 Jan	Dublin		W	4–1 (IYT*)
†1970 4 Feb	Luton		W	10–0 (IYT*)
†1972 15 May	Sabadell		W	4–0 (IYT)
†1975 9 May	Brunnen		W	1–0 (IYT)
†1985 26 Feb	Dublin		L	0–1 (IYT*)
†1986 25 Feb	Leeds		W	2–0 (IYT*)
†1988 17 Feb	Stoke		W	2–0
†1988 20 Sept	Dublin		W	2–0

v Romania

1957 15 Oct	Tottenham		W	4–2
1958 11 April	Luxembourg		W	1–0 (IYT)
1959 31 March	Pazardijc		L	1–2 (IYT)
†1963 15 April	Highbury		W	3–0 (IYT)
†1981 17 Oct	Adelaide		L	0–1 (WYC)

v Saar

1954 13 April	Dortmund		D	1–1 (IYT)
1955 9 April	Prato		W	3–1 (IYT)

v Scotland

1947 25 Oct	Doncaster		W	4–2
1948 30 Oct	Aberdeen		L	1–3
1949 21 April	Utrecht		L	0–1 (IYT)
1950 4 Feb	Carlisle		W	7–1
1951 3 Feb	Kilmarnock		W	6–1
1952 15 March	Sunderland		W	3–1
1953 7 Feb	Glasgow		W	4–3
1954 6 Feb	Middlesbrough		W	2–1
1955 5 March	Kilmarnock		L	3–4
1956 3 March	Preston		D	2–2
1957 9 March	Aberdeen		W	3–1
1958 1 March	Hull		W	2–0
1959 28 Feb	Aberdeen		D	1–1
1960 27 Feb	Newcastle		D	1–1
1961 25 Feb	Elgin		W	3–2
1962 24 Feb	Peterborough		W	4–2
†1963 19 April	White City		W	1–0 (IYT)
1963 18 May	Dumfries		W	3–1
1964 22 Feb	Middlesbrough		D	1–1
1965 27 Feb	Inverness		L	1–2
1966 5 Feb	Hereford		W	5–3
1967 4 Feb	Aberdeen		L	0–1
†1967 1 March	Southampton		W	1–0 (IYT*)
†1967 15 March	Dundee		D	0–0 (IYT*)
1968 3 Feb	Walsall		L	0–5
1969 1 Feb	Stranraer		D	1–1
1970 31 Jan	Derby		L	1–2
1971 30 Jan	Greenock		L	1–2
1972 29 Jan	Bournemouth		W	2–0
1973 20 Jan	Kilmarnock		W	3–2
1974 26 Jan	Brighton		D	2–2
†1981 27 May	Aachen		L	0–1 (IYT)
†1982 23 Feb	Glasgow		L	0–1 (IYT*)
†1982 23 March	Coventry		D	2–2 (IYT*)
†1983 15 May	Birmingham		W	4–2 (IYT)
1983 5 Oct	Middlesbrough		W	3–1
1983 19 Oct	Motherwell		W	4–0
†1984 27 Nov	Fulham		L	1–2 (IYT*)
1985 8 April	Cannes		W	1–0 (IYT*)
†1986 25 March	Aberdeen		L	1–4 (IYT*)

v Spain

1952 15 April	Barcelona		L	1–4 (IYT)
1957 26 Sept	Birmingham		D	4–4
1958 5 April	Saarbrücken		D	2–2 (IYT)
†1958 8 Oct	Madrid		W	4–2
1961 30 March	Lisbon		D	0–0 (IYT)
†1964 27 Feb	Murcia		W	2–1
†1964 5 April	Amsterdam		W	4–0 (IYT)
†1965 17 April	Heilbronn		D	0–0 (IYT)
†1966 30 March	Swindon		W	3–0
†1967 7 May	Manisa		W	2–1 (IYT)
†1971 31 March	Pamplona		L	2–3

107

†1971 20 April	Luton	D	1–1		
†1972 9 Feb	Alicante	D	0–0		
†1972 15 March	Sheffield	W	4–1 (IYT*)		
†1975 25 Feb	Bristol	D	1–1 (IYT*)		
†1975 18 March	Madrid	W	1–0 (IYT*)		
†1976 12 Nov	Monte Carlo	W	3–0		
†1978 7 May	Bukowas	W	1–0 (IYT)		
†1978 17 Nov	Monte Carlo	D	1–1		
†1981 25 May	Siegen	L	1–2 (IYT)		
†1983 13 May	Stoke	W	1–0 (IYT)		
†1990 29 July	Gyula	L	0–1 (IYT)		
†1991 25 May	Wembley	D	1–1		
†1991 15 June	Faro	L	0–1 (WYC)		

v Sweden

†1971 24 May	Poprad	W	1–0 (IYT)
†1981 5 Sept	Pazin	W	3–2
†1984 10 Sept	Rovinj	D	1–1
†1986 10 Nov	West Bromwich	D	3–3
†1988 19 May	Sion	W	2–0

v Switzerland

1950 26 May	Stockerau	W	2–1 (IYT)
1951 27 March	Nice	W	3–1 (IYT)
1952 13 April	Barcelona	W	4–0 (IYT)
1955 11 April	Florence	D	0–0 (IYT)
1956 11 March	Schaffhausen	W	2–0
1956 13 Oct	Brighton	D	2–2
1958 26 May	Zurich	W	3–0
†1960 8 Oct	Leyton	W	4–3
1962 22 Nov	Coventry	W	1–0 *
†1963 21 March	Bienne	W	7–1
1973 2 June	Forte Dei Marmi	W	2–0 (IYT)
†1975 11 May	Buochs	W	4–0 (IYT)
†1980 4 Sept	Rovinj	W	3–0
†1982 6 Sept	Porec	W	2–0
†1983 26 July	Hajduboszormeny	W	4–0
†1983 1 Sept	Porec	W	4–2

v Syria

†1991 18 June	Faro	D	3–3 (WYC)

v Thailand

†1986 7 May	Peking	L	1–2

v Trinidad & Tobago

†1991 25 March	Port of Spain	W	4–0

v Turkey

1959 29 March	Dimitrovo	D	1–1 (IYT)
†1978 5 May	Wodzislaw	D	1–1 (IYT)

v Uruguay

†1977 9 Oct	Las Palmas	D	1–1
†1987 10 June	Montevideo	D	2–2
†1991 20 June	Faro	D	0–0 (WYC)

v USSR

†1963 17 April	Tottenham	W	2–0 (IYT)
†1967 13 May	Istanbul	L	0–1 (IYT)
†1968 11 April	Nimes	D	1–1 (IYT)
†1971 28 May	Prague	D	1–1 (IYT)
†1978 10 Oct	Las Palmas	W	1–0
†1982 4 Sept	Umag	W	1–0
†1983 29 March	Cannes	D	0–0
†1983 17 May	Aston Villa	L	0–2 (IYT)
1984 3 May	Ludwigsburg	L	0–2
†1984 27 May	Moscow	D	1–1 (IYT)
†1984 8 Sept	Porec	W	1–0
†1985 3 April	Cannes	W	2–1
†1985 3 June	Toulon	L	0–2
†1990 26 July	Debrecen	L	1–3 (IYT)

v Wales

1948 28 Feb	High Wycombe	W	4–3
1948 15 April	London	W	4–0
1949 26 Feb	Swansea	D	0–0
1950 25 Feb	Worcester	W	1–0
1951 17 Feb	Wrexham	D	1–1
1952 23 Feb	Plymouth	W	6–0
1953 21 Feb	Swansea	W	4–2
1954 20 Feb	Derby	W	2–1
1955 19 Feb	Milford Haven	W	7–2
1956 18 Feb	Shrewsbury	W	5–1
1957 9 Feb	Cardiff	W	7–1
1958 15 Feb	Reading	W	8–2
1959 14 Feb	Portmadoc	W	3–0
1960 19 March	Canterbury	D	1–1
1961 18 March	Newtown	W	4–0
1962 17 March	Swindon	W	4–0
1963 16 March	Haverfordwest	W	1–0
1964 14 March	Leeds	W	2–1
1965 20 March	Newport	D	2–2
1966 19 March	Northampton	W	4–1
1967 18 March	Cwmbran	D	3–3
1968 16 March	Watford	L	2–3
1969 15 March	Haverfordwest	W	3–1
†1970 25 Feb	Newport	D	0–0 (IYT*)
†1970 18 March	Leyton	L	1–2
1970 20 April	Reading	D	0–0
1971 20 Feb	Aberystwyth	L	1–2
1972 19 Feb	Swindon	W	4–0
1973 24 Feb	Potmadoc	W	4–1
†1974 9 Jan	West Bromwich	W	1–0 (IYT*)
1974 2 March	Shrewsbury	W	2–1
†1974 13 March	Cardiff	L	0–1 (IYT*)
†1976 11 Feb	Cardiff	W	1–0 (IYT*)
†1976 3 March	Manchester	L	2–3 (IYT*)
†1977 9 March	West Bromwich	W	1–0 (IYT*)
†1977 23 March	Cardiff	D	1–1 (IYT*)
†1991 30 April	Wrexham	W	1–0 (IYT*)
†1991 22 May	Yeovil	W	3–0 (IYT*)

v Yugoslavia

1953 2 April	Liège	D	1–1 (IYT)
1958 4 Feb	Chelsea	D	2–2
1962 20 April	Ploesti	L	0–5 (IYT)
†1967 9 May	Izmir	D	1–1 (IYT)
†1971 22 May	Bardejor	W	1–0 (IYT)
†1972 17 May	Barcelona	W	1–0 (IYT)
†1976 16 Nov	Monte Carlo	L	0–3
†1978 20 May	Altenberg	W	2–0
†1981 10 Sept	Pula	W	5–0
†1982 9 Sept	Pula	W	1–0
†1983 25 July	Debrechen	D	4–4
†1983 8 Sept	Pula	D	2–2
1984 5 May	Boblingen	W	1–0
†1984 12 Sept	Buje	L	1–4

World Cup

Results 1930–1990

URUGUAY 1930

POOL 1
France 4, Mexico 1
Argentina 1, France 0
Chile 3, Mexico 0
Chile 1, France 0
Argentina 6, Mexico 3
Argentina 3, Chile 1

	P	W	D	L	F	A	Pts
Argentina	3	3	0	0	10	4	6
Chile	3	2	0	1	5	3	4
France	3	1	0	2	4	3	2
Mexico	3	0	0	3	4	13	0

POOL 2
Yugoslavia 2, Brazil 1
Yugoslavia 4, Bolivia 0
Brazil 4, Bolivia 0

	P	W	D	L	F	A	Pts
Yugoslavia	2	2	0	0	6	1	4
Brazil	2	1	0	1	5	2	2
Bolivia	2	0	0	2	0	8	0

POOL 3
Romania 3, Peru 1
Uruguay 1, Peru 0
Uruguay 4, Romania 0

	P	W	D	L	F	A	Pts
Uruguay	2	2	0	0	5	0	4
Romania	2	1	0	1	3	5	2
Peru	2	0	0	2	1	4	0

POOL 4
USA 3, Belgium 0
USA 3, Paraguay 0
Paraguay 1, Belgium 0

	P	W	D	L	F	A	Pts
USA	2	2	0	0	6	0	4
Paraguay	2	1	0	1	1	3	2
Belgium	2	0	0	2	0	4	0

SEMI-FINALS
Argentina 6, USA 1
Uruguay 6, Yugoslavia 1

FINAL
Uruguay 4 *(Dorado, Cea, Iriarte, Castro)*, **Argentina 2** *(Peucelle, Stabile) (Montevideo, 30 July, 1930. Att: 90,000)*

Uruguay: Ballesteros; Nasazzi, Mascheroni, Andrade, Fernandez, Gestido, Dorado, Scarone, Castro, Cea, Iriarte.

Argentina: Botasso; Della Torre, Paternoster, Evaristo J, Monti, Suarez, Peucelle, Varallo, Stabile, Ferreira, Evaristo M.

Ref: Langenus (Belgium)

ITALY 1934

FIRST ROUND
Italy 7, USA 1
Czechoslovakia 2, Romania 1
Germany 5, Belgium 2
Austria 3, France 2
Spain 3, Brazil 1
Switzerland 3, Holland 2
Sweden 3, Argentina 2
Hungary 4, Egypt 2

SECOND ROUND
Germany 2, Sweden 1
Austria 2, Hungary 1
Italy 1, Spain 1 *(Replay:* Italy 1, Spain 0*)*
Czechoslovakia 3, Switzerland 2

SEMI-FINALS
Czechoslovakia 3, Germany 1 *(Rome)*
Italy 1, Austria 0 *(Milan)*

THIRD PLACE MATCH
Germany 3, Austria 2 *(Naples)*

FINAL
Italy 2 *(Orsi, Schiavio)*, **Czechoslovakia 1** *(Puc) (aet; 1–1 at 90 mins) (Rome, 10 June, 1934. Att: 50,000)*

Italy: Combi; Monzeglio, Allemandi, Ferraris, Monti, Bertolini, Guaita, Meazza, Schiavio, Ferrari, Orsi.

Czechoslovakia: Planicka; Zenisek, Ctyroky, Kostalek, Cambal, Krcil, Junek, Svoboda, Sobotka, Nejedly, Puc.

Ref: Eklind (Sweden)

FRANCE 1938

FIRST ROUND
Switzerland 1, Germany 1 *(Replay:* Switzerland 4, Germany 2*)*
Cuba 3, Romania 3 *(Replay:* Cuba 2, Romania 1*)*
Hungary 6, Dutch East Indies 0
France 3, Belgium 1
Czechoslovakia 3, Holland 0
Brazil 6, Poland 5
Italy 2, Norway 1

SECOND ROUND
Sweden 8, Cuba 0
Hungary 2, Switzerland 0
Italy 3, France 1
Brazil 1, Czechoslovakia 1 *(Replay:* Brazil 2, Czechoslovakia 1*)*

109

SEMI-FINALS
Italy 2, Brazil 1 *(Marseilles)*
Hungary 5, Sweden 1 *(Paris)*

THIRD PLACE MATCH
Brazil 4, Sweden 2 *(Bordeaux)*

FINAL
Italy 4 *(Colaussi 2, Piola 2)*, **Hungary 2** *(Titkos, Sarosi)* *(Paris, 19 June, 1938. Att: 45,000)*

Italy: Olivieri; Foni, Rava, Serantoni, Andreolo, Locatelli, Biavati, Meazza, Piola, Ferrari, Colaussi.

Hungary: Szabo; Polgar, Biro, Szalay, Szucs, Lazar, Sas, Vincze, Sarosi, Szengeller, Titkos.

Ref: Capdeville (France)

BRAZIL 1950
POOL 1
Brazil 4, Mexico 0
Yugoslavia 3, Switzerland 0
Yugoslavia 4, Mexico 1
Brazil 2, Switzerland 2
Brazil 2, Yugoslavia 0
Switzerland 2, Mexico 1

	P	W	D	L	F	A	Pts
Brazil	3	2	1	0	8	2	5
Yugoslavia	3	2	0	1	7	3	4
Switzerland	3	1	1	1	4	6	3
Mexico	3	0	0	3	2	10	0

POOL 2
Spain 3, USA 1
England 2, Chile 0
USA 1, England 0
Spain 2, Chile 0
Spain 1, England 0
Chile 5, USA 2

	P	W	D	L	F	A	Pts
Spain	3	3	0	0	6	1	6
England	3	1	0	2	2	2	2
Chile	3	1	0	2	5	6	2
USA	3	1	0	2	4	8	2

POOL 3
Sweden 3, Italy 2
Sweden 2, Paraguay 2
Italy 2, Paraguay 0

	P	W	D	L	F	A	Pts
Sweden	2	1	1	0	5	4	3
Italy	2	1	0	1	4	3	2
Paraguay	2	0	1	1	2	4	1

POOL 4
Uruguay 8, Bolivia 0

FINAL POOL
Uruguay 2, Spain 2
Brazil 7, Sweden 1
Uruguay 3, Sweden 2
Brazil 6, Spain 1
Sweden 3, Spain 1

	P	W	D	L	F	A	Pts
Uruguay	3	2	1	0	7	5	5
Brazil	3	2	0	1	14	4	4
Sweden	3	1	0	2	6	11	2
Spain	3	0	1	2	4	11	1

FINAL
Uruguay 2 *(Schiaffino, Ghiggia)*, **Brazil 1** *(Friaca)* *(Rio de Janeiro, 16 July, 1950. Att: 199,854)*

Uruguay: Maspoli; Matthias Gonzales, Tejera, Gambetta, Varela, Andrade, Ghiggia, Perez, Miguez, Schiaffino, Moran.

Brazil: Barbosa; Augusto, Juvenal, Bauer, Danilo, Bigode, Friaca, Zizinho, Ademir, Jair, Chico.

Ref: Reader (England)

SWITZERLAND 1954
GROUP 1
Yugoslavia 1, France 0
Brazil 5, Mexico 0
France 3, Mexico 2
Brazil 1, Yugoslavia 1

	P	W	D	L	F	A	Pts
Brazil	2	1	1	0	6	1	3
Yugoslavia	2	1	1	0	2	1	3
France	2	1	0	1	3	3	2
Mexico	2	0	0	2	2	8	0

GROUP 2
Hungary 9, Korea 0
West Germany 4, Turkey 1
Hungary 8, West Germany 3
Turkey 7, Korea 0

	P	W	D	L	F	A	Pts
Hungary	2	2	0	0	17	3	4
West Germany	2	1	0	1	7	9	2
Turkey	2	1	0	1	8	4	2
Korea	2	0	0	2	0	16	0

Play off: West Germany 7, Turkey 2

GROUP 3
Austria 1, Scotland 0
Uruguay 2, Czechoslovakia 0
Austria 5, Czechoslovakia 0
Uruguay 7, Scotland 0

	P	W	D	L	F	A	Pts
Uruguay	2	2	0	0	9	0	4
Austria	2	2	0	0	6	0	4
Czechoslovakia	2	0	0	2	0	7	0
Scotland	2	0	0	2	0	8	0

GROUP 4
England 4, Belgium 4
England 2, Switzerland 0
Switzerland 2, Italy 1
Italy 4, Belgium 1
Play off: Switzerland 4, Italy 1

	P	W	D	L	F	A	Pts
England	2	1	1	0	6	4	3
Italy	2	1	0	1	5	3	2
Switzerland	2	1	0	1	2	3	2
Belgium	2	0	1	1	5	8	1

QUARTER-FINALS
West Germany 2, Yugoslavia 0
Hungary 4, Brazil 2
Austria 7, Switzerland 5
Uruguay 4, England 2

SEMI-FINALS
West Germany 6, Austria 1 *(Basle)*
Hungary 4, Uruguay 2 *(Lausanne)*

THIRD PLACE MATCH
Austria 3, Uruguay 1 *(Zurich)*

FINAL
West Germany 3 *(Morlock, Rahn 2)*, **Hungary 2** *(Puskas, Czibor) (Berne, 4 July, 1954. Att: 60,000)*

West Germany: Turek; Posipal, Kohlmeyer, Eckel, Liebrich, Mai, Rahn, Morlock, Walter O, Walter F, Schaefer.

Hungary: Grosics; Buzanszky, Lantos, Bozsik, Lorant, Zakarias, Czibor, Kocsis, Hidegkuti, Puskas, Toth J.

Ref: Ling (England)

SWEDEN 1958

GROUP 1
West Germany 3, Argentina 1
Northern Ireland 1, Czechoslovakia 0
West Germany 2, Czechoslovakia 2
Argentina 3, Northern Ireland 1
West Germany 2, Northern Ireland 2
Czechoslovakia 6, Argentina 1
Play off: Northern Ireland 2, Czechoslovakia 1

	P	W	D	L	F	A	Pts
West Germany	3	1	2	0	7	5	4
Czechoslovakia	3	1	1	1	8	4	3
Northern Ireland	3	1	1	1	4	5	3
Argentina	3	1	0	2	5	10	2

GROUP 2
France 7, Paraguay 3
Yugoslavia 1, Scotland 1
Yugoslavia 3, France 2
Paraguay 3, Scotland 2
France 2, Scotland 1
Yugoslavia 3, Paraguay 3

	P	W	D	L	F	A	Pts
France	3	2	0	1	11	7	4
Yugoslavia	3	1	2	0	7	6	4
Paraguay	3	1	1	1	9	12	3
Scotland	3	0	1	2	4	6	1

GROUP 3
Sweden 3, Mexico 0
Hungary 1, Wales 1
Wales 1, Mexico 1
Sweden 2, Hungary 1
Sweden 0, Wales 0
Hungary 4, Mexico 0
Play off: Wales 2, Hungary 1

	P	W	D	L	F	A	Pts
Sweden	3	2	1	0	5	1	5
Hungary	3	1	1	1	6	3	3
Wales	3	0	3	0	2	2	3
Mexico	3	0	1	2	1	8	1

GROUP 4
England 2, USSR 2
Brazil 3, Austria 0
Brazil 0, England 0
USSR 2, Austria 0
Brazil 2, USSR 0
England 2, Austria 2
Play off: USSR 1, England 0

	P	W	D	L	F	A	Pts
Brazil	3	2	1	0	5	0	5
England	3	0	3	0	4	4	3
USSR	3	1	1	1	4	4	3
Austria	3	0	1	2	2	7	1

QUARTER-FINALS
France 4, Northern Ireland 0
West Germany 1, Yugoslavia 0
Sweden 2, USSR 0
Brazil 1, Wales 0

SEMI-FINALS
Brazil 5, France 2 *(Stockholm)*
Sweden 3, West Germany 1 *(Gothenburg)*

THIRD PLACE MATCH
France 6, West Germany 3 *(Gothenburg)*

FINAL
Brazil 5 *(Vavà 2, Pelé 2, Zagalo)*, **Sweden 2** *(Liedholm, Simonsson) (Stockholm, 29 June, 1958. Att: 49,737)*

Brazil: Gilmar; Santos D, Santos N, Zito, Bellini, Orlando, Garrincha, Didi, Vavà, Pelé, Zagalo.

Sweden: Svensson; Bergmark, Axbom, Boerjesson, Gustavsson, Parling, Hamrin, Gren, Simonsson, Liedholm, Skoglund.

Ref: Guigue (France)

CHILE 1962

GROUP 1
Uruguay 2, Colombia 1
USSR 2, Yugoslavia 0
Yugoslavia 3, Uruguay 1
USSR 4, Colombia 4
USSR 2, Uruguay 1
Yugoslavia 5, Colombia 0

	P	W	D	L	F	A	Pts
USSR	3	2	1	0	8	5	5
Yugoslavia	3	2	0	1	8	3	4
Uruguay	3	1	0	2	4	6	2
Colombia	3	0	1	2	5	11	1

GROUP 2
Chile 3, Switzerland 1
West Germany 0, Italy 0
Chile 2, Italy 0
West Germany 2, Switzerland 1
West Germany 2, Chile 0
Italy 3, Switzerland 0

	P	W	D	L	F	A	Pts
West Germany	3	2	1	0	4	1	5
Chile	3	2	0	1	5	3	4
Italy	3	1	1	1	3	2	3
Switzerland	3	0	0	3	2	8	0

GROUP 3
Brazil 2, Mexico 0
Czechoslovakia 1, Spain 0
Brazil 0, Czechoslovakia 0
Spain 1, Mexico 0
Brazil 2, Spain 1
Mexico 3, Czechoslovakia 1

	P	W	D	L	F	A	Pts
Brazil	3	2	1	0	4	1	5
Czechoslovakia	3	1	1	1	2	3	3
Mexico	3	1	0	2	3	4	2
Spain	3	1	0	2	2	3	2

GROUP 4

Argentina 1, Bulgaria 0
Hungary 2, England 1
England 3, Argentina 1
Hungary 6, Bulgaria 1
Argentina 0, Hungary 0
England 0, Bulgaria 0

	P	W	D	L	F	A	Pts
Hungary	3	2	1	0	8	2	5
England	3	1	1	1	4	3	3
Argentina	3	1	1	1	2	3	3
Bulgaria	3	0	1	2	1	7	1

QUARTER-FINALS

Yugoslavia 1, West Germany 0
Brazil 3, England 1
Chile 2, USSR 1
Czechoslovakia 1, Hungary 0

SEMI-FINALS

Brazil 4, Chile 2 *(Santiago)*
Czechoslovakia 3, Yugoslavia 1 *(Vina del Mar)*

THIRD PLACE MATCH

Chile 1, Yugoslavia 0 *(Santiago)*

FINAL

Brazil 3 *(Amarildo, Zito, Vavà)*, **Czechoslovakia 1** *(Masopust)* *(Santiago, 17 June, 1962. Att: 68,789)*

Brazil: Gilmar; D Santos, Mauro, Zozimo, N Santos, Zito, Didi, Garrincha, Vavà, Amarildo, Zagalo.

Czechoslovakia: Schroiff; Tichy, Novak, Pluskal, Popluhar, Masopust, Pospichal, Scherer, Kvasniak, Kadraba, Jelinek.

Ref: Latychev (USSR)

ENGLAND 1966

GROUP 1

England 0, Uruguay 0
France 1, Mexico 1
Uruguay 2, France 1
England 2, Mexico 0
Uruguay 0, Mexico 0
England 2, France 0

	P	W	D	L	F	A	Pts
England	3	2	1	0	4	0	5
Uruguay	3	1	2	0	2	1	4
Mexico	3	0	2	1	1	3	2
France	3	0	1	2	2	5	1

GROUP 2

West Germany 5, Switzerland 0
Argentina 2, Spain 1
Spain 2, Switzerland 1
Argentina 0, West Germany 0
Argentina 2, Switzerland 0
West Germany 2, Spain 1

	P	W	D	L	F	A	Pts
West Germany	3	2	1	0	7	1	5
Argentina	3	2	1	0	4	1	5
Spain	3	1	0	2	4	5	2
Switzerland	3	0	0	3	1	9	0

GROUP 3

Brazil 2, Bulgaria 0
Portugal 3, Hungary 1
Hungary 3, Brazil 1
Portugal 3, Bulgaria 0
Portugal 3, Brazil 1
Hungary 3, Bulgaria 1

	P	W	D	L	F	A	Pts
Portugal	3	3	0	0	9	2	6
Hungary	3	2	0	1	7	5	4
Brazil	3	1	0	2	4	6	2
Bulgaria	3	0	0	3	1	8	0

GROUP 4

USSR 3, North Korea 0
Italy 2, Chile 0
Chile 1, North Korea 1
USSR 1, Italy 0
North Korea 1, Italy 0
USSR 2, Chile 1

	P	W	D	L	F	A	Pts
USSR	3	3	0	0	6	1	6
North Korea	3	1	1	1	2	4	3
Italy	3	1	0	2	2	2	2
Chile	3	0	1	2	2	5	1

QUARTER-FINALS

England 1, Argentina 0
West Germany 4, Uruguay 0
Portugal 5, North Korea 3
USSR 2, Hungary 1

SEMI-FINALS

West Germany 2, USSR 1 *(Goodison Park)*
England 2, Portugal 1 *(Wembley)*

THIRD PLACE MATCH

Portugal 2, USSR 1 *(Wembley)*

FINAL

England 4 *(Hurst 3, Peters)*, **West Germany 2** *(Haller, Weber)* *(aet; 2–2 at 90 mins)* (Wembley, 30 July, 1966. Att: 93,802)

England: Banks; Cohen, Wilson, Stiles, Charlton J, Moore, Ball, Hurst, Hunt, Charlton R, Peters.

West Germany: Tilkowski; Höttges, Schulz, Weber, Schnellinger, Haller, Beckenbauer, Overath, Seeler, Held, Emmerich.

Ref: Dienst (Switzerland)

MEXICO 1970

GROUP A
Mexico 0, USSR 0
Belgium 3, El Salvador 0
USSR 4, Belgium 1
Mexico 4, El Salvador 0
USSR 2, El Salvador 0
Belgium 0, Mexico 1

	P	W	D	L	F	A	Pts
USSR	3	2	1	0	6	1	5
Mexico	3	2	1	0	5	0	5
Belgium	3	1	0	2	4	5	2
El Salvador	3	0	0	3	0	9	0

GROUP B
Uruguay 2, Israel 0
Italy 1, Sweden 0
Uruguay 0, Italy 0
Israel 1, Sweden 1
Sweden 1, Uruguay 0
Israel 0, Italy 0

	P	W	D	L	F	A	Pts
Italy	3	1	2	0	1	0	4
Uruguay	3	1	1	1	2	1	3
Sweden	3	1	1	1	2	2	3
Israel	3	0	2	1	1	3	2

GROUP C
England 1, Romania 0
Brazil 4, Czechoslovakia 1
Romania 1, Czechoslovakia 1
Brazil 1, England 0
Brazil 3, Romania 2
England 1, Czechoslovakia 0

	P	W	D	L	F	A	Pts
Brazil	3	3	0	0	8	3	6
England	3	2	0	1	2	1	4
Romania	3	1	0	2	4	5	2
Czechoslovakia	3	0	0	3	2	7	0

GROUP D
Peru 3, Bulgaria 2
West Germany 2, Morocco 1
Peru 3, Morocco 0
West Germany 5, Bulgaria 2
West Germany 3, Peru 1,
Bulgaria 1, Morocco 1

	P	W	D	L	F	A	Pts
West Germany	3	3	0	0	10	4	6
Peru	3	2	0	1	7	5	4
Bulgaria	3	0	1	2	5	9	1
Morocco	3	0	1	2	2	6	1

QUARTER-FINALS
Uruguay 1, USSR 0
Italy 4, Mexico 1
Brazil 4, Peru 2
West Germany 3, England 2

SEMI-FINALS
Italy 4, West Germany 3 *(Mexico City)*
 (aet; 1–1 at 90 mins)
Brazil 3, Uruguay 1 *(Guadalajara)*

THIRD PLACE MATCH
West Germany 1, Uruguay 0 *(Mexico City)*

FINAL
Brazil 4 *(Pelé, Gerson, Jairzinho, Carlos Alberto)*, **Italy 1** *(Boninsegna)* (Mexico City, 21 June, 1970. Att: 107,412)

Brazil: Felix; Carlos Alberto, Brito, Piazza, Everaldo, Gerson, Clodoaldo, Jairzinho, Pelé, Tostao, Rivelino.

Italy: Albertosi; Burgnich, Cera, Rosato, Facchetti, Bertini (Juliano), Riva, Domenghini, Mazzola, De Sisti, Boninsegna (Rivera).

Ref: Glockner (East Germany)

WEST GERMANY 1974

GROUP 1
West Germany 1, Chile 0
East Germany 2, Australia 0
West Germany 3, Australia 0
East Germany 1, Chile 1
East Germany 1, West Germany 0
Chile 0, Australia 0

	P	W	D	L	F	A	Pts
East Germany	3	2	1	0	4	1	5
West Germany	3	2	0	1	4	1	4
Chile	3	0	2	1	1	2	2
Australia	3	0	1	2	0	5	1

GROUP 2
Brazil 0, Yugoslavia 0
Scotland 2, Zaire 0
Brazil 0, Scotland 0
Yugoslavia 9, Zaire 0
Scotland 1, Yugoslavia 1
Brazil 3, Zaire 0

	P	W	D	L	F	A	Pts
Yugoslavia	3	1	2	0	10	1	4
Brazil	3	1	2	0	3	0	4
Scotland	3	1	2	0	3	1	4
Zaire	3	0	0	3	0	14	0

GROUP 3
Holland 2, Uruguay 0
Sweden 0, Bulgaria 0
Holland 0, Sweden 0
Bulgaria 1, Uruguay 1
Holland 4, Bulgaria 1
Sweden 3, Uruguay 0

	P	W	D	L	F	A	Pts
Holland	3	2	1	0	6	1	5
Sweden	3	1	2	0	3	0	4
Bulgaria	3	0	2	1	2	5	2
Uruguay	3	0	1	2	1	6	1

GROUP 4
Italy 3, Haiti 1
Poland 3, Argentina 2
Argentina 1, Italy 1
Poland 7, Haiti 0
Argentina 4, Haiti 1
Poland 2, Italy 1

	P	W	D	L	F	A	Pts
Poland	3	3	0	0	12	3	6
Argentina	3	1	1	1	7	5	3
Italy	3	1	1	1	5	4	3
Haiti	3	0	0	3	2	14	0

SECOND ROUND

GROUP A
Brazil 1, East Germany 0
Holland 4, Argentina 0
Holland 2, East Germany 0
Brazil 2, Argentina 1
Holland 2, Brazil 0
Argentina 1, East Germany 1

113

	P	W	D	L	F	A	Pts
Holland	3	3	0	0	8	0	6
Brazil	3	2	0	1	3	3	4
East Germany	3	0	1	2	1	4	1
Argentina	3	0	1	2	2	7	1

GROUP B

Poland 1, Sweden 0
West Germany 2, Yugoslavia 0
Poland 2, Yugoslavia 1
West Germany 4, Sweden 2
Sweden 2, Yugoslavia 1
West Germany 1, Poland 0

	P	W	D	L	F	A	Pts
West Germany	3	3	0	0	7	2	6
Poland	3	2	0	1	3	2	4
Sweden	3	1	0	2	4	6	2
Yugoslavia	3	0	0	3	2	6	0

THIRD PLACE MATCH

Poland 1, Brazil 0 *(Munich)*

FINAL

West Germany 2 *(Breitner pen, Müller)*, **Holland 1** *(Neeskens pen)* *(Munich, 7 July, 1974. Att: 77,833)*

West Germany: Maier; Vogts, Schwarzenbeck, Beckenbauer, Breitner, Bonhof, Hoeness, Overath, Grabowski, Muller, Holzenbein.

Holland: Jongbloed; Suurbier, Rijsbergen (De Jong), Haan, Krol, Jansen, Van Hanegem, Neeskens, Rep, Cruyff, Rensenbrink,(van der Kerkhof R).

Ref: Taylor (England)

ARGENTINA 1978

GROUP 1

Italy 2, France 1
Argentina 2, Hungary 1
Italy 3, Hungary 1
Argentina 2, France 1
France 3, Hungary 1
Italy 1, Argentina 0

	P	W	D	L	F	A	Pts
Italy	3	3	0	0	6	2	6
Argentina	3	2	0	1	4	3	4
France	3	1	0	2	5	5	2
Hungary	3	0	0	3	3	8	0

GROUP 2

West Germany 0, Poland 0
Tunisia 3, Mexico 1
Poland 1, Tunisia 0
West Germany 6, Mexico 0
Poland 3, Mexico 1
West Germany 0, Tunisia 0

	P	W	D	L	F	A	Pts
Poland	3	2	1	0	4	1	5
West Germany	3	1	2	0	6	0	4
Tunisia	3	1	1	1	3	2	3
Mexico	3	0	0	3	2	12	0

GROUP 3

Austria 2, Spain 1
Brazil 1, Sweden 1
Austria 1, Sweden 0
Brazil 0, Spain 0
Spain 1, Sweden 0
Brazil 1, Austria 0

	P	W	D	L	F	A	Pts
Austria	3	2	0	1	3	2	4
Brazil	3	1	2	0	2	1	4
Spain	3	1	1	1	2	2	3
Sweden	3	0	1	2	1	3	1

GROUP 4

Peru 3, Scotland 1
Holland 3, Iran 0
Scotland 1, Iran 1
Holland 0, Peru 0
Peru 4, Iran 1
Scotland 3, Holland 2

	P	W	D	L	F	A	Pts
Peru	3	2	1	0	7	2	5
Holland	3	1	1	1	5	3	3
Scotland	3	1	1	1	5	6	3
Iran	3	0	1	2	2	8	1

SECOND ROUND

GROUP A

West Germany 0, Italy 0
Holland 5, Austria 1
Italy 1, Austria 0
Holland 2, West Germany 2
Holland 2, Italy 1
Austria 3, West Germany 2

	P	W	D	L	F	A	Pts
Holland	3	2	1	0	9	4	5
Italy	3	1	1	1	2	2	3
West Germany	3	0	2	1	4	5	2
Austria	3	1	0	2	4	8	2

GROUP B

Brazil 3, Peru 0
Argentina 2, Poland 0
Poland 1, Peru 0
Argentina 0, Brazil 0
Brazil 3, Poland 1
Argentina 6, Peru 0

	P	W	D	L	F	A	Pts
Argentina	3	2	1	0	8	0	5
Brazil	3	2	1	0	6	1	5
Poland	3	1	0	2	2	5	2
Peru	3	0	0	3	0	10	0

THIRD PLACE MATCH

Brazil 2, Italy 1 *(Buenos Aires)*

Glenn Hoddle shows the style that made him one of England's most respected players, admired for his smooth skills at the highest levels of the game

FINAL

Argentina 3 *(Kempes 2, Bertoni)*, **Holland 1** *(Nanninga)* *(aet; 1–1 at 90 mins) (Buenos Aires, 25 June, 1978. Att: 77,000)*

Argentina: Fillol; Olguin, Galvan L, Passarella, Tarantini, Ardiles (Larrosa), Gallego, Ortiz (Houseman), Bertoni, Luque, Kempes.

Holland: Jongbloed; Krol, Bortvliet, Brandts, Jansen (Suurbier), Neeskens, Haan, van der Kerkhof W, Rep (Nanninga), van der Kerkhof R, Rensenbrink.

Ref: Gonella (Italy)

SPAIN 1982

GROUP 1
Italy 0, Poland 0
Peru 0, Cameroon 0
Italy 1, Peru 1
Poland 0, Cameroon 0
Poland 5, Peru 1
Italy 1, Cameroon 1

	P	W	D	L	F	A	Pts
Poland	3	1	2	0	5	1	4
Italy	3	0	3	0	2	2	3
Cameroon	3	0	3	0	1	1	3
Peru	3	0	2	1	2	6	2

GROUP 2
Algeria 2, West Germany 1
Austria 1, Chile 0
West Germany 4, Chile 1
Austria 2, Algeria 0
Algeria 3, Chile 2
West Germany 1, Austria 0

	P	W	D	L	F	A	Pts
West Germany	3	2	0	1	6	3	4
Austria	3	2	0	1	3	1	4
Algeria	3	2	0	1	5	5	4
Chile	3	0	0	3	3	8	0

GROUP 3
Belgium 1, Argentina 0
Hungary 10, El Salvador 1
Argentina 4, Hungary 1
Belgium 1, El Salvador 0
Belgium 1, Hungary 1
Argentina 2, El Salvador 0

	P	W	D	L	F	A	Pts
Belgium	3	2	1	0	3	1	5
Argentina	3	2	0	1	6	2	4
Hungary	3	1	1	1	12	6	3
El Salvador	3	0	0	3	1	13	0

GROUP 4

England 3, France 1
Czechoslovakia 1, Kuwait 1
England 2, Czechoslovakia 0
France 4, Kuwait 1
France 1, Czechoslovakia 1
England 1, Kuwait 0

	P	W	D	L	F	A	Pts
England	3	3	0	0	6	1	6
France	3	1	1	1	6	5	3
Czechoslovakia	3	0	2	1	2	4	2
Kuwait	3	0	1	2	2	6	1

GROUP 5

Spain 1, Honduras 1
Northern Ireland 0, Yugoslavia 0
Spain 2, Yugoslavia 1
Honduras 1, Northern Ireland 1
Yugoslavia 1, Honduras 0
Northern Ireland 1, Spain 0

	P	W	D	L	F	A	Pts
Northern Ireland	3	1	2	0	2	1	4
Spain	3	1	1	1	3	3	3
Yugoslavia	3	1	1	1	2	2	3
Honduras	3	0	2	1	2	3	2

GROUP 6

Brazil 2, USSR 1
Scotland 5, New Zealand 2
Brazil 4, Scotland 1
USSR 3, New Zealand 0
Scotland 2, USSR 2
Brazil 4, New Zealand 0

	P	W	D	L	F	A	Pts
Brazil	3	3	0	0	10	2	6
USSR	3	1	1	1	6	4	3
Scotland	3	1	1	1	8	8	3
New Zealand	3	0	0	3	2	12	0

SECOND ROUND

GROUP A

Poland 3, Belgium 0
USSR 1, Belgium 0
Poland 0, USSR 0

	P	W	D	L	F	A	Pts
Poland	2	1	1	0	3	0	3
USSR	2	1	1	0	1	0	3
Belgium	2	0	0	2	0	4	0

GROUP B

West Germany 0, England 0
West Germany 2, Spain 1
Spain 0, England 0

	P	W	D	L	F	A	Pts
West Germany	2	1	1	0	2	1	3
England	2	0	2	0	0	0	2
Spain	2	0	1	1	1	2	1

GROUP C

Italy 2, Argentina 1
Brazil 3, Argentina 1
Italy 3, Brazil 2

	P	W	D	L	F	A	Pts
Italy	2	2	0	0	5	3	4
Brazil	2	1	0	1	5	4	2
Argentina	2	0	0	2	2	5	0

GROUP D

France 1, Austria 0
Northern Ireland 2, Austria 2
France 4, Northern Ireland 1

	P	W	D	L	F	A	Pts
France	2	2	0	0	5	1	4
Austria	2	0	1	1	2	3	1
Northern Ireland	2	0	1	1	3	6	1

SEMI-FINALS

Italy 2, Poland 0 *(Barcelona)*
West Germany 3, France 3 *(Seville)* *(aet; 1–1 at 90 mins, West Germany won 5–4 on pens)*

THIRD PLACE MATCH

Poland 3, France 2 *(Alicante)*

FINAL

Italy 3 *(Rossi, Tardelli, Altobelli)*, **West Germany 1** *(Breitner) (Madrid, 11 July, 1982. Att: 90,080)*

Italy: Zoff; Bergomi, Cabrini, Collovati, Scirea, Gentile, Oriali, Tardelli, Conti, Graziani (Altobelli) (Causio), Rossi.

West Germany: Schumacher; Kaltz, Förster K H, Stielike, Förster B, Breitner, Dremmler (Hrubesch), Littbarski, Briegel, Rummenigge (Müller), Fischer.

Ref: Coelho (Brazil)

MEXICO 1986

GROUP A

Bulgaria 1, Italy 1
Argentina 3, South Korea 1
Italy 1, Argentina 1
South Korea 1, Bulgaria 1
Argentina 2, Bulgaria 0
South Korea 2, Italy 3

	P	W	D	L	F	A	Pts
Argentina	3	2	1	0	6	2	5
Italy	3	1	2	0	5	4	4
Bulgaria	3	0	2	1	2	4	2
South Korea	3	0	1	2	4	7	1

GROUP B

Belgium 1, Mexico 2
Paraguay 1, Iraq 0
Mexico 1, Paraguay 1
Iraq 1, Belgium 2
Paraguay 2, Belgium 2
Iraq 0, Mexico 1

	P	W	D	L	F	A	Pts
Mexico	3	2	1	0	4	2	5
Paraguay	3	1	2	0	4	3	4
Belgium	3	1	1	1	5	5	3
Iraq	3	0	0	3	1	4	0

GROUP C

USSR 6, Hungary 0
Canada 0, France 1
France 1, USSR 1
Hungary 2, Canada 0
Hungary 0, France 3
USSR 2, Canada 0

	P	W	D	L	F	A	Pts
USSR	3	2	1	0	9	1	5
France	3	2	1	0	5	1	5
Hungary	3	1	0	2	2	9	2
Canada	3	0	0	3	0	5	0

GROUP D

Spain 0, Brazil 1
Algeria 1, Northern Ireland 1
Northern Ireland 1, Spain 2
Brazil 1, Algeria 0
Algeria 0, Spain 3
Northern Ireland 0, Brazil 3

	P	W	D	L	F	A	Pts
Brazil	3	3	0	0	5	0	6
Spain	3	2	0	1	5	2	4
Northern Ireland	3	0	1	2	2	6	1
Algeria	3	0	1	2	1	5	1

GROUP E

Uruguay 1, West Germany 1
Scotland 0, Denmark 1
Denmark 6, Uruguay 1
West Germany 2, Scotland 1
Scotland 0, Uruguay 0
Denmark 2, West Germany 0

	P	W	D	L	F	A	Pts
Denmark	3	3	0	0	9	1	6
West Germany	3	1	1	1	3	4	3
Uruguay	3	0	2	1	2	7	2
Scotland	3	0	1	2	1	3	1

GROUP F

Morocco 0, Poland 0
Portugal 1, England 0
England 0, Morocco 0
Poland 1, Portugal 0
England 3, Poland 0
Portugal 1, Morocco 3

	P	W	D	L	F	A	Pts
Morocco	3	1	2	0	3	1	4
England	3	1	1	1	3	1	3
Poland	3	1	1	1	1	3	3
Portugal	3	1	0	2	2	4	2

SECOND ROUND

Mexico 2, Bulgaria 0
USSR 3, Belgium 4 (*aet*; 2–2 at 90 mins)
Brazil 4, Poland 0
Argentina 1, Uruguay 0
France 2, Italy 0
Morocco 0, West Germany 1
England 3, Paraguay 0
Denmark 1, Spain 5

QUARTER-FINALS

Brazil 1, France 1 (*aet*; 1–1 at 90 mins, France won 4–3 on pens)
West Germany 0, Mexico 0 (*aet*; West Germany won 4–1 on pens)
Argentina 2, England 1
Spain 1, Belgium 1 (*aet*; 1–1 at 90 mins, Belgium won 5–4 on pens)

SEMI-FINALS

Argentina 2, Belgium 0 *(Mexico City)*
France 0, West Germany 2 *(Guadalajara)*

THIRD PLACE MATCH

France 4, Belgium 2 *(Puebla)*

FINAL

Argentina 3 *(Brown, Valdano, Burruchaga)*, **West Germany 2** *(Rummenigge, Völler)* *(Mexico City, 29 June, 1986. Att: 114,580)*

Argentina: Pumpido; Cuciuffo, Olarticoechea, Ruggeri, Brown, Giusti, Burruchaga (Trobbiani), Batista, Valdano, Maradona, Enrique.

West Germany: Schumacher; Berthold, Briegel, Jakobs, Förster, Eder, Brehme, Matthäus, Allofs (Völler), Magath (Hoeness), Rummenigge.

Ref: Filho (Brazil)

ITALY 1990

GROUP A

Italy 1, Austria 0
Czechoslovakia 5, USA 1
Italy 1, USA 0
Austria 0, Czechoslovakia 1
Italy 2, Czechoslovakia 0
Austria 2, USA 1

	P	W	D	L	F	A	Pts
Italy	3	3	0	0	4	0	6
Czechoslovakia	3	2	0	1	6	3	4
Austria	3	1	0	2	2	3	2
USA	3	0	0	3	2	8	0

GROUP B

Argentina 0, Cameroon 1
USSR 0, Romania 2
Argentina 2, USSR 0
Cameroon 2, Romania 1
Argentina 1, Romania 1
USSR 4, Cameroon 0

	P	W	D	L	F	A	Pts
Cameroon	3	2	0	1	3	5	4
Romania	3	1	1	1	4	3	3
Argentina	3	1	1	1	3	2	3
USSR	3	1	0	2	4	4	2

GROUP C

Brazil 2, Sweden 1
Costa Rica 1, Scotland 0
Brazil 1, Costa Rica 0
Scotland 2, Sweden 1
Brazil 1, Scotland 0
Costa Rica 2, Sweden 1

	P	W	D	L	F	A	Pts
Brazil	3	3	0	0	4	1	6
Costa Rica	3	2	0	1	3	2	4
Scotland	3	1	0	2	2	3	2
Sweden	3	0	0	3	3	6	0

GROUP D

Colombia 2, UAE 0
Yugoslavia 1, West Germany 4
Yugoslavia 1, Colombia 0
West Germany 5, UAE 1
West Germany 1, Colombia 1
Yugoslavia 4, UAE 1

	P	W	D	L	F	A	Pts
West Germany	3	2	1	0	10	3	5
Yugoslavia	3	2	0	1	6	5	4
Colombia	3	1	1	1	3	2	3
UAE	3	0	0	3	2	11	0

GROUP E

Belgium 2, South Korea 0
Spain 0, Uruguay 0
Spain 3, South Korea 1
Belgium 3, Uruguay 1
Spain 2, Belgium 1
Uruguay 1, South Korea 0

	P	W	D	L	F	A	Pts
Spain	3	2	1	0	5	2	5
Belgium	3	2	0	1	6	3	4
Uruguay	3	1	1	1	2	3	3
South Korea	3	0	0	3	1	6	0

GROUP F

England 1, Republic of Ireland 1
Egypt 1, Holland 1
England 0, Holland 0
Republic of Ireland 0, Egypt 0
England 1, Egypt 0
Holland 1, Republic of Ireland 1

	P	W	D	L	F	A	Pts
England	3	1	2	0	2	1	4
Rep of Ireland*	3	0	3	0	2	2	3
Holland	3	0	3	0	2	2	3
Egypt	3	0	2	1	1	2	2

*Republic of Ireland finished second courtesy of drawing lots

SECOND ROUND
Cameroon 2, Colombia 1 (*aet*; 0–0 at 90 mins)
Czechoslovakia 4, Costa Rica 1
Argentina 1, Brazil 0
West Germany 2, Holland 1
Republic of Ireland 0, Romania 0 (*aet*; Republic of Ireland won 5–4 on pens)
Italy 2, Uruguay 0
Spain 1, Yugoslavia 2 (*aet*; 1–1 at 90 mins)
England 1, Belgium 0 (*aet*)

QUARTER-FINALS
Yugoslavia 0, Argentina 0 (*aet*; Argentina won 3–2 on pens)
Republic of Ireland 0, Italy 1
Czechoslovakia 0, West Germany 1
Cameroon 2, England 3 (*aet*; 2–2 at 90 mins)

SEMI-FINALS
Argentina 1, Italy 1 *(Naples)* (*aet*; 1–1 at 90 mins, Argentina won 4–3 on pens)
England 1, West Germany 1 *(Turin)* (*aet*; 1–1 at 90 mins, West Germany won 4–3 on pens)

THIRD PLACE MATCH
Italy 2, England 1 *(Bari)*

FINAL
West Germany 1 *(Brehme pen)*, **Argentina 0** *(Rome, 8 July, 1990. Att: 73,603)*

West Germany: Illgner; Berthold (Reuter), Kohler, Augenthaler, Buchwald, Brehme, Littbarski, Hässler, Matthäus, Völler, Klinsmann.

Argentina: Goycochea; Lorenzo, Serrizuela, Sensini, Ruggeri (Monzon†), Simon, Basualdo, Burruchaga (Calderon), Maradona, Troglio, Dezotti†.

Ref: Codesal (Mexico)

† *sent off*

Other Facts

Statistics

		Matches	Goals	Attendance
1930	Uruguay	18	70	434,500 (av. 24,138)
1934	Italy	17	68	395,000 (av. 23,235)
1938	France	18	83	483,000 (av. 26,833)
1950	Brazil	22	88	1,337,000 (av. 60,772)
1954	Switzerland	26	140	943,000 (av. 36,270)
1958	Sweden	35	126	868,000 (av. 24,800)
1962	Chile	32	89	776,000 (av. 24,250)
1966	England	32	89	1,614,677 (av. 50,458)
1970	Mexico	32	95	1,673,975 (av. 52,311)
1974	W Germany	38	97	1,774,022 (av. 46,684)
1978	Argentina	38	102	1,610,215 (av. 42,374)
1982	Spain	52	146	1,766,277 (av. 33,967)
1986	Mexico	52	132	2,199,941 (av. 42,307)
1990	Italy	52	115	2,510,686 (av. 48,282)

Leading scorers

1930	8	Stabile (Argentina)
1934	4	Schiavio (Italy), Nejedly (Czechoslovakia), Conen (Germany)
1938	8	Leonidas (Brazil)
1950	9	Ademir (Brazil)
1954	11	Kocsis (Hungary)
1958	13	Fontaine (France)
1962	5	Jerkovic (Yugoslavia)
1966	9	Eusebio (Portugal)
1970	10	Müller (West Germany)
1974	7	Lato (Poland)
1978	6	Kempes (Argentina)
1982	6	Rossi (Italy)
1986	6	Lineker (England)
1990	6	Schillaci (Italy)

England lose their World Cup semi-final on a penalty shoot-out and Paul Gascoigne cannot hide his tears of disappointment. But he became an international star in Italy and returned home a hero

European Nations' Cup/European Championship

Results 1958–1992

FRANCE 1958–60

PRELIMINARY ROUND
Republic of Ireland 2, Czechoslovakia 0
Czechoslovakia 4, Republic of Ireland 0

FIRST ROUND
France 7, Greece 1
Greece 1, France 1
USSR 3, Hungary 1
Hungary 0, USSR 1
Romania 3, Turkey 0
Turkey 2, Romania 0
Norway 0, Austria 1
Austria 5, Norway 2

Yugoslavia 2, Bulgaria 0
Bulgaria 1, Yugoslavia 1
Portugal 3, East Germany 2
East Germany 0, Portugal 2
Denmark 2, Czechoslovakia 2
Czechoslovakia 5, Denmark 1
Poland 2, Spain 4
Spain 3, Poland 0

QUARTER-FINALS
Portugal 2, Yugoslavia 1
Yugoslavia 5, Portugal 1
France 5, Austria 2

Austria 2, France 4
Romania 0, Czechoslovakia 2
Czechoslovakia 3, Romania 0
USSR w.o. *(Spain withdrew)*

SEMI-FINALS
Yugoslavia 5, France 4 *(Paris)*
USSR 3, Czechoslovakia 0 *(Marseilles)*

THIRD PLACE MATCH
Czechoslovakia 2, France 0 *(Marseilles)*

FINAL
USSR (0) 2 *(Metreveli, Ponedelnik)*, **Yugoslavia (1) 1** *(Netto o.g.)* (aet; 1–1 at 90 mins) *(Paris, 10 July, 1960. Att: 17,966)*

USSR: Yashin; Tchekeli, Kroutilov, Voinov, Maslenkin, Netto, Metreveli, Ivanov, Ponedelnik, Bubukin, Meshki.

Yugoslavia: Vidinic; Durkovic, Jusufi, Zanetic, Miladinovic, Perusic, Sekularac, Jerkovic, Galic, Matus, Kostic.

Ref: Ellis (England)

SPAIN 1962–64

FIRST ROUND
Spain 6, Romania 0
Romania 3, Spain 1
Poland 0, Northern Ireland 2
Northern Ireland 2, Poland 0
Denmark 6, Malta 1
Malta 1, Denmark 3
Republic of Ireland 4, Iceland 2
Iceland 1, Republic of Ireland 1
Albania w.o. (Greece withdrew)
East Germany 2, Czechoslovakia 1
Czechoslovakia 1, East Germany 1
Hungary 3, Wales 1
Wales 1, Hungary 1
Italy 6, Turkey 0
Turkey 0, Italy 1
Holland 3, Switzerland 1
Switzerland 1, Holland 1
Norway 0, Sweden 2
Sweden 1, Norway 1
Yugoslavia 3, Belgium 2
Belgium 0, Yugoslavia 1
Bulgaria 3, Portugal 1

Portugal 3, Bulgaria 1
Bulgaria 1, Portugal 0
England 1, France 1
France 5, England 2

SECOND ROUND
Spain 1, Northern Ireland 1
Northern Ireland 0, Spain 1
Denmark 4, Albania 0
Albania 1, Denmark 0
Austria 0, Republic of Ireland 0
Republic of Ireland 3, Austria 2
East Germany 1, Hungary 2
Hungary 3, East Germany 3
USSR 2, Italy 0
Italy 1, USSR 1
Holland 1, Luxembourg 1
Luxembourg 2, Holland 1
Yugoslavia 0, Sweden 0
Sweden 3, Yugoslavia 2
Bulgaria 1, France 0
France 3, Bulgaria 1

QUARTER-FINALS
Luxembourg 3, Denmark 3
Denmark 2, Luxembourg 2
Denmark 1, Luxembourg 0
Spain 5, Republic of Ireland 1
Republic of Ireland 0, Spain 2
France 1, Hungary 3
Hungary 2, France 1
Sweden 1, USSR 1
USSR 3, Sweden 1

SEMI-FINALS
USSR 3, Denmark 0 *(Barcelona)*
Spain 2, Hungary 1 *(Madrid)*

THIRD PLACE MATCH
Hungary 3, Denmark 1 (aet; 1–1 at 90 mins) *(Barcelona)*

FINAL
Spain (1) 2 *(Pereda, Marcellino)*, **USSR (1) 1** *(Khusainov)* *(Madrid, 21 June, 1964. Att: 120,000)*

Spain: Iribar; Rivilla, Calleja, Fuste, Olivella, Zoco, Amancio, Pereda, Marcellino, Suarez, Lapetra.

USSR: Yashin; Chustikov, Mudrik, Voronin, Shesternjev, Anitchkin, Chislenko, Ivanov, Ponedelnik, Kornaev, Khusainov.

Ref: Holland (England)

ITALY 1966-68

GROUP 1
Republic of Ireland 0, Spain 0
Republic of Ireland 2, Turkey 1
Spain 2, Republic of Ireland 0
Turkey 0, Spain 0
Turkey 2, Republic of Ireland 1
Republic of Ireland 0, Czechoslovakia 2
Spain 2, Turkey 0
Czechoslovakia 1, Spain 0
Spain 2, Czechoslovakia 1
Czechoslovakia 3, Turkey 0
Turkey 0, Czechoslovakia 0
Czechoslovakia 1, Republic of Ireland 2

GROUP 2
Norway 0, Bulgaria 0
Portugal 1, Sweden 2
Bulgaria 4, Norway 2
Sweden 1, Portugal 1
Norway 1, Portugal 2
Sweden 0, Bulgaria 2
Norway 3, Sweden 1
Sweden 5, Norway 2
Bulgaria 3, Sweden 0
Portugal 2, Norway 1
Bulgaria 1, Portugal 0
Portugal 0, Bulgaria 0

GROUP 3
Finland 0, Austria 0
Austria 2, Finland 1
Greece 2, Finland 1
Greece 4, Austria 1
Finland 1, Greece 1
Austria 1, USSR 0
USSR 4, Austria 3
Greece 0, USSR 1
USSR 2, Finland 0
Austria 1, Greece 1
Finland 2, USSR 5
USSR 4, Greece 0

GROUP 4
Albania 0, Yugoslavia 2
West Germany 6, Albania 0
Yugoslavia 1, West Germany 0
West Germany 3, Yugoslavia 1
Yugoslavia 4, Albania 0
Albania 0, West Germany 0

GROUP 5
Holland 2, Hungary 2
Hungary 6, Denmark 0
Holland 2, Denmark 0
East Germany 4, Holland 3
Hungary 2, Holland 1
Denmark 0, Hungary 2
Denmark 1, East Germany 1
Holland 1, East Germany 0
Hungary 3, East Germany 1
Denmark 3, Holland 2
East Germany 3, Denmark 2
East Germany 1, Hungary 0

GROUP 6
Cyprus 1, Romania 5
Romania 4, Switzerland 2
Italy 3, Romania 1
Cyprus 0, Italy 2
Romania 7, Cyprus 0
Switzerland 7, Romania 1
Italy 5, Cyprus 0
Switzerland 5, Cyprus 0
Switzerland 2, Italy 2
Italy 4, Switzerland 0
Cyprus 2, Switzerland 1
Romania 0, Italy 1

GROUP 7
Poland 4, Luxembourg 0
France 2, Poland 1
Luxembourg 0, France 3
Luxembourg 0, Bulgaria 5
Luxembourg 0, Poland 0
Poland 3, Belgium 1
Belgium 2, France 1
Poland 1, France 4
Belgium 2, Poland 4
France 1, Belgium 1
Belgium 3, Luxembourg 0
France 3, Luxembourg 1

GROUP 8
Northern Ireland 0, England 2
Wales 1, Scotland 1
England 5, Wales 1
Scotland 2, Northern Ireland 1
Northern Ireland 0, Wales 0
England 2, Scotland 3
Wales 0, England 3
Northern Ireland 1, Scotland 0
England 2, Northern Ireland 0
Scotland 3, Wales 2
Scotland 1, England 1
Wales 2, Northern Ireland 0

QUARTER-FINALS
England 1, Spain 0
Spain 1, England 2
Bulgaria 3, Italy 2
Italy 2, Bulgaria 0
France 1, Yugoslavia 1
Yugoslavia 5, France 1
Hungary 2, USSR 0
USSR 3, Hungary 0

SEMI-FINALS
Yugoslavia 1, England 0 *(Florence)*
Italy 0, USSR 0 (Italy won on *toss of coin*) *(Naples)*

THIRD PLACE MATCH
England 2, USSR 0 *(Rome)*

FINAL
Italy (0) 1 *(Domenghini)*, **Yugoslavia (1) 1** *(Dzajic)* (aet; 1–1 at 90 mins) *(Rome, 8 June, 1968. Att: 60,000)*

Italy: Zoff; Burgnich, Facchetti, Ferrini, Guarneri. Castano, Domenghini, Juliano, Anastasi, Lodetti, Prati.

Yugoslavia: Pantelic; Fazlagic, Damjanovic, Pavlovic, Paunovic, Holcer, Petkovic, Acimovic, Musemic, Trivic, Dzajic.

Ref: Dienst (Switzerland)

REPLAY
Italy (2) 2 *(Riva, Anastasi)*, **Yugoslavia (0) 0** *(Rome, 10 June, 1968. Att: 75,000)*

Italy: Zoff; Burgnich, Facchetti, Rosato, Guarneri, Salvadore, Domenghini, Mazzola, Anastasi, De Sisti, Riva.

Yugoslavia: Pantelic; Fazlagic, Damjanovic, Pavlovic, Paunovic, Holcer, Hosic, Acimovic, Musemic, Trivic, Dzajic.

Ref: Dienst (Switzerland)

BELGIUM 1970–72

GROUP 1
Czechoslovakia 1, Finland 1
Romania 3, Finland 0
Wales 0, Romania 0
Wales 1, Czechoslovakia 3
Finland 0, Wales 1
Czechoslovakia 1, Romania 0
Finland 0, Czechoslovakia 4
Finland 0, Romania 4
Wales 3, Finland 0
Czechoslovakia 1, Wales 0
Romania 2, Czechoslovakia 1
Romania 2, Wales 0

GROUP 2
Norway 1, Hungary 3
France 3, Norway 1
Bulgaria 1, Norway 1
Hungary 1, France 1
Bulgaria 3, Hungary 0
Norway 1, Bulgaria 4
Norway 1, France 3
Hungary 2, Bulgaria 0
France 0, Hungary 2
Hungary 4, Norway 0
France 2, Bulgaria 1
Bulgaria 2, France 1

GROUP 3
Greece 0, Switzerland 1
Malta 1, Switzerland 2
Malta 0, England 1
England 3, Greece 0
Switzerland 5, Malta 0
England 5, Malta 0
Malta 1, Greece 1
Switzerland 1, Greece 0
Greece 2, Malta 0
Switzerland 2, England 3
England 1, Switzerland 1
Greece 0, England 2

GROUP 4
Spain 3, Northern Ireland 0

Cyprus 0, Northern Ireland 3
Northern Ireland 5, Cyprus 0
Cyprus 1, USSR 3
Cyprus 0, Spain 2
USSR 2, Spain 1
USSR 6, Cyprus 1
USSR 1, Northern Ireland 0
Northern Ireland 1, USSR 1
Spain 0, USSR 0
Spain 7, Cyprus 0
Northern Ireland 1, Spain 1

GROUP 5
Denmark 0, Portugal 1
Scotland 1, Denmark 0
Belgium 2, Denmark 0
Belgium 3, Scotland 0
Belgium 3, Portugal 0
Portugal 2, Scotland 0
Denmark 1, Scotland 0
Portugal 5, Denmark 0
Denmark 1, Belgium 2
Scotland 2, Portugal 1
Scotland 1, Belgium 0
Portugal 1, Belgium 1

GROUP 6
Republic of Ireland 1, Sweden 1
Sweden 1, Republic of Ireland 0
Austria 1, Italy 2
Italy 3, Republic of Ireland 0
Republic of Ireland 1, Italy 2
Republic of Ireland 1, Austria 4
Sweden 1, Austria 0
Sweden 0, Italy 0
Austria 1, Sweden 0
Italy 3, Sweden 0
Austria 6, Republic of Ireland 0
Italy 2, Austria 2

GROUP 7
Holland 1, Yugoslavia 1
East Germany 1, Holland 0
Luxembourg 0, East Germany 5

Yugoslavia 2, Holland 0
East Germany 2, Luxembourg 1
Luxembourg 0, Yugoslavia 2
Holland 6, Luxembourg 0
East Germany 1, Yugoslavia 2
Holland 3, East Germany 2
Yugoslavia 0, East Germany 0
Yugoslavia 0, Luxembourg 0
Luxembourg 0, Holland 8

GROUP 8
Poland 3, Albania 0
West Germany 1, Turkey 1
Turkey 2, Albania 1
Albania 0, West Germany 1
Turkey 0, West Germany 3
Albania 1, Poland 1
West Germany 2, Albania 0
Poland 5, Turkey 1
Poland 1, West Germany 3
Albania 3, Turkey 0
West Germany 0, Poland 0
Turkey 1, Poland 0

QUARTER-FINALS
England 1, West Germany 3
Italy 0, Belgium 0
Hungary 1, Romania 1
Yugoslavia 0, USSR 0
West Germany 0, England 0
Belgium 2, Italy 1
USSR 3, Yugoslavia 0
Romania 2, Hungary 2
Play off: Hungary 2, Romania 1

SEMI-FINALS
USSR 1, Hungary 0 *(Brussels)*
West Germany 2, Belgium 1 *(Antwerp)*

THIRD PLACE MATCH
Belgium 2, Hungary 1 *(Liège)*

FINAL
West Germany (1) 3 *(Müller 2, Wimmer)*, **USSR (0) 0** *(Brussels, 18 June, 1972. Att: 43,437)*

West Germany: Maier; Hottges, Schwarzenbeck, Beckenbauer, Breitner, Hoeness, Wimmer, Netzer, Heynckes, Müller, Kremers.

USSR: Rudakov; Dzodzuashvili, Khurtsilava, Kaplichny, Istomin, Troshkin, Kolotov, Baidachni, Konkov (Dolmatov), Banishevski (Kozinkievits), Onishenko.

Ref: Marschall (Austria)

YUGOSLAVIA 1974–76

GROUP 1
England 3, Czechoslovakia 0
England 0, Portugal 0
England 5, Cyprus 0
Czechoslovakia 4, Cyprus 0
Czechoslovakia 5, Portugal 0

Cyprus 0, England 1
Cyprus 0, Portugal 2
Czechoslovakia 2, England 1
Portugal 1, Czechoslovakia 1
Portugal 1, England 1
Cyprus 0, Czechoslovakia 3

Portugal 1, Cyprus 0

GROUP 2
Austria 2, Wales 1
Luxembourg 2, Hungary 4
Wales 2, Hungary 0

121

Wales 5, Luxembourg 0
Luxembourg 1, Austria 2
Austria 0, Hungary 0
Hungary 1, Wales 2
Luxembourg 1, Wales 3
Hungary 2, Austria 1
Austria 6, Luxembourg 2
Hungary 8, Luxembourg 1
Wales 1, Austria 0

GROUP 3
Norway 2, Northern Ireland 1
Yugoslavia 3, Norway 1
Sweden 0, Northern Ireland 2
Northern Ireland 1, Yugoslavia 0
Sweden 1, Yugoslavia 2
Norway 1, Yugoslavia 3
Sweden 3, Norway 1
Norway 0, Sweden 2
Northern Ireland 1, Sweden 2
Yugoslavia 3, Sweden 0
Northern Ireland 3, Norway 0
Yugoslavia 1, Northern Ireland 0

GROUP 4
Denmark 1, Spain 2
Denmark 0, Romania 0
Scotland 1, Spain 2
Spain 1, Scotland 1
Spain 1, Romania 1
Romania 6, Denmark 1
Romania 1, Scotland 1
Denmark 0, Scotland 1
Spain 2, Denmark 0
Scotland 3, Denmark 1
Romania 2, Spain 2
Scotland 1, Romania 1

GROUP 5
Finland 1, Poland 2
Finland 1, Holland 3
Poland 3, Finland 0
Holland 3, Italy 1
Italy 0, Poland 0
Finland 0, Italy 1
Holland 4, Finland 1
Poland 4, Holland 1
Italy 0, Finland 0
Holland 3, Poland 0
Poland 0, Italy 0
Italy 1, Holland 0

GROUP 6
Republic of Ireland 3, USSR 0
Turkey 1, Republic of Ireland 1
Turkey 2, Switzerland 1
USSR 3, Turkey 0
Switzerland 1, Turkey 1
Republic of Ireland 2, Switzerland 1
USSR 2, Republic of Ireland 1
Switzerland 1, Republic of Ireland 0
Switzerland 0, USSR 1
Republic of Ireland 4, Turkey 0
USSR 4, Switzerland 1
Turkey 1, USSR 0

GROUP 7
Iceland 0, Belgium 2
East Germany 1, Iceland 1
Belgium 2, France 1
France 2, East Germany 2
East Germany 0, Belgium 0
Iceland 0, France 0
Iceland 2, East Germany 1
France 3, Iceland 0
Belgium 1, Iceland 0
Belgium 1, East Germany 2
East Germany 2, France 1
France 0, Belgium 0

GROUP 8
Bulgaria 3, Greece 3
Greece 2, West Germany 2
Greece 2, Bulgaria 1
Malta 0, West Germany 1
Malta 2, Greece 0
Bulgaria 1, West Germany 1
Greece 4, Malta 0
Bulgaria 5, Malta 0
West Germany 1, Greece 1
West Germany 1, Bulgaria 0
Malta 0, Bulgaria 2
West Germany 8, Malta 0

QUARTER-FINALS
Spain 1, West Germany 1
Yugoslavia 2, Wales 0
Czechoslovakia 2, USSR 0
Holland 5, Belgium 0
West Germany 2, Spain 0
USSR 2, Czechoslovakia 2
Wales 1, Yugoslavia 1
Belgium 1, Holland 2

SEMI-FINALS
Czechoslovakia 3, Holland 1
  (aet; 1–1 at 90 mins) (Zagreb)
West Germany 4, Yugoslavia 2
  (aet; 2–2 at 90 mins) (Belgrade)

THIRD PLACE MATCH
Holland 3, Yugoslavia 2
  (aet; 2–2 at 90 mins) (Zagreb)

FINAL
Czechoslovakia (2) 2 *(Svehlic, Dobias)*, **West Germany (1) 2** *(Müller, Holzenbein)* (aet; 2–2 at 90 mins; Czechoslovakia won 5–3 on pens) (Belgrade, 20 June, 1976. Att: 30,790)

Czechoslovakia: Viktor; Dobias (Vesely F), Pivarnik, Ondrus, Capkovic, Gogh, Moder, Panenka, Svehlic (Jurkemik), Masny, Nehoda.

West Germany: Maier; Vogts, Beckenbauer, Schwarzenbeck, Dietz, Bonhof, Wimmer (Flohe), Müller D, Beer (Bongartz), Hoeness, Holzenbein.

Ref: Gonella (Italy)

ITALY 1978–80

GROUP 1
Denmark 3, Republic of Ireland 3
Denmark 3, England 4
Republic of Ireland 0, Northern Ireland 0
Denmark 2, Bulgaria 2
Republic of Ireland 1, England 1
Northern Ireland 2, Denmark 1
Bulgaria 0, Northern Ireland 2
England 4, Northern Ireland 0
Northern Ireland 2, Bulgaria 0
Republic of Ireland 2, Denmark 0
Bulgaria 1, Republic of Ireland 0
Denmark 4, Northern Ireland 0
Bulgaria 0, England 3
England 1, Denmark 0
Republic of Ireland 3, Bulgaria 0
Northern Ireland 1, England 5
Bulgaria 3, Denmark 0
Northern Ireland 1, Republic of Ireland 0
England 2, Bulgaria 0
England 2, Republic of Ireland 0

GROUP 2
Norway 0, Austria 2
Belgium 1, Norway 1
Austria 3, Scotland 2
Portugal 1, Belgium 1
Scotland 3, Norway 2
Austria 1, Portugal 2
Portugal 1, Scotland 0
Belgium 1, Austria 1
Austria 0, Belgium 0
Norway 0, Portugal 1
Norway 0, Scotland 4
Austria 4, Norway 0
Norway 1, Belgium 2
Belgium 2, Portugal 0
Scotland 1, Austria 1

Portugal 3, Norway 1
Belgium 2, Scotland 0
Portugal 1, Austria 2
Scotland 1, Belgium 3
Scotland 4, Portugal 1

GROUP 3

Yugoslavia 1, Spain 2
Romania 3, Yugoslavia 2
Spain 1, Romania 0
Spain 5, Cyprus 0
Cyprus 0, Yugoslavia 3
Romania 2, Spain 2
Cyprus 1, Romania 1
Spain 0, Yugoslavia 1
Yugoslavia 2, Romania 1
Yugoslavia 5, Cyprus 0
Romania 2, Cyprus 0
Cyprus 1, Spain 3

GROUP 4

Iceland 0, Poland 2
Holland 3, Iceland 0
East Germany 3, Iceland 1
Switzerland 1, Holland 3
Holland 3, East Germany 0
Poland 2, Switzerland 0
Holland 3, Switzerland 0
East Germany 2, Poland 1
Poland 2, Holland 0
Switzerland 0, East Germany 2
Switzerland 2, Iceland 0
Iceland 1, Switzerland 2
Iceland 0, Holland 4
Switzerland 0, Poland 2

Iceland 0, East Germany 3
Poland 1, East Germany 1
Poland 2, Iceland 0
East Germany 5, Switzerland 2
Holland 1, Portugal 1
East Germany 2, Holland 3

GROUP 5

France 2, Sweden 2
Sweden 1, Czechoslovakia 3
Luxembourg 1, France 3
France 3, Luxembourg 0
Czechoslovakia 2, France 0
Luxembourg 0, Czechoslovakia 3
Sweden 3, Luxembourg 0
Sweden 1, France 3
Czechoslovakia 4, Sweden 1
Luxembourg 1, Sweden 1
France 2, Czechoslovakia 0
Czechoslovakia 4, Luxembourg 0

GROUP 6

Finland 3, Greece 0
Finland 2, Hungary 1
USSR 2, Greece 0
Hungary 2, USSR 0
Greece 8, Finland 1
Greece 4, Hungary 1
Hungary 0, Greece 0
USSR 2, Hungary 2
Finland 1, USSR 1
Greece 1, USSR 0
Hungary 3, Finland 1
USSR 2, Finland 2

GROUP 7

Wales 7, Malta 0
Wales 1, Turkey 0
Malta 0, West Germany 0
Turkey 2, Malta 1
Turkey 0, West Germany 0
Wales 0, West Germany 2
Malta 0, Wales 2
West Germany 5, Wales 1
Malta 1, Turkey 2
Turkey 1, Wales 0
West Germany 2, Turkey 0
West Germany 8, Malta 0

GROUP 1 (FINALS)

West Germany 1, Czechoslovakia 0
Greece 0, Holland 1
West Germany 3, Holland 2
Czechoslovakia 3, Greece 1
Czechoslovakia 1, Holland 1
West Germany 0, Greece 0

GROUP 2 (FINALS)

Belgium 1, England 1
Spain 0, Italy 0
Spain 1, Belgium 2
Italy 1, England 0
England 2, Spain 1
Italy 0, Belgium 0

THIRD PLACE MATCH

Italy 1, Czechoslovakia 1 (*aet;* 1–1 at 90 mins; Czechoslovakia won 9–8 on pens) *(Naples)*

FINAL

West Germany (1) 2 *(Hrubesch 2)*, **Belgium (0) 1** *(Van der Eycken)* *(Rome, 22 June, 1980. Att: 47,864)*

West Germany: Schumacher; Briegel (Cullmann), Förster K, Dietz, Schuster, Rummenigge, Hrubesch, Müller, Allofs, Stielike, Kaltz.

Belgium: Pfaff; Gerets, Millecamps, Meeuws, Renquin, Cools, Van der Eycken, Van Moer, Mommens, Van der Elst, Ceulemans.

Ref: Rainea (Romania)

FRANCE 1982–84

GROUP 1

Belgium 3, Switzerland 0
Scotland 2, East Germany 0
Switzerland 2, Scotland 0
Belgium 3, Scotland 2
East Germany 1, Belgium 2
Scotland 2, Switzerland 2
Belgium 2, East Germany 1
Switzerland 0, East Germany 0
East Germany 3, Switzerland 0
Scotland 1, Belgium 1
Switzerland 3, Belgium 1
East Germany 2, Scotland 1

GROUP 2

Finland 2, Poland 3
Finland 0, Portugal 2
Portugal 2, Poland 1

USSR 2, Finland 0
Poland 1, Finland 1
USSR 5, Portugal 0
Poland 1, USSR 1
Finland 0, USSR 1
Portugal 5, Finland 0
USSR 2, Poland 0
Poland 0, Portugal 1
Portugal 1, USSR 0

GROUP 3

Denmark 2, England 2
Luxembourg 0, Greece 2
Luxembourg 1, Denmark 2
Greece 0, England 3
England 9, Luxembourg 0
Luxembourg 2, Hungary 6
England 0, Greece 0

Hungary 6, Luxembourg 2
Denmark 1, Greece 0
England 2, Hungary 0
Hungary 2, Greece 3
Denmark 3, Hungary 1
England 0, Denmark 1
Denmark 6, Luxembourg 0
Hungary 0, England 3
Hungary 1, Denmark 0
Greece 0, Denmark 2
Luxembourg 0, England 4
Greece 2, Hungary 2
Greece 1, Luxembourg 0

GROUP 4

Wales 1, Norway 0
Norway 3, Yugoslavia 1
Bulgaria 2, Norway 2

Bulgaria 0, Yugoslavia 1
Yugoslavia 4, Wales 4
Wales 1, Bulgaria 0
Norway 1, Bulgaria 2
Norway 0, Wales 0
Yugoslavia 2, Norway 1
Bulgaria 1, Wales 0
Wales 1, Yugoslavia 1
Yugoslavia 3, Bulgaria 2

GROUP 5
Romania 3, Cyprus 1
Romania 2, Sweden 0
Czechoslovakia 2, Sweden 2
Cyprus 0, Sweden 1
Italy 2, Czechoslovakia 2
Italy 0, Romania 0
Cyprus 1, Italy 1
Cyprus 1, Czechoslovakia 1
Czechoslovakia 6, Cyprus 0
Romania 1, Italy 0
Sweden 5, Cyprus 0
Romania 0, Czechoslovakia 1
Sweden 2, Italy 0
Sweden 0, Romania 1
Sweden 1, Czechoslovakia 0
Italy 0, Sweden 3
Cyprus 0, Romania 1
Czechoslovakia 2, Italy 0
Czechoslovakia 1, Romania 1
Italy 3, Cyprus 1

GROUP 6
Austria 5, Albania 0
Austria 2, Northern Ireland 0
Turkey 1, Albania 0
Austria 4, Turkey 0
Northern Ireland 1, West Germany 0
Albania 0, Northern Ireland 0
Albania 1, West Germany 2
Northern Ireland 2, Turkey 1
Turkey 0, West Germany 3
Austria 0, West Germany 0
Northern Ireland 1, Albania 0
Albania 1, Turkey 1
Albania 1, Austria 2
Northern Ireland 3, Austria 1
West Germany 3, Austria 0
Turkey 1, Northern Ireland 0
West Germany 5, Turkey 1
Turkey 3, Austria 1
West Germany 0, Northern Ireland 1
West Germany 2, Albania 1

GROUP 7
Malta 2, Iceland 1
Iceland 1, Holland 1
Holland 2, Republic of Ireland 1
Republic of Ireland 2, Iceland 0
Spain 1, Iceland 0
Republic of Ireland 3, Spain 3
Malta 0, Holland 6
Spain 1, Holland 0
Malta 0, Republic of Ireland 1
Spain 2, Republic of Ireland 0
Malta 2, Spain 3
Iceland 0, Spain 1
Iceland 1, Malta 0
Holland 3, Iceland 0
Iceland 0, Republic of Ireland 3
Republic of Ireland 2, Holland 3
Holland 2, Spain 1
Republic of Ireland 8, Malta 0
Holland 5, Malta 0
Spain 12, Malta 1

GROUP 1 (FINALS)
France 1, Denmark 0
Belgium 2, Yugoslavia 0
France 5, Belgium 0
Denmark 5, Yugoslavia 0
France 3, Yugoslavia 2
Denmark 3, Belgium 2

GROUP 2 (FINALS)
West Germany 0, Portugal 0
Spain 1, Romania 1
Spain 1, Portugal 1
West Germany 2, Romania 1
West Germany 0, Spain 1
Portugal 1, Romania 0

SEMI-FINALS
France 3, Portugal 2 *(Marseilles)*
Denmark 1, Spain 1 *(aet;* 1–1 at 90 mins; Spain won 5–4 on pens) *(Lyon)*

FINAL
France (0) 2 *(Platini, Bellone),* **Spain (0) 0** *(Paris, 27 June, 1984. Att: 47,368)*

France: Bats; Battiston (Amoros), Le Roux, Bossis, Domergue, Giresse, Platini, Tigana, Fernandez, Lacombe (Genghini), Bellone.

Spain: Arconada; Urquiaga, Salva (Roberto), Gallego, Camacho, Francisco, Julio Alberto (Sarabia), Senor, Victor, Carrasco, Santillana.

Ref: Christov (Czechoslovakia)

WEST GERMANY 1986-88

GROUP 1
Romania 4, Austria 0
Austria 3, Albania 0
Spain 1, Romania 0
Albania 1, Spain 2
Romania 5, Albania 1
Austria 2, Spain 3
Albania 0, Austria 1
Romania 3, Spain 1
Spain 2, Austria 0
Albania 0, Romania 1
Spain 5, Albania 0
Austria 0, Romania 0

GROUP 2
Sweden 2, Switzerland 0
Portugal 1, Sweden 1
Switzerland 1, Portugal 1
Italy 3, Switzerland 2
Malta 0, Sweden 5
Malta 0, Italy 2
Italy 5, Malta 0
Portugal 0, Italy 1
Portugal 2, Malta 2
Switzerland 4, Malta 1
Sweden 1, Malta 0
Sweden 1, Italy 0
Switzerland 1, Sweden 1
Sweden 0, Portugal 1
Switzerland 0, Italy 0
Portugal 0, Switzerland 0
Italy 2, Sweden 1
Malta 1, Switzerland 1
Italy 3, Portugal 0
Malta 0, Portugal 1

GROUP 3
Iceland 0, France 0
Iceland 1, USSR 1
Norway 0, East Germany 0
France 0, USSR 2
USSR 4, Norway 0
East Germany 2, Iceland 0
East Germany 0, France 0
France 2, Iceland 0
USSR 2, East Germany 0
Norway 0, USSR 1
Iceland 0, East Germany 6
Norway 2, France 0
USSR 1, France 1
Iceland 2, Norway 1
Norway 0, Iceland 1
East Germany 1, USSR 1
France 1, Norway 1
USSR 2, Iceland 0
East Germany 3, Norway 1
France 0, East Germany 1

GROUP 4
England 3, Northern Ireland 0
Yugoslavia 4, Turkey 0
England 2, Yugoslavia 0
Turkey 0, Northern Ireland 0

Northern Ireland 0, England 2
Northern Ireland 1, Yugoslavia 2
Turkey 0, England 0
Yugoslavia 3, Northern Ireland 0
England 8, Turkey 0
Yugoslavia 1, England 4
Northern Ireland 1, Turkey 0
Turkey 2, Yugoslavia 3

GROUP 5

Hungary 0, Holland 1
Poland 2, Greece 1
Greece 2, Hungary 1
Holland 0, Poland 0
Cyprus 2, Greece 4
Cyprus 0, Holland 2
Greece 3, Cyprus 1
Cyprus 0, Hungary 1
Holland 1, Greece 1
Poland 0, Cyprus 0
Greece 1, Poland 0
Holland 2, Hungary 0
Hungary 5, Poland 3
Poland 3, Hungary 2
Hungary 3, Greece 0
Poland 0, Holland 2
Cyprus 0, Poland 1
Hungary 1, Cyprus 0
Holland 4, Cyprus 0
Greece 0, Holland 3

GROUP 6

Finland 1, Wales 1
Czechoslovakia 3, Finland 0
Denmark 1, Finland 0
Czechoslovakia 0, Denmark 0
Wales 4, Finland 0
Finland 0, Denmark 1
Wales 1, Czechoslovakia 1
Denmark 1, Czechoslovakia 1
Wales 1, Denmark 0
Finland 3, Czechoslovakia 0
Denmark 1, Wales 0
Czechoslovakia 2, Wales 0

GROUP 7

Scotland 0, Bulgaria 0
Belgium 2, Republic of Ireland 2
Luxembourg 0, Belgium 6
Republic of Ireland 0, Scotland 0
Scotland 3, Luxembourg 0
Belgium 1, Bulgaria 1
Scotland 0, Republic of Ireland 1
Belgium 4, Scotland 1

David Batty of Leeds United offers an incentive to all aspiring Under-21 players, having graduated with honours to play for the England senior side

Bulgaria 2, Republic of Ireland 1
Republic of Ireland 0, Belgium 0
Luxembourg 1, Bulgaria 4
Bulgaria 3, Luxembourg 0
Luxembourg 0, Republic of Ireland 2
Republic of Ireland 2, Luxembourg 1
Bulgaria 2, Belgium 0
Scotland 2, Belgium 0
Republic of Ireland 2, Bulgaria 0
Belgium 3, Luxembourg 0
Bulgaria 0, Scotland 1
Luxembourg 0, Scotland 0

GROUP 1 (FINALS)

West Germany 1, Italy 1
Spain 3, Denmark 2

West Germany 2, Denmark 0
Italy 1, Spain 0
West Germany 2, Spain 0
Italy 2, Denmark 0

GROUP 2 (FINALS)

England 0, Republic of Ireland 1
Holland 0, USSR 1
Holland 3, England 1
Republic of Ireland 1, USSR 1
England 1, USSR 3
Holland 1, Republic of Ireland 0

SEMI-FINALS

West Germany 1, Holland 2 *(Hamburg)*
USSR 2, Italy 0 *(Stuttgart)*

FINAL

Holland (1) 2 *(Gullit, van Basten)*, **USSR (0) 0** *(Munich, 25 June, 1988. Att: 72,308)*

Holland: van Breukelen; van Aerle, van Tiggelen, Wouters, Koeman R, Rijkaard, Vanenburg, Gullit, van Basten, Muhren, Koeman E.

USSR: Dassayev; Khidiatulin, Aleinikov, Mikhailichenko, Litovchenko, Demianenko, Belanov, Gotsmanov (Baltacha), Protasov (Pasulko), Zavarov, Rats.

Ref: Vautrot (France)

British Home International Championships 1883–1984

Year	Champions	Year	Champions
1883–84	Scotland	1936–37	Wales
1884–85	Scotland	1937–38	England
1885–86	England / Scotland	1938–39	England / Scotland / Wales
1886–87	Scotland	1946–47	England
1887–88	England	1947–48	England
1888–89	Scotland	1948–49	Scotland
1889–90	Scotland / England	1949–50	England
1890–91	England	1950–51	Scotland
1891–92	England	1951–52	Wales / England
1892–93	England	1952–53	England / Scotland
1893–94	Scotland	1953–54	England
1894–95	England	1954–55	England
1895–96	Scotland	1955–56	England / Scotland / Wales / Northern Ireland
1896–97	Scotland	1956–57	England
1897–98	England	1957–58	England / Northern Ireland
1898–99	England	1958–59	Northern Ireland / England
1899–1900	Scotland	1959–60	England / Scotland / Wales
1900–01	England	1960–61	England
1901–02	Scotland	1961–62	Scotland
1902–03	England / Ireland / Scotland	1962–63	Scotland
1903–04	England	1963–64	Scotland / England / Northern Ireland
1904–05	England	1964–65	England
1905–06	England / Scotland	1965–66	England
1906–07	Wales	1966–67	Scotland
1907–08	Scotland / England	1967–68	England
1908–09	England	1968–69	England
1909–10	Scotland	1969–70	England / Scotland / Wales
1910–11	England	1970–71	England
1911–12	England / Scotland	1971–72	England / Scotland
1912–13	England	1972–73	England
1913–14	Ireland	1973–74	England / Scotland
1919–20	Wales	1974–75	England
1920–21	Scotland	1975–76	Scotland
1921–22	Scotland	1976–77	Scotland
1922–23	Scotland	1977–78	England
1923–24	Wales	1978–79	England
1924–25	Scotland	1979–80	Northern Ireland
1925–26	Scotland	1980–81	not completed
1926–27	Scotland / England	1981–82	England
1927–28	Wales	1982–83	England
1928–29	Scotland	1983–84	Northern Ireland
1929–30	England		
1930–31	Scotland / England		
1931–32	England		
1932–33	Wales		
1933–34	Wales		
1934–35	England / Scotland		
1935–36	Scotland		

Above: Alf Ramsey shows a serious hand-on-heart approach to his work as he builds a side that was to bring England World Cup glory in 1966

Below: Walter Winterbottom, England's first post-war manager, directs operations during an England training session

FA FIXTURES FOR 1992-93

August
Sat   1   Opening of Season
Sat   8   Tennents FA Charity Shield
Sat 15   FA Premier League and Football League programmes begin
Sat 29   FA Cup Preliminary Round

September
Sat   5   FA Vase Extra Preliminary Round
Wed   9   Spain v England (Friendly)
Sat 12   FA Cup First Qualifying Round
           FA Youth Cup Preliminary Round
Wed 16   European club competitions: First Round, First Leg
Sat 19   FA Trophy First Qualifying Round
Sat 26   FA Cup Second Qualifying Round
Wed 30   European club competitions: First Round, Second Leg

October
Sat   3   FA Vase Preliminary Round
           FA Youth Cup First Qualifying Round
Sat 10   FA Cup Third Qualifying Round
Sun 11   FA Sunday Cup First Round
Wed 14   England v Norway (World Cup)
Sat 17   FA Trophy Second Qualifying Round
           FA Youth Cup Second Qualifying Round
           FA County Youth Cup First Round
Wed 21   European club competitions: Second Round, First Leg
Sat 24   FA Cup Fourth Qualifying Round
Sat 31   FA Vase First Round

November
Wed   4   European club competitions: Second Round, Second Leg
Sun   8   FA Sunday Cup Second Round
Sat 14   FA Cup First Round
           FA Youth Cup First Round
Wed 18   England v Turkey (World Cup)
Sat 21   FA Vase Second Round
Wed 25   European Cup group matches; UEFA Cup Third Round, First Leg
Sat 28   FA Trophy Third Qualifying Round
           FA County Youth Cup Second Round

December
Sat   5   FA Cup Second Round
Sun   6   FA Sunday Cup Third Round
Wed   9   European Cup group matches; UEFA Cup Third Round, Second Leg
Sat 12   FA Vase Third Round
           FA Youth Cup Second Round

January 1993
Sat   2   FA Cup Third Round
Sat   9   FA Trophy First Round
Sat 16   FA Vase Fourth Round

127

	FA Youth Cup Third Round
Sun 17	FA Sunday Cup Fourth Round
Sat 23	FA Cup Fourth Round
Sat 30	FA Trophy Second Round

February

Sat 6	FA Vase Fifth Round
	FA Youth Cup Fourth Round
Sat 13	FA Cup Fifth Round
Sun 14	FA Sunday Cup Fifth Round
Wed 17	England v San Marino (World Cup)
Sat 20	FA Trophy Third Round
	FA County Youth Cup Fourth Round
Sat 27	FA Vase Sixth Round

March

Wed 3	European Cup group matches; ECWC & UEFA Cup Quarter-final, First Leg
Sat 6	FA Cup Sixth Round
	FA Youth Cup Fifth Round
Sat 13	FA Trophy Fourth Round
Wed 17	European Cup group matches; ECWC & UEFA Cup Quarter-final, Second Leg
Sat 20	FA Vase Semi-final, First Leg
	FA County Youth Cup Semi-final
Sun 21	FA Sunday Cup Semi-final
Sat 27	FA Vase Semi-final, Second Leg
Wed 31	Turkey v England (World Cup)

April

Sat 3	FA Trophy Semi-final, First Leg
	FA Youth Challenge Cup Semi-final
Sun 4	FA Cup Semi-finals
Wed 7	European Cup group matches; ECWC & UEFA Cup Semi-final, First Leg
Sat 10	FA Trophy Semi-final, Second Leg
Wed 21	European Cup group matches; ECWC & UEFA Cup Semi-final, Second Leg
Wed 28	England v Holland (World Cup)

May

Sat 1	**FA County Youth Cup Final**
Sun 2	**FA Sunday Cup Final**
Wed 5	**UEFA Cup Final,** First Leg
Sat 8	**FA Vase Final**
	FA Youth Cup Final
Sun 9	**FA Trophy Final**
Wed 12	**European Cup Winners' Cup Final**
Sat 15	**FA Cup Final**
Wed 19	**UEFA Cup Final,** Second Leg
Wed 26	**European Cup Final**
Sat 29	Poland v England (World Cup)

June

Wed 2	Norway v England (World Cup)